La Güera Rodríguez

The publisher and the University of California Press Foundation gratefully acknowledge the generous support of the Constance and William Withey Endowment Fund in History and Music.

La Güera Rodríguez

THE LIFE AND LEGENDS OF A MEXICAN INDEPENDENCE HEROINE

Silvia Marina Arrom

UNIVERSITY OF CALIFORNIA PRESS

University of California Press
Oakland, California

Permission to reprint has been sought from rights holders for images and
text included in this volume, but in some cases it was impossible to clear
formal permission because of coronavirus-related institution closures.
The author and the publisher will be glad to do so if and when contacted
by copyright holders of third-party material.

Library of Congress Cataloging-in-Publication Data

Names: Arrom, Silvia Marina, 1949- author.
Title: La Güera Rodríguez : the life and legends of a Mexican
    independence heroine / Silvia Marina Arrom.
Description: Oakland, California : University of California Press, [2021] |
    Includes bibliographical references and index.
Identifiers: LCCN 2020056078 (print) | LCCN 2020056079 (ebook) |
    ISBN 9780520383425 (cloth) | ISBN 9780520383432 (epub)
Subjects: LCSH: Rodríguez de Velasco y Osorio, María Ignacia,
    1778-1851. | Women—Mexico—Mexico City—19th century—
    Biography. | Mexico—History—Wars of Independence, 1810-1821.
Classification: LCC F1232.R7 A77 2021 (print) | LCC F1232.R7 (ebook) |
    DDC 972/.03092 [B]—dc23
LC record available at https://lccn.loc.gov/2020056078
LC ebook record available at https://lccn.loc.gov/2020056079

Manufactured in the United States of America

30 29 28 27 26 25 24 23 22 21
10 9 8 7 6 5 4 3 2 1

For my grandsons Max and Alex, with the hope that they will learn to be critical readers and avoid being seduced by attractive narratives full of false facts and apocryphal stories

Si lo que relatamos no sucedió exactamente, nos hubiera
gustado que así hubiese sucedido.
If what we depict did not actually happen, it is the way we
would have liked it to occur.

Emilio Carballido and Julio Alejandro, handwritten note
on the script for the movie *La Güera Rodríguez* (1977)

Contents

Illustrations

Acknowledgments

This book has benefited from the extraordinary generosity of scholars both in Mexico and the United States. Rodrigo Amerlinck, Linda Arnold, Alfredo Ávila, Ann G. Carmichael, William Christian, María José Esparza Liberal, Juan Martín Gama Jaramillo, Nina Gerassi Navarro, Pilar Gonzalbo, Guadalupe Jiménez Codinach, Marcela López Arellano, María Dolores Lorenzo, James Mandrell, María Dolores Morales, Erika Pani, Sonia Pérez Toledo, John Frederich Schwaller, Anne Staples, Ibrahim Sundiata, Angélica Velázquez Guadarrama, Judith Weiss Tayar, and Verónica Zárate Toscano answered my questions, shared relevant sources, or commented on parts of the draft. I owe special thanks to Marjorie Agosín, Gene Bell-Villada, Francie Chassen-López, June Erlick, and Susie Porter for reading the complete manuscript; to my son Daniel Oran for assisting me with the preparation of the map and illustrations; to Julia Tuñón Pablos for helping me locate the film *La Güera Rodríguez* and arranging for me to see it at the Filmoteca of the National University; and to Nelly Ramírez Delgado for serving as an exemplary assistant in copying documents and obtaining reproduction permissions in Mexico City. I am deeply grateful to all of them.

I also received valuable feedback on early versions of this project from participants in the Boston Area Workshop on Latin American and

Caribbean History and members of the Latin American Historians of Northern California and the Seminario Permanente de Historia Social in Mexico. The papers I presented at their seminars resulted in an article that preceded this book, "La Güera Rodríguez: La construcción de una leyenda," *Historia Mexicana* 274, vol. LXIX, no. 2 (October–December 2019): 471–510.

In addition, I owe a large debt to two departed observers of Mexican life. The first is Fanny Calderón de la Barca, whose *Life in Mexico* I read as an undergraduate. Her lively travel account not only introduced me to La Güera but was instrumental in keeping her memory alive for future generations. The second is Artemio de Valle-Arizpe, whose marvelous novelized biography of María Ignacia Rodríguez sparked my interest in her so many decades ago and made her an icon of Mexican history.

Finally, I thank my husband, David Oran, who welcomed La Güera into our daily lives as she became part of our conversations, and who served as a thoughtful sounding board during the years that I was working on this project.

NOTE TO THE READER

All translations into English are mine. I have followed the naming practices in the original documents, which were not always consistent. Thus, for example, La Güera is sometimes Ignacia and sometimes María; and the surname of her first husband and children is usually Villamil, sometimes Villar Villamil.

Introduction

María Ignacia Rodríguez de Velasco y Osorio Barba (1778–1850). Known to history simply as "La Güera Rodríguez"—in English, "the Fair" or perhaps "Blonde" Rodríguez. A household name in Mexico yet barely known in the rest of the world. The witty beauty who allegedly charmed Simón Bolívar, Alexander von Humboldt, and Agustín de Iturbide. Banished from Mexico City for her part in a political intrigue. Involved in messy lawsuits with her first husband and then married twice more. The topic of malicious gossip as well as admiration during her lifetime. Later remembered in historical chronicles and in the press, as well as in novels, plays, comic books, movies, an opera, and a telenovela. Her fame exploded in 2010 during the bicentennial of the Grito de Dolores that initiated Mexico's struggle for independence. That year saw revivals and reprints of earlier works as well as new representations in popular publications, radio and television programs, a corrido, blogs, and lectures and performances uploaded to YouTube. Since then she has continued to be a darling of popular culture. Yet, until now, she has not received the scholarly biography she so richly deserves.

La Güera Rodríguez has fascinated me ever since, fifty years ago, I read *Life in Mexico* (1843) by Fanny Calderón de la Barca, the Scottish wife of

Spain's first minister in republican Mexico. Her lively account of living in Mexico City during 1840 and 1841 mentions La Güera repeatedly because the two women became fast friends who shared many pleasurable times together. Fanny reported—among other intriguing anecdotes—that Humboldt had pronounced La Güera the most beautiful woman he had ever seen.[1] Later I read the biographical novel by Artemio de Valle-Arizpe, *La Güera Rodríguez* (1949), which painted an unforgettable portrait of "one of the most brilliant figures" in Mexican history, a clever and rebellious woman who defied many conventions of the day.[2] And when, as a young graduate student, I stumbled upon several documents about her in the archives, I published a long excerpt from her 1802 divorce suit with her first husband and filed my notes away for future use.[3] Through all these years my well-worn copies of *Life in Mexico* and *La Güera Rodríguez* had an honored place on my bookshelf. So, when I started this project, I felt that I was going back to an old friend, one of the few Mexican women who left enough of a documentary trace for a solid biography, one whose life offered a unique window into the neglected social history of her day and who broke so many "rules" that we have to question whether those rules existed outside of our deeply ingrained stereotypes.

Yet as I looked at what had been written about La Güera Rodríguez over the past few decades, I barely recognized her. She had gone from playing a minor role in the independence movement to becoming a major protagonist. In the twentieth century not a single statue, avenue, or school was named for her—the recognition given several other heroines. Neither was she part of the official history taught to Mexican schoolchildren and enshrined in the exhibits at the Museum of National History.[4] In contrast, by 2010 posters announcing the play and opera bearing her name were all over Mexico City. When her glamorous image was paraded during street processions commemorating the bicentennial, bystanders immediately recognized her as one of Mexico's beloved patriots.[5] The Museo de la Mujer, a museum of Mexican women's history that opened in 2011, placed her as one of only four women in the room of "insurgent women," alongside the famous Leona Vicario, Josefa Ortiz de Domínguez (La Corregidora), and Mariana Rodríguez del Toro de Lazarín.[6] And Mexican writers made increasingly outlandish claims: "The Mother of the Patria" who as Iturbide's "adviser" was "the most politically powerful woman in the entire history of Mexico." "It is probable that without her, Mexico's independence never would have been consummated."[7] Some authors blithely asserted that she had affairs with many men, including Bolívar, Humboldt, and Iturbide. She was dubbed "a sex addict," "the Marilyn Monroe of her day," and even "one of the ten most famous prostitutes in history."[8]

At this point I realized that her afterlife in the 170 years since her death was worth studying in its own right. As I followed her rise from relative obscurity to fame, I saw her change before my very eyes, from a Proper Aristocratic Lady, to a Naughty Patriot Finally Tamed by a Man, to a Wise Woman, to a Feminist, and, finally, to a Fully Liberated Heroine. In trying to find the real Güera Rodríguez, I discovered that much of what I thought I knew about her was mistaken. And I noticed that once a false detail appeared it was subsequently repeated as if true in later works— sometimes even those written by scholars.

I therefore decided to expand the focus of my research from my initial attempt to write the definitive biography of doña María Ignacia Rodríguez— in any case an impossible task, given the lacunae in the documentation—to analyzing her many representations in historical, literary, and artistic narratives that variously labeled her as "remarkable," "magnificent and extraordinary," "astute," "mischievous," "seductive," "libertine," "depraved," "docile," a "nymphomaniac," and a "feminist." As I learned, she has been the subject of so many myths that it is exceedingly difficult to disentangle the woman from the legend.

I have nonetheless tried to separate fact from fiction. The first part of this book presents what I have been able to document about her life, much of it missing from—or distorted by—later representations. The picture that emerges is of a beautiful, vivacious socialite who confronted many vicissitudes with great resilience, but who did not defy the social norms of her day or play a central role in the struggle for independence. Yet even when shorn of the many myths that have clouded our vision, her true story is so fascinating that it does not need embellishment. Along with moments of high drama, comedy, and tragedy, it provides insight into one woman's life during a period for which we have few biographies. And it confirms the findings of historians who have questioned many stereotypes about women and gender in the late colonial and early republican periods.[9]

The second part of the book explores her journey after death, beginning with her disappearance from Mexican arts and letters in the second half of the nineteenth century and continuing through her resurrection and transformation in the twentieth century until, by the bicentennial of 2010, she had become an iconic figure. By examining these representations in chronological order, I show how her portrayal shifted over time and how each of her new identities reflected the cultural context and ideology of the narrators who recounted her tale with gusto. I also consider why she has exerted such a magnetic hold on generations of Mexicans.

Although the two sections of the book may be read independently, each one informs the other. The accounts published long after her death provided hypotheses for me to test as I pieced together her life story, and it, in turn, allowed me to determine which parts of the posthumous accounts were fictional. For example: Did she really have love affairs with Bolívar, Humboldt, and Iturbide? Was she really the author of the Plan de Iguala that ushered in Mexican independence? Was she really the model that the famous sculptor Manuel Tolsá used for the Virgen de los Dolores in Mexico City's famed La Profesa church? It turns out that none of these statements—nor many others—can be corroborated with historical documents, and some are demonstrably false. By tracing the emergence of falsehoods that became part of La Güera's legend, I demonstrate how, gradually, her mythical personage was created.

I could not have written this book forty-five years ago, when I began collecting information about doña María Ignacia Rodríguez. I was part of a generation of social historians that reacted against studying the elites to focus instead on the lower classes. I suppose I have mellowed with time. And I have been inspired by the resurgence of scholarly interest in the genre of biography, which has shown how much we can learn about myriad subjects from the detailed study of an individual life.[10] I have also become more self-conscious about the historian's craft and the difficulty of freeing ourselves from stereotypes and myths. In thinking about this problem, I have benefited from reading numerous works that examine the changing interpretations of historical figures.[11] By analyzing historical memory as distinct from what actually happened, these works reveal how present-day concerns shape the way we represent—and misrepresent—the past.

This book thus serves as a meditation on the construction of history. The successive transformations of La Güera Rodríguez highlight the large gap between memory and history, for her persona in popular culture is a far cry from the woman who lived long ago. It also shows that historical memory is never definitive and final, for the stories we tell about the past are constantly refashioned to reflect changing ideas about gender, race, class, politics, and nation. And it reminds us of the need to evaluate historical narratives carefully by paying close attention to who created each text, when, on the basis of what sources, and for what purpose. My hope is that this study of both the woman and the legend will help us sharpen our skills as critical readers who are not taken in by false facts and apocryphal stories.

PART ONE The Life

1 La Güera as a Young Woman, 1778–1808

Many readers have been introduced to La Güera Rodríguez—as I was—in the now classic *Life in Mexico* by Fanny Calderón de la Barca. So impressed was she with her new friend that, on the very same day they met, she wrote to a relative recounting the details of the visit. Fanny's oft-cited letter of February 1, 1840, gushed:

> Before I conclude this letter, I must tell you that I received a visit this morning from a very remarkable character, well known here by the name of La Güera Rodríguez, or the Fair Rodríguez. [She] is the celebrated beauty mentioned by Humboldt as the most beautiful woman he had seen in the whole course of his travels forty or fifty years ago. Considering the lapse of time which has passed since that distinguished traveller visited these parts, I was almost astonished when her card was sent up with a request for admission, and still more so to find that in spite of years and of the furrows which it pleases Time to plough in the loveliest faces, La Güera retains a profusion of fair curls without one gray hair, a set of beautiful white teeth, very fine eyes . . . and great vivacity.
>
> I found La Güera very agreeable, a great talker, and a perfect living chronicle. She must have been more pretty than beautiful—lovely hair, complexion and figure, and very gay and witty. She is lately married to her third husband, and had three daughters, all celebrated beauties: the Countess de Regla, who died in New York and was buried in the cathedral there; the

Marquesa de Guadalupe, also dead; and the Marquesa de Aguayo, now a handsome widow, to be seen every day in the Calle San Francisco, standing smiling in her balcony—fat and fair.

We spoke of Humboldt and, talking of herself as of a third person, she related to me all the particulars of his first visit, and his admiration of her; that she was then very young, about eighteen, though married and the mother of three children; and that when he came to visit her mother she was sitting sewing in a corner where the baron did not perceive her until, talking very earnestly on the subject of cochineal, he inquired if he could visit a certain district where there was a plantation of nopals.

"To be sure," said La Güera from her corner, "we can take M. De Humboldt there today."

Whereupon he, first perceiving her, stood amazed, and at length exclaimed: "*Válgame Dios!* [God protect me!] Who is that girl?"

Afterwards he was constantly with her, and, she says, more captivated by her wit than by her beauty, considering her a sort of western Madame de Staël . . . which leads me to suspect that the grave traveller was considerably under the influence of her fascinations, and that neither mines, mountains, geography, geology, geometry, petrified shells nor *alpenkalkstein* had occupied him to the exclusion of a slight *stratum* of flirtation. So I have caught him—it is a comfort to think that "sometimes even the great Humboldt nods!"

Her Mexican contemporaries did not need a foreign visitor to know about doña María Ignacia Rodríguez. Besides being a prominent member of high society, she was the subject of gossip on several occasions: in 1801 and 1802 during three very public marital disputes that included a scandalous ecclesiastical divorce suit; in 1810 when she was banished from the Mexican capital for her part in a political intrigue; and in 1822 when Emperor Iturbide's enemies attempted to discredit him by linking him to her romantically. The distinguished statesman and chronicler Carlos María de Bustamante mentioned "the famous Güera Rodríguez" several times in the diary he kept from December 1822 until his death in September 1848.[1] In 1840 Fanny Calderón pronounced her "a celebrated character" in Mexico City, "never called by any other name than La Güera Rodríguez."[2] Indeed, she was already known by that nickname at least as early as 1811, when insurgent leader Ignacio Allende referred to her at his trial as "the astute and famous *cortesana* [courtier] La Güera Rodríguez."[3] And her daughters were often identified first and foremost as "the daughters of La Güera," even though they were interesting and accomplished women in their own right.[4]

It is difficult to piece together a complete portrait of her life. The secondary literature, written long after her death, is full of inaccurate and contradictory information—even about such basic facts as how many children she had (seven, two of whom died in infancy), the name of her second husband (Juan Ignacio Briones), or what year she died (1850). The primary sources also leave much to be desired. Because her personal papers have not survived, I have been forced to rely on the few brief impressions of contemporary observers and the abundant but fragmented public records. Although she appeared in notarial protocols, birth and marriage registers, wills, ecclesiastical and civil court cases, and Inquisition files, these leave enormous gaps in her history. For some years we know a great deal about her and for others we know nothing at all. Most of the available documents were filtered through lawyers, notaries, or scribes and shaped to further a particular agenda. Aside from an occasional dramatic detail, they are dry and formulaic. They privilege male actors, thus making it difficult to reconstruct her female networks (and, still, many questions remain about her three husbands and her son; we even lack portraits of these men who played such an important part in her life). Moreover, few of these documents shed light on her inner thoughts and feelings. Despite their limitations, these sources nonetheless paint a fascinating picture of her life. They do not, however, support her later portrayals as a libertine rebel or a major independence heroine.

CHILDHOOD, 1778–1794

María Ignacia (Ygnacia, as she spelled it) Xaviera Raphaela Rodríguez de Velasco y Osorio Barba was born in Mexico City on November 20, 1778 and baptized that same day in the parish of the Sagrario. She was the first child of Licenciado don Antonio Rodríguez de Velasco and doña María Ignacia Osorio Barba, both members of illustrious families. Her father held the prestigious position of *regidor perpetuo* in the *ayuntamiento* (councillor in perpetuity of the city council). He also had an appointment as *alcalde honorario* of the Sala del Crimen de la Real Audiencia (officer of the royal criminal court) and was a member of the Consejo de su Majestad (king's council) and the Ilustre y Real Colegio de Abogados

(royal lawyers' association). Her maternal grandfather, Captain don
Gaspar Osorio, was a wealthy landowner and knight (*caballero*) in the
chivalrous Order of Calatrava. Her well-placed uncles included her mother's brother, don Luis Osorio Barba, who was the administrator of the
Casa de Moneda (royal mint), and the husband of her father's sister, don
Silvestre Díaz de la Vega, a member of the Real y Supremo Consejo de
Hacienda (royal treasury) and director of the Renta de Tabaco (tobacco
monopoly).[5] Her family was therefore part of the Mexican elite in which
aristocrats and highly educated professionals mixed in what Doris Ladd
called "a great extended family whose members occupied a privileged
position in society."[6]

We know very little about La Güera's childhood. She grew up with two
sisters. Josefa, a year younger, married Antonio Manuel Cosío Acevedo,
the fifth Marqués de Uluapa, in 1796. Vicenta, five years younger, married
José Marín y Muros, an employee of the Real Aduana (royal customs
house), in 1808.[7] Her parents' house on the street of San Francisco—today
the glorious Madero street, lined with elegant colonial mansions such as
the spectacular House of Tiles—put her in the center of Mexico City, a few
blocks from the cathedral and viceregal palace and a few doors from the
residences of several counts and marquises. Subsequent documents reveal
the family's excellent connections to members of the nobility, the Catholic
Church, and the royal government.

La Güera lived in the comfortable world of high society where families
resided close to each other, visited often, attended church regularly, and
enjoyed a rich social life. The available sources reveal that she frequented
theater performances, dinner parties, and dances. She joined in the singing and card playing at animated *tertulias* (social gatherings). Following
the old Spanish tradition, she received visits from friends on her saint's
day (July 31, the feast of St. Ignatius) and corresponded by calling on
them on their days. The family also traveled to nearby villages for entertainment, for example, attending the annual summer fiesta at San Agustín
de las Cuevas that featured grand festivities as well as gambling and cockfights. And she was a guest at her friends' country homes, among them the
Casa de la Bola, today a beautiful museum in Tacubaya.

The Catholic religion was an integral part of the fabric of daily life.
Several witnesses in the ecclesiastical divorce case declared that she had

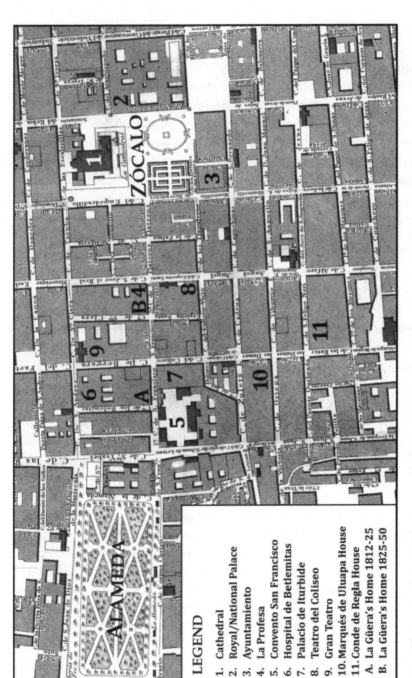

Map of the center of Mexico City. Prepared by Silvia Arrom and Daniel Oran based on Diego García Conde, *Plan general de la Ciudad de México* (London: Eduardo Mogg, 1811). Benson Latin American Collection, University of Texas at Austin, http://www.lib.utexas .edu/maps/historical/garcia_conde-mexico-1811.jpg.

LEGEND

1. Cathedral
2. Royal/National Palace
3. Ayuntamiento
4. La Profesa
5. Convento San Francisco
6. Hospital de Betlemitas
7. Palacio de Iturbide
8. Teatro del Coliseo
9. Gran Teatro
10. Marqués de Uluapa House
11. Conde de Regla House

A. La Güera's Home 1812-25
B. La Güera's Home 1825-50

been raised with the "best" Christian and moral values and that her virtue was "sustained by frequenting religious acts."[8] One witness described an incident that occurred as La Güera was leaving the cathedral after receiving communion, and others mentioned her regular prayers and confession. They also show that she spent considerable time in the company of priests, several of whom had known her since she was a child.

A curious document in the Inquisition records indicates how seriously her mother took religious precepts and propriety. On May 17, 1800, she turned to Friar Manuel Arévalo, an old family friend, to ask whether she should denounce certain indecent prints she had found in the house of one of her daughters (either Josefa or Ignacia, since Vicenta still lived at home). The prints were images of the latest French fashions provided by their Italian hairdresser, Carlos Franco. Presumably because they showed low-cut necklines, the prudish mother considered them "very scandalous and conducive to sin." Arévalo decided to report them to the Holy Office. After interviewing the *peinador de damas,* the Inquisitors confiscated the fashion plates in his salon as well as those in the daughter's house and let the matter end there.[9] The incident not only shows that the women in La Güera's social circle followed the styles popular in Europe, but also reveals the close ties between the aristocracy and Church officials, to whom they regularly turned for help in family matters.

The girls must have received some formal instruction, if not in a school then at home, as was the custom in their social class. By the late colonial period elite women studied reading, writing, arithmetic, and at least a smattering of geography and history. Evidence of La Güera's education is that she signed her name with a sure hand and penned several letters and petitions, conserved as part of long judicial files, without the help of an attorney. She would also have learned fine sewing and embroidery as well as the musical skills that were considered essential for women of refinement. Later events show that she knew her rights and had been well prepared for the responsibilities of protecting her family's interests. Yet we cannot know if she was one of the well-educated women of her generation like Leona Vicario (who was so learned that she translated Fénelon's *Aventures de Télémaque* from the French) or whether she was one of the "ignorant" society ladies decried by Fanny Calderón, who claimed that many of her Mexican friends never opened a book besides their missals.[10]

FIRST MARRIAGE, 1794–1805

When she was but fifteen years old, María Ignacia became engaged to a military officer twelve years her senior: don José Gerónimo López de Peralta de Villar Villamil y Primo, a lieutenant in the Primer Batallón del Regimiento de Milicias Provinciales. This was a good match for La Güera. Her future husband's family was part of the untitled nobility of New Spain because they traced their descent from the conqueror Gerónimo López and had a *mayorazgo* (entail) that kept much of their wealth in an indivisible trust. Its holdings were quite valuable, consisting of the corn and barley producing Hacienda de Bojay near Atitalaquia (today in the state of Hidalgo) as well as several additional properties.[11] Villamil's widowed father was the possessor of the *mayorazgo*; a knight of the Real Maestranza de Ronda; and served at times in the Mexico City government as *alcalde honorario*.[12]

The couple first had to overcome the opposition of Villamil's father. In objecting to the union, the elder José Gerónimo Villamil (for they shared the same name) cited his twenty-eight-year-old son's failure to obtain paternal permission before contracting *esponsales* (the promise to marry), as well as his failure to present proof of his bride's pure lineage (*limpieza de sangre e hidalguía*). The real reason, as suggested by a subsequent lawsuit, was that the father did not believe his son was in a position to support a family. The younger Villamil turned to the Real Audiencia, the royal court that had jurisdiction over affairs related to *mayorazgos* by virtue of their being granted by the king of Spain. The judges found no merit in the father's complaint and authorized the marriage. Indeed, the court noted that the father had not raised any objection to "la niña" herself and that her "illustrious birth" was well known.[13]

The wedding took place in the chapel of the Hospital de los Bethlemitas in Mexico City on September 7, 1794. La Güera was just shy of sixteen. The witnesses on the bride's side were her parents. On the groom's side they were don José María Otero y Castillo, the captain of Villamil's regiment, and Doctor don Ignacio del Rivero Casal y Alvarado, Villamil's cousin and a member of the Colegio de Abogados who would later represent him in the lawsuit against his father.[14] In a sign of the bad blood that existed between father and son, the former did not attend the ceremony

Figure 1. This portrait of doña María Ignacia Rodríguez is the only known image of her. The miniature, by an unknown artist, may have been created around the time of her wedding in 1794. Reproduced in the exhibit catalogue *Veinte mujeres notables en la vida de México.*

and only found out about it after the fact, when his son informed him by letter.[15]

Despite the Villamil family's wealth, the newlyweds lived in straitened circumstances because he had not yet inherited his father's *mayorazgo.* Thus, three weeks after the wedding, Villamil sued his father for an allowance from his anticipated inheritance in order to maintain his young wife in the style to which she was accustomed—and to which he, as the future holder of the *mayorazgo*, believed that he was entitled. He also claimed that his father still owed him his deceased mother's *legítima* (the portion of a parent's estate guaranteed by law to each child).

The acrimonious lawsuit lasted over three years. On January 30, 1795, the *audiencia* ordered the father to provide his son with an annual stipend of 1,500 pesos, retroactive to January 1. The father protested in long, flowery petitions but reluctantly obeyed. The son countered that this allowance was not only insufficient but irregularly paid and that it should be retroactive to September 8, 1794 (the day after his wedding). The court ultimately backed the son and raised his stipend to 2,000 pesos a year. Because the judges did not trust the father to comply, they approved an arrangement whereby doña Eugenia López Rodena, the tenant who leased the Hacienda de Bojay, was to pay 2,000 pesos directly to the son and send the rest of the rent (120 *cargas* of barley) to his father until 1799, when her contract expired and the younger Villamil could take over the property himself.

By 1802 Villamil's position had improved. Although he would not receive the entire *mayorazgo* until after his father's death in 1803, he identified himself in court proceedings as a captain of the regiment of Granaderos de las Milicias Provinciales de México and knight of both the Orden de Calatrava and of the Real Maestranza de Ronda. The honorific positions were unpaid, however. His principal salary derived from his position as *subdelegado* of the district of Tacuba, close to Mexico City, where the couple made their home.[16] He supplemented this revenue with the profits from Bojay, which would have varied depending on the weather and markets. In addition, Villamil's economic situation was complicated by mortgages on his holdings and by ongoing litigation with nearby indigenous villagers whom he charged with "insolently" and unlawfully occupying a quarter of the estate.[17]

Although they were far from poor, Villamil's income barely covered the expenses of the growing family. Their house in Tacuba was apparently comfortable: according to a description in the divorce case, it was the venue for elegant parties and included a lovely patio, outfitted with a swing, where they entertained friends. The family was attended to by at least four servants, who testified in the lawsuit. There were nonetheless times when La Güera complained to her confessor, Fray José Herrera, that she lacked sufficient money for basic necessities. Meanwhile, the couple was running through the dowry that María Ignacia brought to the marriage and which, according to later documents, would be completely consumed.[18] And Villamil was borrowing money to fill in the gaps.[19] It is indeed likely that these financial difficulties contributed to their marital strife.

During their eleven-year union the couple had six children, the first five in quick succession. María Josefa, named after La Güera's sister, was born on July 7, 1795; María Antonia, named after her maternal grandfather, was born on May 14, 1797; Gerónimo Mariano, named after his father, was born on September 9, 1798; Agustín Gerónimo arrived on March 2, 1800; María Guadalupe, named after her paternal aunt, on May 28, 1801; and María de la Paz on June 12, 1805 (see appendix B).

The children's baptismal records provide information about where their mother was when they were born, for at a time when babies often died soon after birth, baptisms usually took place on the same day that they came into the world. Antonia was baptized in Orizaba (Veracruz), an indication that in the early part of their marriage María Ignacia may have accompanied her husband on his military assignments. By 1800 they had established their residence in Tacuba, where Agustín was baptized. The other children were baptized in Mexico City, perhaps because La Güera went to her parents' house to give birth. Despite their access to the best medical care, however, two of the children perished before reaching adulthood. Agustín died when he was eight months old and Guadalupe, still a single *doncella*, died at the age of fifteen.

The couple's choice of their children's godparents provides a glimpse of their social network. For their first-born, Josefa, they chose La Güera's mother to serve as her *madrina;* and for the second-born, Antonia, they chose as *padrinos* her aunt and uncle, doña Bárbara Rodríguez de Velasco and her husband don Silvestre Díaz de la Vega. For the other children, the couple reached outside the family. For example, Gerónimo's godparents were the Mariscales de Castilla and Marqueses de Ciria; and Guadalupe's godfather was the Conde de Contramina. Villamil's father was notably absent from the list of those so honored.

The marriage was quite stormy and because the couple aired their conflicts publicly, they left a rich documentary trail. Their quarrels seem to have been fueled by Villamil's jealousy, exacerbated by long absences during which he attended to affairs on his remote properties or served with his regiment in provincial cities. On October 21, 1801, he accused his wife of adultery with a Frenchman, don Luis Ceret, and demanded his imprisonment or expulsion from Mexico; but he withdrew the charges ten days later. His suspicions continued, however. On July 4, 1802, he returned from the Hacienda de Bojay to find his wife outside the house talking to two priests, José Mariano Beristáin and Ramón Cardeña y Gallardo, and in a fit of rage (and in plain view of the Conde de Contramina) fired his gun at her. Although it failed to go off—and he later claimed he only meant to scare her—La Güera fled Tacuba for her parents' house in Mexico City. That very night she appeared with her father before Viceroy Félix Berenguer de Marquina (who as captain-general had jurisdiction over men with military privileges, or *fueros*) and filed a criminal case against her husband for attempted murder.[20]

Villamil was placed under house arrest the next day, released on bail eight weeks later on August 29, and immediately filed for an ecclesiastical divorce—a separation of bed and board, since absolute divorce would not be legal in Mexico until the twentieth century. His petition cited his wife's "sacrilegious adultery" with three unnamed subjects, whom he subsequently identified as the distinguished priests José Mariano Beristáin, a canon of the metropolitan cathedral and author of the monumental *Biblioteca hispano-americana septentrional*; Ramón Cardeña y Gallardo, the newly appointed canon of the Guadalajara cathedral; and Ignacio Ramírez, a cleric in the archdiocese of Mexico.

The records of the divorce case are nearly four hundred pages long, full of bitter recriminations and obstructionist legal maneuvers. The couple fought about where La Güera should live and who should keep the children. Villamil spread the rumor that his wife was pregnant, which a doctor found to be false, and refused to pay her expenses during the trial, the source of yet more petitions. The case became bogged down in jurisdictional squabbles, because although divorce cases were normally handled by ecclesiastical authorities, viceregal officials had intervened in this one from the start.

The majority of the filings related to the *depósito*, the residence where the court placed a woman during such proceedings, as much to protect the husband's honor as to safeguard the wife. The viceroy had ordered La Güera's "deposit" in the house of her maternal uncle, don Luis Osorio, on July 5, 1802, immediately after she initiated the criminal case against her husband and before he requested the divorce. From that refuge she petitioned for custody of her children. Since mothers normally had custody of children under three years of age, she would have taken one-year-old Guadalupe with her. She also "wrested from my arms" (in Villamil's words) another daughter who was "not even in the age of lactation," probably Antonia, then five. Seven-year-old Josefa was already boarding at the Colegio de la Enseñanza, the best girls' school in Mexico City, which, following the custom in her social class, she attended from the age of six to fourteen.[21] Only four-year-old Gerónimo may have remained in his father's care.

Complaining that his wife enjoyed excessive liberty in her uncle's house, Villamil asked that she be moved to a convent or *colegio* where she could be kept in strict seclusion. He accused her of receiving visitors, "walking freely in the streets," dressing immodestly even when going to the cathedral, spending too much time with her lawyer, the Licenciado Juan Francisco Azcárate, and even hosting a party where "Italian singers" were brought for her entertainment—allegations that she roundly denied.

The ecclesiastical authorities nonetheless believed them and acceded to Villamil's petition. On the morning of September 30, when La Güera learned that the *provisor vicario* (ecclesiastical judge) had ordered her removal from Osorio's house with a troop of eight to twelve men, she considered it such an emergency that she immediately wrote the viceroy without waiting for her lawyer to arrive, imploring him to prevent the move. This letter, one of the few I have found that are written in her own hand, reveals her unmediated voice. Although it lacks the flowery language used by her attorneys, it shows that she was not only literate but familiar with the formal greetings, closings, and abbreviations used by well-educated Mexicans. It also shows how the rumor mill worked in her social network, as well as how she fought back against her husband by using her connections to important people, including the viceroy.

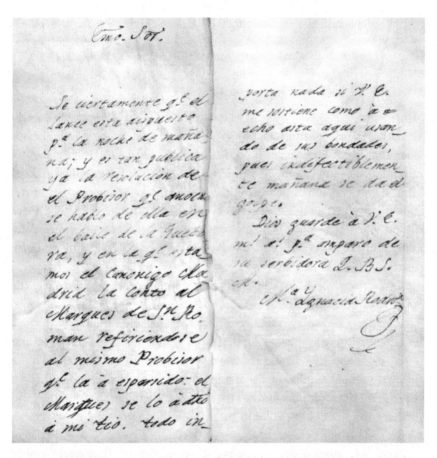

Figure 2. Letter written in La Güera's own hand to the viceroy, September 30, 1802, in the case file of the ecclesiastical divorce between María Ignacia Rodríguez and José Gerónimo Villamil. Archivo General de la Nación, Criminal, vol. 582, exp. 1 (1802), cuaderno 3, ff. 146–146v.

Your Excellency:

I know with certainty that the move is planned for tomorrow night. The resolution of the provisor is so public that last night the news was the talk of *la Guevara's* dance [Michaela Guevara, the daughter of the regent of the *audiencia*], and today the canon Madrid told the Marqués de San Román, referring to what the provisor himself had said; and the marqués told my uncle. Everything is lost unless Your Excellency supports me as you have kindly done until now, because otherwise the attack will inevitably take place tomorrow.

God give Your Excellency many years for the benefit of your servant

Q.B.S.M. [Who Kisses Your Hand]

Mª *Ygnacia Rodrig^z*

With this brief petition La Güera succeeded in stopping what she considered an assault on her person, for the provisor desisted when he was reminded that the viceroy had ordered her *depósito*. Eventually the king himself was consulted as to whether the regal or ecclesiastical authority should prevail when they disagreed in such cases. The answer—that it was the province of the ecclesiastical officers to decide matters concerning matrimonial cases—arrived from Spain in August of 1803, long after the case had been abandoned.[22]

Before the divorce suit could proceed, the viceroy tried to reconcile the couple (the standard attempt at *conciliación*). His efforts failed, however. Villamil proposed such severe conditions for a reunion—that his wife obey him in everything and be prohibited from seeing her sisters, parents, and other "persons who have been the cause of our conflicts"—that La Güera rejected them as totally unacceptable. Indeed, her attorney labeled them "the infamous conditions under which a prostitute might be reunited" and further evidence of how Villamil "treated her not as a companion but as a *sierva* [servant]."

Each side presented witnesses whose testimony, not surprisingly, conflicted. La Güera's witnesses—nine highly respected gentlemen: six priests, two military officers, and the family doctor[23]—claimed that she was the innocent and long-suffering victim of Villamil's jealousy, quick temper, and violence. Several gentlemen testified to the *mala vida* she endured. The curate of Atitalaquia, Doctor don Alejandro García Jove, declared that when she arrived at the Hacienda de Bojay a year earlier, her mother—"afflicted by the separation from her daughter"—had asked him to keep an eye on her because she feared "the mistreatment that here, far from her parents and relatives, her husband might inflict on her." The mother had ample reason to worry. The eminent doctoral canon of Guadalupe, Franciso Beye Cisneros, an old friend of both families, declared that Villamil treated his wife badly, "beating and abusing her, such that she was many times bathed in her blood." One of her confessors, Vicar Francisco Manuel Arévalo, likewise testified that he had more than once seen her "bathed in blood and covered with bruises." García Jove added that he had found "the afflicted lady . . . crying because of her deplorable situation." And she had often sought their advice about what she should do.

All but one of her witnesses pronounced her completely blameless and testified to her "proper, pure, and Christian" comportment. The Franciscan priest Juan Francisco Domínguez, who had known both spouses since they were children, believed that she bore some responsibility for the couple's discord because she dressed "with profanity" and treated her admirers with too much familiarity. Yet he emphatically denied that she had committed adultery. The other gentlemen described her good conduct, prudence, and attempts to please her husband. According to García Jove, she had even accompanied Villamil on the long ride to Bojay while she was bleeding, "perhaps risking her life" only to satisfy him. Yet when she sought treatment for her ailments by going to bathe in a "very beneficial spring" about one league from the hacienda, he let her go alone, a sign of his total indifference. (When word got out, a kind lady from a neighboring town, doña Mariana Díaz Gorráez, took pity and went along to assist her.)

Her witnesses unanimously blamed Villamil for starting their fights. Lieutenant Colonel don Mariano Soto Carrillo, a friend of both spouses, explained that Villamil couldn't deal with the fact that his young wife, "whom nature has adorned with many gifts," attracted the attention of many men. Soto added that "there is little consonance between Villamil's thoughts and actions": on the one hand, he "retired to Tacuba to keep his wife from seeing people," and, on the other, "he organized dance parties to which he invited the principal residents of Mexico." He showed her off at card-playing evenings, "even insisting that she lead the group in singing an *ejercicio acantonado* and making sure that she dressed in a way that was sure to inspire passions." Then he would fly into a rage when men noticed her and even complained that "he feared that his wife was a prostitute." Thus "doña María Ignacia had to put up great resistance to liberate herself from a multitude of admirers who sought her out because of her husband's false charges." Indeed, Villamil's humors were so "disordered" that, as she confided to the parish priest García Jove, if her husband saw

Figure 3. A *tertulia,* or social gathering in a private home, such as those that incited the jealousy of La Güera's husband when she attracted the attention of their guests by leading the singing. Cumplido, *Album mexicano,* vol. 1, p. 401. Harvard Library.

her praying, he would ask: "What are you doing? Praying against me?" So he was hardly a model spouse.

But she didn't leave him, even after several friends recommended that she seek what was known at the time as the "unhappy remedy" of a legal separation. Indeed, the vicar Arévalo praised her discreet attempts to hide her difficult economic and personal situation in order "to avoid upsetting her parents and dishonoring her husband." When Villamil threatened her life, however, she reached the end of her patience. As Soto Carrillo explained, "Seeing that she was alive only because of the good fortune that a pistol failed to fire, she fears and resists a reunion to preserve her life." Even then, it was her husband—not she—who initiated the divorce proceedings, for if turning to priests and civil authorities to resolve marital problems was a normal strategy for Mexican women, seeking a divorce was a last resort that carried considerable stigma.

Villamil's witnesses were four servants, a dependent, and a scribe. Despite being mostly "lowly people" who were, according to her lawyer, "susceptible to pressure," they could not confirm the adultery. They nonetheless suspected it might be true because La Güera was so sociable and fun loving. She evidently continued attending parties and entertaining visitors during her husband's absences. Not only did she host her little sister, "la niña Vicentina," but she received visits from three priests: the canon Beristáin, who, as Villamil's *compadre* was a fictive relative; Beristáin's nephew, the canon Cardeña; and the cleric Ramírez. Moreover, Beristáin and Ramírez stayed overnight on at least one occasion. She also attended a dinner party at Beristáin's house in Tacuba, taking dishes prepared by her cook. On the Wednesday of the Fiesta del Espíritu Santo she accompanied him to San Agustín de las Cuevas (against her husband's orders, he later claimed) and did not return until dawn. Beristáin did not deny these facts. On the contrary, in a long letter to his *compadre*, he explained that these incidents were public knowledge and proved nothing except his close friendship with the family. (He also reminded Villamil that he had always brought important visitors to the Villamil home to introduce them, as a sign of his esteem.) Lieutenant Juan de Roa, Villamil's assistant, declared that he had heard that doña María Ignacia "loves dances, diversions at all hours of the night, and being courted." Despite living in his employer's house, however, he had not seen anything amiss with her behavior. The household cook, the widowed mestiza Juana Marcelina Campos, only criticized her mistress for failing to make sure the servants fulfilled their religious obligations. The seamstress, the single *castiza* María Marcelina Salinas, declared that she held her mistress in high esteem.

In the end, Villamil was unable to prove his charges. Even his own relatives, friends, and colleagues took La Güera's side—and they would remain her lifelong friends, appearing periodically in later documents. A close reading of the case files suggests that he initiated the lawsuit to get back at her for accusing him of attempted murder and causing him to be detained. Both the timing of the suit—immediately after his release from house arrest—and his failure to give the names of her alleged lovers in his first petition are highly suspicious. His proposed conditions for reuniting with his wife also show his overriding concern with his honor and reputation: in addition to demanding her total obedience, he offered to drop the divorce suit if the authorities would publicly proclaim his honor unsullied and if those who knew of the case (the Rodríguezes, Uluapas, and the Conde de Contramina) promised never to speak of it again. Beye Cisneros had another theory: that Villamil's charges against her were concocted "to excuse the abominable fact of his having beaten her many times." The preponderance of evidence indeed points to her innocence and suggests that she was a battered wife and he a volatile, vain, and hot-tempered individual who was consumed by jealousy.

After four months the paper trail went cold, an indication that the suit was dropped (as often happened in Mexican divorce cases). A few notes in the military archives reveal that on December 23, 1802, La Güera, still chafing in her forced enclosure, petitioned to be allowed out occasionally to take some exercise, per her doctor's orders. Arguing that the *depósito* was never meant to be "a prison" and that there was nothing "illicit" in her outings, she promised always to go out in the company of her uncle, aunt, or other relatives. Her request was granted on January 12, 1803, yet the *depósito* was not immediately lifted because the case against Villamil for attempted murder was still open. By June 1803 she had nonetheless left her uncle's house and may have gone to live with her parents, where Humboldt found her sewing in a corner when he visited. The last entry in the criminal file, dated March 24, 1804, noted that the case against Villamil had not yet been resolved.[24]

La Güera appears to have continued her active social life during this interlude. If we are to believe the story that she later told Fanny Calderón, she spent much time in the company of the famed Prussian scientist during his stay in Mexico City, which he visited from April 12, 1803, to January 9, 1804. Even if she was exaggerating the degree of their friendship, it is quite plausible that (as she said) she took Humboldt to visit a plantation of nopal cactuses on the outskirts of the capital and that they saw each other on several occasions. This friendship would not have raised eyebrows in her social circle. Elite Mexicans were known for their gracious hospitality to foreign visitors, and—contrary to the prevalent stereotype—men and women frequently interacted outside of marriage. Indeed, even the jealous Villamil had regularly sent his wife to the theater in the company of his cousin, Doctor don Ignacio del Rivero—though he later charged that on these outings, Rivero covered up her adulterous behavior.[25] In any case, La

Güera's friendship with Humboldt was probably more episodic than constant because he spent long hours examining papers in the viceregal archive and also left the capital on scientific expeditions. Moreover, their visits most likely included her parents, sisters, or Humboldt's traveling companions Carlos Montúfar and Aimé Bonpland.

At some point La Güera reunited with her husband who, according to the Licenciado Andrés de Alcántara, another of her lawyers, had "himself admitted that he cannot live without my minor client forever." By then he had inherited the full Villamil *mayorazgo*. His improved financial situation may have contributed to domestic peace: the couple's last child, Paz—perhaps named for the new phase in the marriage—was born on June 12, 1805. But the captain never met her because he had died on January 26, at the age of thirty-nine. Death had overtaken him in Querétaro, where he may have been visiting his mother's relatives or was perhaps stationed with his regiment. In his will he named doña María Ignacia Rodríguez as the guardian of their children and directed "that all the papers, letters and other documents concerning the divorce case I filed against my wife shall be immediately burned to obliterate any memory of the matter." As the historian Fernando Muñoz Altea concluded, had there been any truth to Villamil's accusations in that lawsuit, "he would not have granted her the custody of his children or ordered the destruction of those papers."[26]

Thus the difficult marriage came to an end. Because their ecclesiastical divorce was never granted, María Ignacia became the widow of the *mayorazgo* Villamil, not a divorcée, after his death.

WIDOWHOOD AND SECOND MARRIAGE, 1805–1807

Widowed at age twenty-six with five young children, La Güera moved back to Mexico City, where her parents and sisters lived. Although twentieth-century authors would portray her as a merry widow, her life was not in fact easy. For one thing, she was saddled with a chronically ill daughter. When Guadalupe finally died in July 1816, her aunt Josefa lamented that "the poor innocent child has been sickly for the space of eleven years."[27] That would have put the onset of her illness in 1805, just as Villamil was dying and baby Paz was making her appearance. Perhaps four-year-old

Guadalupe had contracted tuberculosis, the dreaded wasting disease that could drag on for many years and killed a large proportion of people in all social classes in the early nineteenth century.

La Güera's financial situation was also precarious, because she had no property of her own. Colonial law was designed to protect widows by guaranteeing them a share of their spouse's estate and allowing them to recover the dowry they had brought to the marriage, but that did not help in this case. *Mayorazgos,* as indivisible family foundations, were excluded from the community property from which a widow automatically inherited; there had been no *gananciales* (accrued assets) in the marriage; and there was nothing left of her dowry. Villamil had only left debts and his property, tied up in entail, could not be sold. In addition, she had to fend off his creditors. The magnitude of his debts is referenced in a response she gave in 1808 to a demand for payment of a 2,000-peso obligation: she could not pay, she insisted, because her late husband had left debts totaling more than 30,000 pesos which, because he did not leave any *bienes libres* (property outside the entail), could not be repaid.[28]

Villamil's *mayorazgo* was nonetheless quite valuable, and their six-year-old son Gerónimo stood to inherit it when he reached the age of majority (twenty-five). Until then, La Güera served as his guardian and managed his properties—one of the responsibilities of being a good mother. As a woman, she had to appoint male attorneys to represent her in court, and her choice of representatives was critical to her success—or, at times, difficulties, since some of these men unfortunately let her down. In 1805, "in the instant that I became a widow," she chose her father and her uncle José Miguel Rodríguez de Velasco to manage her affairs.[29] In later years she relied on a series of important men, including Villamil's cousin, Ignacio del Rivero, and family friends Domingo Malo e Iturbide and José María Guridi y Alcocer. For her part, she apparently discharged her duties with such honesty that "no one can say that she ever misappropriated even the smallest quantity."[30]

Meanwhile, she and her children were assigned an annual stipend from the *mayorazgo*: 2,000 pesos for the mother and four daughters and 2,000 for the male heir apparent.[31] Although this sum represented less than half of what the properties produced each year, it was a generous allowance at a time when a high government functionary, such as her uncle Luis Osorio, earned some 6,000 pesos a year.[32] Still, 4,000 pesos barely allowed her to maintain a fine house with many servants and to raise five children in the manner that was customary among the Mexican elites. Moreover, her stipend would end when Gerónimo came of age. La Güera therefore borrowed 9,500 pesos against the entailed property. No doubt she pinched pennies as well.[33]

Within two years she had found a new husband, a wealthy widower who was twenty-five years older than she. We know almost nothing about her second marriage except that it was very brief. The groom was the distinguished Doctor don Juan Ignacio Briones Fernández de Ricaño y Bustos. A native of Guanajuato, he had served as *vicerector* of the Colegio de San Ildefonso in Mexico City from 1779 to at least 1781. He then moved to Querétaro, where he served as *comisario de guerra honorario, alcalde ordinario,* and *censor regi de conclusiones.* By 1807 he was back in the viceregal capital, a lawyer of the *audiencia* and Colegio de Abogados.[34] Thus, the second time around, instead of a dashing military officer, La Güera chose to marry a highly educated and well-connected member of the colonial bureaucracy.

The couple wed on February 10, 1807. The bride was twenty-eight years old and the groom fifty-three. The nuptials took place at seven in the evening at their house on Coliseo street. Her old friend, Canon José Mariano Beristáin, officiated. La Güera's uncle Silvestre Díaz de la Vega and her brother-in law, the Marqués de Uluapa, served as witnesses. According to the marriage certificate, the wedding was attended by many "distinguished persons of this vicinity and commerce."[35]

Yet death again intervened. Briones died only six months after the wedding, on August 16, 1807, leaving his widow pregnant with her seventh (and last) child. His posthumous daughter, Victoria, was born on April 22, 1808. As with the other children, her full name was much longer: Victoria Rita Juana Nepomuceno Josefa Ygnacia Luisa Gonzaga Briones Rodríguez. But her life was short: she perished at the age of a year and a half, in the fall of 1809.[36]

Briones's death embroiled La Güera in a nasty dispute with his family over the estate, for he had named his brother and two sisters as his "universal heirs" in an earlier will—probably made before he married and certainly before he knew that his wife was expecting a child.[37] The litigation was complicated because, according to law, a widow was guaranteed a portion of the estate and the birth of a posthumous child added another compulsory heir. Because the young widow apparently held onto her deceased husband's property, his siblings took her to court. They even questioned whether the child was their brother's. Indeed, on May 31, 1808, after receiving news of Victoria's birth, they sent a request to Mexico City to have a priest certify whether María Ignacia had truly been pregnant and given birth. The answer was affirmative. In fact, two weeks after Briones died, when she appointed Rivero as her representative to go to Querétaro to retrieve Briones's will from the family's *casa mortuaria*, she explained that she could not do so herself "because she was with child and could not walk."[38] When Victoria lived long enough to break his will, she became her father's sole heir. Then, when Victoria died, La Güera inherited everything (although she eventually agreed to give the Briones family a fifth of the estate to end the lawsuit).[39]

Doña María Ignacia Rodríguez became the prosperous owner of cash, gold and silver jewelry, a house in San Luis de la Paz, two houses in Querétaro, and the haciendas of San Isidro and Santa María in the state of Guanajuato. These holdings were worth the substantial sum of 320,000 pesos—today the equivalent of several million pesos. Her economic position was thus notably improved. Although this legacy could not compare with the enormous wealth of the richest families of the realm, it is certainly true, as Carlos María de Bustamante noted years later, that her second marriage to a rich man left her heir to a "not inconsiderable fortune."[40] Having entered the union with no property to her name, she emerged a wealthy widow.

CONCLUSION

When Briones died in 1807, La Güera was twenty-eight years old. She had come through some difficult times with remarkable resilience. With support from her family, friends, and clergy, she had weathered an abusive first marriage and scandalous accusations without incurring any evident stigma, successfully defended herself in court, managed a household with limited funds for many years, and buried two husbands. She had endured repeated pregnancies to bear six children in ten years, lost one in infancy, and faced a new widowhood pregnant with another and fighting for her inheritance. Although she would subsequently live quite comfortably, she would encounter unforeseen headaches caused by the independence wars. Her life was also complicated by the responsibilities of motherhood. And she would raise her brood on her own, waiting the better part of two decades before remarrying.

2 La Güera on Her Own, 1808–1820

Following Victoria's birth on April 22, 1808, the widowed doña María Ignacia Rodríguez had six children to look after, ranging in age from a baby to a teenager. She had considerable property to manage, both hers and her minor children's. She lived in the sophisticated City of Palaces, a major metropolis with some 150,000 residents and a rich cultural life. And she had a large extended family and many friends to keep her occupied. Yet she did not just devote herself to private life, for the period between 1808 and 1824 that encompassed her second widowhood also coincided with the tumultuous years of the independence struggle that would change her world in unexpected ways. Like many Mexican women, she too entered the fray, for she was fully engaged in the world around her. She faced banishment from Mexico City for her part in an early political intrigue, saw her fortune diminish, suffered the death and grave illnesses of several loved ones, was involved in lengthy litigation, and—as always—kept malicious tongues wagging.

A WIDOW ONCE MORE, 1808–1809

After Briones died in August 1807, La Güera did not return to live with her parents. Instead, she stayed in the house on Coliseo street, raising her children and attending to the legal and financial responsibilities that came with widowhood. By April 8, 1808, she was managing her deceased husband's estate and defending herself in the lawsuit brought by his siblings. The confusion over the legacy was resolved when Victoria lived long enough to break her father's will. When La Güera inherited the entire estate because of the death of her infant daughter, she turned her attention to investing—and thus safeguarding—her fortune. Thus, on December 29, 1809, she expanded her real estate holdings by buying the Hacienda de la Patera and the adjacent Rancho del Rosario in the district of Tacuba, close to the village of Guadalupe. Because she lacked the cash to buy them outright, she put down 18,000 pesos toward the approximately 70,000-peso cost and took out mortgages from the Colegio de San Gregorio and the Convento de Santa Clara to complete the purchase.[1]

There was nothing unusual about these activities. It was normal for Mexican women to own and manage property, as attested to in notarial records and court cases, where they appeared regularly. Widows were particularly active because they enjoyed full juridical capacity and therefore did not have to submit to anyone's authority, as was required of married women. Since real estate was considered the safest investment in colonial times, the acquisition of property close to the capital was a wise decision. La Patera was an especially advantageous purchase because it was next to the Hacienda de la Escalera, owned by La Güera's uncle José Miguel Rodríguez de Velasco, thereby expanding the area controlled by the extended family—another common strategy at a time when individuals identified their interests with those of their kin. It was also normal for properties to be heavily mortgaged to the Church institutions that served as the principal banks during this period. And bitter lawsuits between family members over the division of estates were quite common, for this was an extremely litigious society, at least when it came to the propertied classes.

The Inquisition archives also show La Güera's concern with another aspect of her family's future. On June 6, 1809, she gave her power of attorney to her old friend, the priest Ramón Cardeña y Gallardo (one of the men her husband had accused of being her lover), to represent her in the royal court, where he served as honorary chaplain to the king of Spain. The document, replete with fulsome praise of his royal Catholic majesty, requested that he grant her and her son Gerónimo "all the honors, appointments, and favors that please your Sovereign."[2] Thus María Ignacia—who socialized in the highest circles but lacked a title of nobility—was attempting to obtain more honors, if not for herself, then for her son, to augment the prestige that accompanied his *mayorazgo*. Such a request reflects the constant maneuvering of people attempting to enhance their family's social standing in a world where aristocratic titles and privileges were taken very seriously.

At the same time, La Güera was dealing with the sickness of two of her daughters. In the fall of 1809, one-and-a-half-year-old Victoria died from unknown causes. We can only guess at the mother's grief in losing a child who was already walking and beginning to talk, because the documents are completely silent on this tragedy. As if this were not enough, eight-year-old Guadalupe alternated between periods of chronic weakness and acute attacks during which she "clamored to see me at all hours."[3] Indeed, disease and death were ever-present in the nineteenth century: mothers faced mortal peril every time they gave birth; child mortality was high in all social classes; and it was women who bore most of the responsibility for caring for the sick and dying.

La Güera nonetheless continued receiving visitors. We can document this with two rare letters that have been preserved because they were written by the future Liberator of Mexico, don Agustín de Iturbide, to his *compadre*, the jurist and future statesman don Juan Gómez Navarrete. On March 31, 1809, Iturbide reported that he had visited "my lady doña Ignacia who had come to see the [Holy Week] procession from her parents' house," and she excused herself for not having written because she was so busy with religious exercises. A week later, on April 7, he wrote that he "had been with my lady doña Ignacia, and I brought up, if only superficially, the matter you and I discussed, and it seems that she is not in agreement with our ideas although she did not say so with clarity. . . . Let's see when these things can be formalized."[4]

Although these brief references do not explain what was discussed, they point to the long-standing friendship between the two. In 1809 Iturbide was an aristocratic military officer who had not yet made his fame; he was also an old family friend, their relationship perhaps dating to when her first husband sold his father-in-law some property.[5] Both families continued to have some business dealings, two of which coincidentally came to light in later documents. On September 22, 1817, Iturbide's cousin, Captain Domingo Malo e Iturbide, leased the Molino Prieto, a wheat- and flour-producing estate that was part of her son Gerónimo's entail. Malo committed himself to paying an annual rent of 4,600 pesos for seven years and listed Agustín de Iturbide as his guarantor (*fiador*).[6] At some point Malo also began to manage her Hacienda de la Patera. The only thing we know about the arrangement is that he hired an administrator, Pablo Cortés, to oversee the day-to-day operations and that Cortés later claimed that Malo did not regularly pay his 600-peso annual salary.[7] La Güera's 1819 will listed Captain Malo as the attorney to whom she had given broad powers over her affairs, so he may have controlled several of her properties.[8]

It is thus likely that Iturbide's two visits to La Güera in the spring of 1809 concerned the formalization of some financial arrangements, for the bonds of friendship and family included economic and legal matters. Since their meetings occurred in the midst of mounting political unrest, they may also have discussed public affairs. What is clear is that their conversations went beyond social pleasantries. It is also evident that she had excellent relationships with men who would later play important roles in Mexican history.

POLITICAL CONSPIRATOR, 1809

Doña María Ignacia Rodríguez was soon drawn into the political maelstrom that began in the spring of 1808 when Napoleon's troops occupied Spain and placed a French ruler on the Spanish throne. When news reached New Spain, local elites were thrown into a quandary about who should rule while Fernando VII was in captivity. On July 19, 1808, the *ayuntamiento* of Mexico City—composed of creole gentlemen, including La Güera's father—presented a plan to form a provisional government of New Spain with Viceroy José de Iturrigaray at its head. Although the plan was cloaked in protestations of loyalty to the rightful Spanish king and backed by the viceroy, many saw it as a dangerous declaration of home rule because the government in Mexico City was to consist of representatives from city councils throughout New Spain and would be independent from the popular juntas created in the mother country to maintain

Spanish sovereignty. The *audiencia* of Mexico—largely composed of peninsular-born Spaniards—opposed the plan and backed a coup d'état to prevent the creation of the Junta de México. On the night of September 15, 1808, the "peninsular" faction, led by the wealthy merchant Gabriel de Yermo, arrested the viceroy and detained several supporters of the autonomist project.

The coup eroded the legitimacy of the colonial regime and exacerbated the tensions between the *criollos* and the *peninsulares*—and thus between the *ayuntamiento* and the *audiencia*. Although the new viceroy tried to placate the disaffected *criollos*, by then Pandora's box had been opened. In the fall of 1809 the situation was complicated by rumors of a possible French invasion of New Spain, of suspected French collaborators in Mexico, and of various plots against the viceregal authorities, including a planned *criollo* military uprising in the city of Valladolid.

La Güera was in the middle of this ferment because of her close ties with many of the men involved on the creole side. Besides her father, there was her brother-in-law, the Marqués de Uluapa, as well as several other city councilmen. The Licenciado Juan Francisco Azcárate, one of two lawyers who had represented her in the 1802 marital dispute, was the *regidor* who co-authored the 1808 proposal for a provisional autonomous government and was subsequently imprisoned until 1811. Two old friends who had testified on her behalf in the divorce suit, Canon José Mariano Beristáin and Abbot Francisco Beye Cisneros, were also among those detained in the wake of the Yermo coup.

As tensions continued to mount, La Güera herself was at the center of a conspiracy to discredit the pro-peninsular (or "European," as they called it) faction led by *audiencia* judge don Guillermo de Aguirre y Viana. The details of this incident are exceedingly confusing. The only thing known for certain is that La Güera—and several other *criollos*—accused Aguirre of plotting against the interim viceroy (who was also the archbishop), Francisco Lizana y Beaumont. Their allegations were so believable that on October 31 Lizana ordered Aguirre to leave town, but the expulsion of the *oidor* Aguirre led to such an outcry that the viceroy was forced to allow him to return a few days later. The incident also led to an investigation of María Ignacia Rodríguez, who was brought in for questioning in October 1809 and banished from Mexico City in March 1810.

Figure 4. A *criollo* city councilman, like La Güera's father and
son, as well as other friends and relatives who served in the
Mexico City *ayuntamiento* and were involved in the plan to
establish provisional home rule for New Spain in 1808. Theubet
de Beauchamp, *Regidor*, in Lombardo de Ruiz and Beauchamp,
Trajes y vistas. Harvard Library.

At his trial in May 1811, captured insurgent leader Ignacio Allende
referred to this conspiracy by declaring that he had heard that "the astute
and famous" Güera Rodríguez was part of a group of people close to the
viceroy that "seduced him by different means and made him commit grave
errors."[9] Decades later the chroniclers Carlos María de Bustamante and
Lucas Alamán mentioned in their histories that she had been the author of

the plot against Aguirre. According to Alamán, "It was known for certain that this entire incident originated in the intrigue crafted by a lady from a distinguished family, celebrated at the time for her beauty, whom the Archbishop immediately banished to Querétaro." According to Bustamante, "It was said that a certain Mexican lady, a widow who because of her loveliness has attained a place among our fabled beauties, played a large part in the secret proceedings; she paid a heavy price, but banished to fifty leagues from Mexico City, she married a rich man from whom she inherited a not inconsiderable fortune."[10]

Apart from their brevity, these references contain mistakes that serve as a reminder of how facts become confused with the passage of time. For starters, La Güera was not banished from the Mexican capital "immediately," as Alamán asserted, but rather after four and a half months. Neither was she banished to fifty leagues from the capital, as Bustamante claimed, but only forty. Nor did she marry Briones following her exile to Querétaro; he had died more than two years earlier. Moreover, Allende's statement, entirely based on hearsay, merely confirms that he had heard rumors that she gave the viceroy bad advice.

The thick file arising from the investigation by the *inquisidor decano*, Bernardo de Prado y Obejero, provides little clarity about what La Güera was up to.[11] According to her own testimony, on October 28, 1809, she went to see don Juan Miguel Riego, an official in the viceregal government, to declare that she had overheard a conversation about a plot to kill the viceroy. That very evening, at seven o'clock, Viceroy Lizana called her to the royal palace to obtain more information. Her testimony was sensational. She claimed that while visiting Oidor Aguirre's house to see a painting, she heard voices in the next room and, listening through the keyhole, "clearly and distinctly" heard Aguirre tell the Marqués de San Román (the superintendent of the royal mint) and don Joaquín Gutiérrez de los Ríos (a colonel in the Provincial Infantry of Puebla) that they should find a way to remove the "despotic" viceroy from his post—even poisoning him if necessary. Respectfully signing her deposition, she swore that she was telling the truth "owing to her sentiments of honor, religion, fidelity, and patriotism." The plot thickened the next day when several gentlemen testified that they had heard that two medical doctors had been offered

50,000 pesos to poison the viceroy, and that another subject was offered 2,000 ounces in gold to perform the task.[12]

By November 11 Prado had concluded that the allegations were false and that the entire incident was motivated by "resentments and personal hatreds." On January 18, 1810, he presented his written report to the viceroy and on February 6 reminded him of La Güera's false denunciation. Prado recommended that she be punished so as to discourage "the powerful" (*los poderosos*) from continuing to spread rumors that stirred up "the lowly people" (*el pueblo ínfimo*), thereby "perturbing the public tranquility."[13] It is hard to know what to believe, however, because the inquisitor was far from impartial in the matter; having vociferously opposed the 1808 proposal for home rule, he likely favored Aguirre and the peninsular party.

On March 9, 1810, Archbishop Viceroy Lizana, convinced of the need to take some action to soothe tensions in the Mexican capital, decreed that María Ignacia Rodríguez be banished from Mexico City: "Because it is not desirable in the current circumstances for doña María Ignacia Rodríguez de Velasco to remain in this city, she is to be informed, without manifesting the motive, that she should depart within twenty-four hours without any excuse or pretext and remain at a distance of at least forty leagues, informing me of the town or place where she plans to reside and remaining there until receiving further orders from this Supreme Government." With this decree the investigation into her role in the plot was suspended—without her being formally charged or tried—and the case was closed.[14] She thus got off easy; the penalty for sedition could be quite severe.

Because the viceroy did not explain his decision, the reasons for La Güera's actions remain unclear. It is possible that the intrigue was part of the early movement for home rule championed by so many of her creole friends and relatives—though that was not the same as supporting a full separation from Spain, a position that few Mexicans favored at the time. It could also be, however, that as Prado asserted, her denunciation of Aguirre was merely caused by personal resentments against the leader of the pro-peninsular faction that had promoted the coup against Iturrigaray. Either way, she was clearly allied with the *criollo* side.[15] She herself did not provide any clues to help us understand her actions. Petitioning a week later for permission to return to Mexico City, she claimed that she had never done anything wrong, was only trying to protect the viceroy, and had no idea why she had been punished.[16]

BANISHED FROM MEXICO CITY, 1810

After receiving the viceroy's deportation order on March 9, La Güera obediently left the capital. The next day she informed him that she would be living in Querétaro because, as she later explained, her poor health prevented her from continuing to her distant haciendas, and she had "good friends and relatives" in that city who could help her. Indeed, her first husband's mother came from Querétaro and her second husband had made his career there. In fact, Villamil's uncle don José Luis Primo Villanueva (his mother's brother) had succeeded Briones as *censor regi* of Querétaro after the latter died in 1807.[17] La Güera also owned two houses in Querétaro that she had inherited as part of Briones's estate.

Yet she did not accept her banishment lightly. In three melodramatic petitions of March 17, April 14, and April 28 she beseeched the viceroy to reconsider his decision. These missives provide a rare glimpse of her thoughts and feelings because they are written in the first person, without the acknowledged intervention of an attorney. It is impossible to tell how much of the language was hers, because the handwriting does not match her signature, an indication that she hired a scribe to assist her. Yet they nonetheless shed considerable light on the difficult situation she endured in exile. And they demonstrate her strong will and persistence—or perhaps her desperation—because she did not stop petitioning until the viceroy agreed, on May 5, 1810, to allow her to return to the outskirts of Mexico City, as long as she did not set foot inside it.[18]

If her exile in Querétaro was relatively short—just under two months— it was hardly sweet, as several twentieth-century writers have portrayed it. Describing herself as a "poor defenseless widow" who was the sole support of "five innocent children who are young and without a father," her first petition of March 17 lamented the "scandalous blow that I have received without knowing why" and the "misfortune" of "being calumnied, insulted, and despised throughout the Realm," as people assumed the worst of her in order to explain her banishment. Her only consolation, she declared, was "knowing in my heart that I am innocent and have not committed any crime," having only served the viceroy to the best of her abilities.

Her stay in Querétaro was marked by severe illness. Her first petition requested permission to return to Mexico City because her health had taken a turn for the worse, but did not elaborate on the details. When the viceroy denied her request, reminding her that the causes for her punishment "are well known ... even though I did not formally notify you of them," she petitioned again, on April 14. This time she appended a certificate signed by three medical doctors who had examined her two days earlier. Listing an alarming array of symptoms, they argued that she risked imminent death unless she could return to the viceregal capital for treatment. The distinguished "professors of medicine" reported that La Güera suffered from *homoptisis* (coughing up blood), *expixtaxis* (nosebleeds), *hemi-crania intermitente* (headaches), *inedia* (loss of appetite), fevers, an oozing rash, liver pain, nausea, vomiting, diarrhea, fatigue, and anxiety. It is of course possible that the doctors were exaggerating her symptoms to make a convincing case for their patient, yet they would not have invented them completely because they had their reputations to uphold.

La Güera's petition elaborated on these ailments. Her health had recently deteriorated to the point that she was now "battling with death." She was coughing up bloody sputum that contained blood clots. She suffered almost continuous nosebleeds, terrible diarrhea, a pain in the side, and a rash on her arm and hands. Unable to keep food or medicine down, she was rapidly weakening. Her maladies were aggravated by the "heat of the climate, the poor water, and ... the lack of resources to treat her complicated afflictions in this place, because of the difficulty of bringing them from so far away." Reminding the viceroy of her "five fatherless children, ... some still so little that they clamor to see me at all hours" and who badly needed their mother "for their education and establishment," she begged him to take pity on this "wretched widow" and to allow her to return to her *patria* (Mexico City) to be cured. The viceroy's reply came four days later: although denying her permission to return to the capital, he authorized her to move from Querétaro to a healthier environment of her choosing, as long as it was the required distance from Mexico City—a response that did not satisfy the supplicant.

La Güera's third petition of April 28 was the charm. This time she modified her request, only asking to be allowed to move to the environs of Mexico City where her "elderly parents" could send her "everything I need" and her doctors could visit on a weekly basis. She explained that she could not find another distant location where she would be properly cared for because she was "utterly alone" in the world, "with no other company than two small children who, instead of helping me, I have to attend, especially the older one who lies in one bed while I lie in another, both of us continually dying." (This statement suggests that she only took her two youngest daughters, five-year-old Paz and the ailing nine-year-old Guadalupe, with her to Querétaro. Since fourteen-year-old Josefa had been boarding at La Enseñanza since she was six, it is likely that Gerónimo and Antonia, then eleven and twelve, were attending Mexico City convent schools as well.) Finally, she appealed to the mercy of the viceroy who, as a "pastor who loves his sheep," would surely want to prevent her death and that of her innocent daughter. A week later he acceded to her request and permitted her to move to a "place that is better for her health with the exception of Mexico City." Thus, on May 5, 1810, her exile in Querétaro was over.

It is difficult to diagnose La Güera's medical condition retrospectively. Early nineteenth-century doctors were still Galenists who believed that illnesses were caused by an imbalance of the four humors, and their certificate attributed most of the afflictions of this "young widow of sanguineous temperament" to a disordered liver. Yet many of her symptoms are consistent with tuberculosis, especially the coughing up of bloody sputum, nosebleeds, fever, weight loss, fatigue, headaches, and chest pains. Even a rash could be a symptom of cutaneous tuberculosis. If, in fact, Guadalupe was suffering from tuberculosis, it would have been difficult for the mother to avoid contagion during the many years that she cared for her sick daughter. And they could have been suffering from more than one malady simultaneously, as was common in past times.[19]

Even though we will never be able to definitively confirm this diagnosis, the picture that emerges of that period in La Güera's life is far from glamorous. Sickness and death were her constant companions. In addition to her own ailments, her thirty-year-old brother-in-law, the Marqués de Uluapa, died while she was in exile, on April 3, 1810, "after inspecting the city's garbage dumps." Her "ancient" father died on December 5 at the age of sixty-three.[20] Her daughter Guadalupe continued to languish for another six years before finally succumbing to death in July 1816. Although their doctors prescribed medicines, until antibiotics were discovered in the twentieth century, there was little that could be done for their suffering beyond palliative care and prayer.

Still, La Güera must have had a strong constitution. Owing more to luck than to medical treatment, she recovered—or at least, her disease went into remission, as often occurred with tuberculosis. She would survive another forty years, albeit with at least two other major bouts of illness: one in March 1819 that was so severe that she dictated her last will and testament from her sick bed, and another in June 1825 that led her to temporarily release her family's private box in the Coliseo theater because she was too sick to attend performances.[21]

BACK IN TOWN, 1811–1820

By the beginning of 1811—if not earlier—La Güera was back in Mexico City, renting a house across from the Alameda park.[22] It was not unusual for wealthy residents of the capital to rent their homes, for in a city where real estate was concentrated in the hands of the Church and a few noble families, the best houses were not for sale. And, although La Güera owned several rural properties, she would never own her own dwelling in Mexico City.

On January 22, 1811, she was officially informed "in her abode" that before he died, her father had requested that his grandson, Gerónimo, inherit his position as *regidor* of the city council and that she, as her son's guardian, was to name someone else to serve until he came of age. Doña María Ignacia Rodríguez signed *lo oye* (I hear) to indicate that she had received the notification and accepted the responsibility. She later named her old friend Doctor don Ignacio Rivero to serve in the interim.[23]

In March 1811 she moved from the first rental, which her doctor considered unhealthy, to the "magnificent" *casa grande* on the corner of Damas and Ortega streets owned by her sister Josefa—or more precisely, by the Uluapa *mayorazgo* that the newly widowed Josefa managed for her minor son. (It was, coincidentally, the same house that Aguirre had rented until his death in December 1810, where La Güera alleged to have

Figure 5. The Alameda park facing the house rented by María Ignacia Rodríguez at the beginning of 1811, where she no doubt took her five children to play. Drawing by Moritz Rugendas in Sartorius, *Mexico about 1850*. Harvard Library.

overheard the plot to poison the viceroy.) The two sisters signed a five-year contract on May 1, 1811, retroactive to March 1, that committed María Ignacia to paying an annual rent of 1,200 pesos (400 more than Aguirre had paid) and to conducting some needed repairs. She spent the next few months renovating the house by, among other things, installing a new interior railing, replacing the decrepit window grills with wrought iron balconies, and painting the exterior. Their uncle, José Rodríguez, and several neighbors later remembered seeing both sisters happily conversing while they observed the repairs. These witnesses also concurred that the changes were a decided improvement to the old rundown structure, giving the "ancient building" the "splendor and distinction befitting a title of Castile."[24] Yet La Güera only stayed there fourteen months before moving to another rental on the elegant street of San Francisco—which was both more centrally located and probably cheaper—and subletting her sister's house for the remainder of the contract.[25]

By the fall of 1811 La Güera was feeling settled enough to attend to other business. On October 4 she reached an extrajudicial settlement with the Briones siblings to resolve the "extremely intricate lawsuit" over his estate, a matter that had been put on the back burner while she was in exile. According to a later summary of the case, the Briones family was "persuaded . . . that justice was on her side." She, to "honor . . . the memory of Doctor don Juan Ignacio Briones, her late husband," agreed to give his siblings José, Vicenta, and Manuela the fifth of his estate that he would have been free to bequeath (the disposition of the other four-fifths being regulated by law—and all hers, after the death of Victoria). Their share, worth 64,000 pesos plus 5 percent interest retroactive to April 8, 1808, was to be paid over a period of years from the revenues of the haciendas of San Isidro and Santa María in Guanajuato. This arrangement was meant to put the matter to rest once and for all, thereby "conserving the harmony that should unite those bound together by family ties."[26]

La Güera also found time for frivolity. On July 16, 1811, the Count of Santa María Guadalupe del Peñasco appeared in the office of the Inquisition to denounce a scandalous portrait in wax of his wife's cousin, doña Ignacia Rodríguez de Velasco. The count testified that the artist, don Francisco Rodríguez (no relation), had shown him pictures of several distinguished ladies—even though these had been ordered by the women themselves for their personal use. The women were allegedly depicted from the waist up with such a low décolleté that "their breasts were quite uncovered." He claimed that the portrait of La Güera was particularly shocking because "her breasts were entirely visible" in a blouse so low-cut that "you could even see her belly button." The count explained that he thought he should let the Inquisitor know because this was not the only "indecent portrait" of said lady, and his predecessor had "destroyed another likeness of the same Rodríguez" made by the same artist. This time the authorities did not act on the tip, and indeed noted that they did not believe the story.[27]

The count's motives for coming forward are mysterious. He may sincerely have been concerned that the ladies' attire violated Archbishop Lizana's 1808 decree prohibiting women from wearing low-cut dresses that bared their arms in the Empire style that was in vogue at the time.[28] Or this could have been some sort of payback for the role La Güera had played in the conspiracy that led to Oidor Aguirre's banishment. Either way, the denunciation reveals that she and her friends were sitting for

Figure 6. Low-cut dresses in the Empire style that was fashionable at the beginning of the nineteenth century and that scandalized La Güera's mother as well as Archbishop Lizana y Beaumont. Depicted on a canoe ride on a canal crossing through Mexico City. Theubet de Beauchamp, *Promenade en canot à México,* in Lombardo de Ruiz and Beauchamp, *Trajes y vistas.* Harvard Library.

their portraits and keeping up with the latest fashions, to the great dismay of their parents' generation.

Meanwhile, La Güera was busy raising her five children. Caring for chronically ill Guadalupe was a constant concern, and the mother's anguish emerges even in otherwise dry documents. La Güera had already lamented her daughter's grave sickness when she petitioned the viceroy on April 28, 1810, for permission to return to Mexico City. Then, in an undated letter of 1814, she excused herself from a meeting because she had to attend to a "daughter who is dying."[29] As her daughter's condition deteriorated in 1816, La Güera explained—in a July 19 document in which her attorney, Ignacio del Rivero, appears to have transcribed her words—that she had neglected her legal affairs "because of the terrible blow, and my grief, because at that time my daughter was gravely ill and on the verge of death." Rivero later reiterated that his client had not responded to a judicial notification "because she was distracted while nursing a daughter of about fifteen years who was dying." Indeed, court officials were unable to deliver a legal notice because when they arrived the girl was "in a moribund state with the Santo Cristo and two Fernandino friars by her bedside."[30] She died a few days later, on July 24. If Guadalupe's death may not have been unexpected, it appears to have been quite traumatic.

Her other four children flourished. Foreign visitors repeatedly remarked on her three daughters' beauty, charm, kindness, and intelligence.[31] La Güera gave them excellent educations and positioned them to marry three of the most eligible men in the realm. On January 15, 1812, when she was sixteen, Josefa married the third Count of Regla, Pedro José Romero de Terreros, who praised the "fine, honest, Christian education" his bride had received in the Colegio de la Enseñanza.[32] That same year, on June 6, her fifteen-year-old daughter Antonia married the widowed fifth Marqués de Aguayo, José María Valdivielso. In 1820 the youngest child, Paz—then fifteen—married the second Marqués de Guadalupe Gallardo, José María Rincón Gallardo.[33] Thus, in this status-conscious society, La Güera's daughters moved up in the world by acquiring titles of nobility, which had always eluded their mother. Moreover, their husbands were all multi-millionaires.[34] Indeed, the Reglas were so wealthy that, according to Fanny Calderón de la Barca, when Josefa's husband Pedro was christened in 1788, "The whole party walked from his house to the Church upon ingots of silver."[35]

La Güera provided Antonia and Paz with dowries each worth approximately 6,000 pesos—substantial sums, though not large by the standards of the Mexican aristocracy. (For example, Villamil's mother had married with a dowry of 23,754 pesos and Pedro's mother with one worth 200,000.)[36] Antonia's husband, in turn, gave her a splendid wedding gift (called *arras* at the time) of a coach worth 2,000 pesos.[37] In contrast, Josefa married without a dowry or *arras* because she and Pedro wed in defiance of his mother.

The story of their romance is worthy of a novel. The Marquesa de Villahermosa (also the widowed countess of Regla) opposed the marriage because of her son's youth and limited income, since he was still twenty-three and had not yet inherited his deceased father's *mayorazgo de Regla*. She also wanted him to wait until the family's financial situation improved, because many of their mines and rural estates had been looted by marauding troops after the independence war broke out in 1810. But the lovestruck

Pedro insisted on following his heart. Although his mother grounded him to prevent him from seeing his beloved, he "escaped" one morning at dawn, despite the family chaplain's effort to stop him, and ran the two blocks straight to his beloved's abode—that is, La Güera's house—where he remained until 6:30 in the evening. When she found out, the furious marquesa had the viceroy place Pedro under house arrest, on December 10, 1811, to prevent any "precipitous" move on the part of her son, who was "blinded" by "an excess of passionate love." After his house arrest was lifted three days later, he petitioned the viceroy to authorize him to marry without his mother's permission. His petition noted that she had not raised any objections to the bride or to her family and that Josefa's illustrious ancestors and "exemplary conduct and virtuous manner" were known to all. He also insisted (though it proved to be false) that he had sufficient funds from his father's *bienes libres* "to live with the decorum and luster corresponding to his station." After consulting eight of his ministers, the viceroy sided with the young count and on January 14, 1812, granted him permission to marry.[38]

The couple wed the next day at eight o'clock in the evening at La Güera's home on the corner of Damas and Ortega streets.[39] Pedro would later declare that Josefa "brought no property to the marriage" except for one valuable jewel, a diamond medallion worth about 1,400 pesos, plus her clothes and a few inexpensive sundries.[40] They married without a dowry, perhaps because, after receiving a visit from the Conde de Xala (the marquesa's father) with the news that his daughter opposed his grandson's marriage, La Güera had warned the young lovebirds to wait until they could obtain his mother's blessing.[41] In retaliation, Pedro's mother cut off his allowance and refused to let them live in the Regla mansion. Instead, they moved in with La Güera, who ended up paying the couple's expenses during the first year of their marriage, until Pedro came into his inheritance. A month after the wedding, in a letter to a local merchant explaining why she could not pay a debt, La Güera claimed that supporting her daughter and son-in-law was such a heavy financial burden that she had been forced to sell jewelry and other goods, and was "even left without a bed to sleep in"—presumably because she lent her bedroom with the double bed to the newly-married couple.[42]

The scandal soon passed, and Pedro's mother warmed to his new bride. Six months after the wedding, on July 4, 1812, she wrote to her close friend,

Figure 7. Portrait of La Güera's oldest daughter, the Countess of Regla. Unknown artist, *Doña María Josefa Villamil de Terreros*, ca. 1810–1825. Graphite on paper, 15 × 13 in. (38.1 × 33 cm). Brooklyn Museum, Museum Collection Fund and Dick S. Ramsay Fund, 52.166-8.

doña Inés de Jáuregui (wife of the deposed Viceroy José de Iturrigaray) to inform her that "Pedrito" had married and that her young daughter-in-law had won her over. "The girl is the daughter of La Güera, very pretty, a good person, extremely well educated, with a great deal of prudence and modesty; qualities that sweetened my initial displeasure that made me resist the union to the point of appealing to the authorities to prevent it, since, owing to the current circumstances of my son's estate, I considered it imprudent to think of marriage and urged him to delay it; but I repeat, I am pleased with my new daughter, who loves and respects me with the greatest tenderness."[43] A portrait of the young countess shows that she was, in effect, quite pretty and bore a strong resemblance to her mother.

We know much less about La Güera's son, Gerónimo. He undoubtedly obtained an excellent education befitting his gender and social standing. In November 1816, when he was eighteen, he "received the Hacienda de Bojay belonging to his entail . . . and has taken its products since then."[44] In 1817 he paid 2,393 pesos for the privilege of inheriting his grandfather's position on the city council.[45] He may just have served for one year, however, as he only appeared on the lists of *regidores* in 1818.[46] In 1823 he inherited the rest of his father's *mayorazgo* (just as entails were being abolished, which would have benefited him by allowing him to freely sell or encumber his properties).[47] Unlike his sisters, who married so young, he waited until he was twenty-seven and well established. On March 19, 1826—the feast day of San José—he wed María Guadalupe Díaz de Godoy in the church of San Miguel Arcangel in Atitalalquia, near his Hacienda de Bojay.[48] He must have spent considerable time there overseeing his property, which may explain why foreign visitors like Fanny Calderón only remarked on his three beautiful sisters and did not appear to know of his existence. Yet his principal residence was in Mexico City, where he served as a courtier to Emperor Iturbide in 1822–1823 and as a representative in the republican Chamber of Deputies, at least in the 1830s. At that time, he was also identified in notarial records as a colonel in the Mexican army.[49]

The widowed doña María Ignacia would have been kept busy attending—and often organizing—family events. First came her children's weddings, then the births of seventeen grandchildren. Josefa had seven children; Antonia and Paz each four; and Gerónimo two—although each lost one child in infancy (see appendix B). Many of them are pictured in the family history written in 1909 by La Güera's great-great-grandson, the Marqués de San Francisco, Manuel Romero de Terreros y Vinent. La Güera not only attended their baptisms but served as godmother for some.[50] The family likewise gathered for funerals, such as that of her elderly mother in 1818 and those of her three young grandchildren. In 1815 family members also received news from Paris that Pedro's uncle, the Marqués de San Cristóbal, had died of a drug overdose—"killing himself by taking *arrobas*

Figure 8. Portrait of the children of the third Count of Regla, four of La Güera's many grandchildren, ca. 1820. Reproduced in Romero de Terreros, *Condes de Regla,* between pp. 88 and 89. Library of Congress.

de quina to get high"[51]—which served as additional proof that death was ever present and life could never be taken for granted.

ECONOMIC TROUBLES, 1811–1820

Wealth could not be taken for granted, either, for the independence war that raged in the countryside destroyed many fortunes. As both royalist and insurgent armies ransacked property and disrupted trade routes, the economy went into a tailspin. Because most of La Güera's holdings were in rural real estate, they were particularly vulnerable. As her haciendas ceased producing the steady income she relied on, she attempted to cope with the changing situation by buying, selling, and renting properties, renegotiating mortgages, selling silver pieces and jewelry, and even trying her hand at business. Her affairs were complicated by lawsuits and by the difficulty of calling in more than 50,000 pesos that were owed to her, apparently because her predicament was shared by many of her peers, who likewise faced enormous losses during this period. Despite her best efforts, however, her once comfortable financial position became increasingly precarious.

The largest liability came from her bachelor uncle, José Miguel Rodríguez de Velasco, whose financial problems had been building for years. He was already deeply in debt before the war began. In May 1810 La Güera agreed to let her father take 13,000 pesos that she had given him to pay down the mortgage on La Patera and instead loan it to his brother, who provided a guarantee on his Hacienda de la Escalera. At various times she also gave him smaller quantities to help keep him afloat and lent him some of her silver that he apparently pawned with a friend, don Ignacio Paz Tagle.[52] The debt grew even larger when José served as the executor of his brother's estate. Both brothers held their property in a common *compañía* that must have had little liquidity. After Antonio died in December 1810, his brother lacked the cash to pay his niece the 3,400 pesos due as her portion of the *legítima paterna*. Finally, on January 16, 1818, when his total debt plus interest had ballooned to 30,533 pesos, José signed a *convenio* (contract) agreeing to repay her over a nine-year term with 5 percent interest, and to secure the debt with a 25,864-peso mortgage on his Hacienda de la Escalera.[53] When La Güera dictated her last will and testament in 1819, however, her uncle still owed her more than 30,000 pesos and had not yet returned her silver service.

Another liability was that of her old friend, the priest Ramón Cardeña. In better times she had loaned him 25,000 pesos, perhaps in return for the favors she had asked him to obtain on his trip to Spain in 1809. (This could explain the mystery of how the cleric supported himself during that journey.) In her 1819 will La Güera explained that he "obligated himself to repay me with the income from his position as canon, which he has not done, and thus I direct that the debt be collected; although there is no written record of this obligation, . . . he cannot deny it; and if he does both Mariano and don Tomás Murphy can vouch for me." Because Cardeña died the following year, she may have had to write off the loan as a total loss despite her evident ties to the important merchant brothers.[54]

Warfare compounded these problems. In 1811 the rebels occupied La Güera's most valuable assets, the formerly profitable haciendas of San Isidro and Santa María in Guanajuato. Three surviving letters inserted in an 1816 court case brought by a creditor show how quickly her economic situation deteriorated. On December 8, 1811, she excused herself from paying a debt of 1,012 pesos by explaining that "I absolutely cannot pay . . . because the funds I had here have run out, and also those from *Tierra Adentro* [the interior of the realm], since I have received no income from them for eleven months, and do not expect to receive any more while my two haciendas are in the hands of the enemy, which is using them as a general barracks."[55] The reference to "eleven months" indicates that the rebels had taken those properties by February 1811. They apparently kept them for several years—until 1820, according to an 1827 document, though the precise date could have become confused over time (especially because the figure is suspiciously rounded). In any case, the damage "due to the war for the independence of this America" was real enough: the haciendas not only stopped producing income but were left "in ruins."[56]

These were not the only estates affected by the fighting. The insurgents also occupied two cattle ranches that belonged to her son's entail: Cabezones in Monterrey and La Soledad in the pueblo of Dolores. By 1818 Cabezones was already free of the rebels, but "it had suffered from such looting that there were no cattle left." La Güera nonetheless had to continue paying 700 pesos annually to the workers who remained on the property. That year she obtained permission to sell the distant Cabezones and buy the Rancho del Cristo adjacent to the entail's Molino Prieto, thus consolidating her son's investments closer to home.[57] But by then even the properties close to Mexico City were impacted by the ongoing crisis.

As her economic situation became increasingly critical, La Güera tried various ways to make ends meet. The December 1811 letter lamented that in October she had been forced to obtain a loan of 200 pesos a month "to be able to continue eating" and had sold the silver plate that she ate off at a loss. According to the letter of February 10, 1812, she also had to part with some of her jewelry. By March she was so distraught that for two weeks her children hid a letter from her creditor demanding payment "to avoid upsetting her, when she was already overwhelmed with her illnesses and troubles."

Yet she did not give up. In 1813 she renegotiated the mortgage on La Patera with the Colegio de San Gregorio.[58] In 1817, in an attempt to secure a steady income from her son's *mayorazgo*, she contracted with Domingo Malo to rent her son's Molino Prieto for 4,600 pesos a year. By then she had stopped relying on her uncle José Rodríguez, instead appointing Malo as her attorney with broad powers to manage her Hacienda de la Patera as well. The next year she signed the compact with her uncle, no doubt assuming that his situation would improve with the end of the fighting. In 1818 she also petitioned the government to exempt her from special wartime taxes on her son's Hacienda de Bojay because of financial hardship.[59]

At the same time, she was trying to find a new way to pay the amount she owed the Briones siblings, for as the fighting dragged on it became clear that she could not depend on the revenues from San Isidro and Santa María as originally planned. As she explained in her 1819 will, the debt had grown enormously because it had been accruing interest: "Because of the harm the rebellion of the Kingdom has caused me, principally on those haciendas, that debt has grown due to the unpaid interest to a very considerable sum."[60] She therefore tried to convince them to take the two haciendas in lieu of payment so she could "be freed from the accumulating interest." When they refused, she sold the Hacienda de Santa María (the least valuable of the two estates), put the Hacienda de San Isidro under new management, and sold her two houses in Querétaro. Although she was able to give them 36,201 pesos, that barely covered half of what she owed.[61]

Apparently in desperation, she tried her hand at retail business— something that a woman of her social standing would normally avoid. In 1817 she bought twenty-four cases of cigarettes on credit from the royal tobacco factory, valued at 6,543 pesos, with the plan to sell the 103,200 *cajillas* (packs) individually. Her bill came due on January 10, 1818; the document does not say whether she had managed to sell her stock or whether she had turned a profit. Although foreign travelers repeatedly noted that Mexican women of all social classes smoked cigarettes, we do not know if La Güera shared this habit; it is nevertheless inconceivable that this quantity of cigarettes was entirely for her personal use.[62]

She may also have tried to profit from another business venture as early as March 1811, when she allegedly purchased twenty-two dozen stockings made of fine British cotton—again, too many for her personal use. We know of this project only because the merchant don Juan Manuel Lama took her to court in May 1816 demanding that she pay him the 1,012 pesos that were five years overdue. Before initiating the lawsuit, Lama sent his representative, don Pedro Gutiérrez Salcedo, to collect the debt. The three letters that La Güera sent Gutiérrez, in December 1811 and February and March 1812, suggest that the obligation was real, for instead of denying the purchase she replied that she simply did not have the means to pay. By 1816 she had changed her tune, insisting that she had never purchased any stockings and variously claiming that the signed receipt exhibited by Lama was a forgery or that, because she had trusted his agent, she had indeed signed it but without reading the contents or knowing what she had agreed to, that she had never received said stockings, and that Gutiérrez must have stolen them using her signature. A lower court ruled in favor of Lama, who produced considerable evidence to back his case. Yet the decision was overturned upon appeal. On December 4, 1818, the *audiencia* ruled that the lawsuit should be dropped without prejudice to "the good reputation and honor of said Lady" or to "the excellent credit of don Juan Manuel Lama." The only stated reason was "to avoid the agitation that these lawsuits bring, even for a small amount of money." It thus appears that La Güera used her connections with the powerful judges to get out of paying a legitimate debt.[63]

Another money-making project got her into trouble with her sister and ultimately led to another lawsuit. When, in 1812, La Güera decided to sublet the house she had rented from Josefa, she divided it into two units to increase her income. Taking the stables and a patio of the large house, she created a *casa chica* where the tenant installed offices and ovens to convert it into a bakery. When María Ignacia's rental contract expired on March 1, 1816, Josefa refused to accept the keys and took her sister to court to demand that she restore the dwelling to its original condition and continue paying rent until she had done so. La Güera replied that she was returning the house in much better shape than she had found it, that Josefa had approved the construction, and that because her rent was completely paid up through the end of the contract, she owed nothing more.[64]

The case dragged on for two years and became quite contentious. In July 1816, when La Güera stopped responding to legal notifications because her daughter was dying, Josefa even accused her of inventing the girl's illness as an excuse—a low blow to a mother whose child perished soon thereafter, on the twenty-fourth of that month. Five days later Josefa was back at it, insisting that her sister should have recovered from the loss of her daughter. (The court was more compassionate and gave the grieving mother a fifteen-day extension.) As the lawsuit continued, Josefa accused her sister of lying and malice. As an example of her deviousness, Josefa reminded the judges that "your honored Regent Aguirre was a victim of her intrigues, which were so amply proven . . . that they resulted in her banishment."[65]

La Güera offered to give her sister 400 additional pesos, later raised to 500, to end the litigation—which she haughtily dismissed as *una ratera cantidad* ("a trifling sum") that she could easily cover by selling some jewelry. But Josefa wanted more, eventually insisting that her sister owed her 4,000 pesos and threatening to embargo her furniture in order to, according to La Güera, "just satisfy her whim" and subject me to "the shame of having them auctioned." Meanwhile, as witnesses were brought in and lawyers filed numerous motions, the empty rental was deteriorating, especially because there had been some water damage when no one cleaned the hail off the roof during the rainy season.

The *audiencia* heard the case (because the house belonged to the Uluapa *mayorazgo*) and on March 10, 1818—"considering the distinguished circumstances of the two litigating sisters, whose relationship, and harmony, has been interrupted . . . and whose discord grows every day"—ordered María Ignacia to pay 1,000 pesos plus the two years of rent she had continued collecting on the *casa chica* since July 1816 (122 pesos a year). La Güera's lawyer petitioned for a moratorium, alleging that his client could not afford to pay because "at the moment she does not have a thousand pesos, due to a delay in the revenues she expected from her haciendas, the 4,000-peso sales tax she has just paid on the purchase of a nearby property . . . , and the aid she is giving her mother, who is on the verge of death." The request was denied, and on April 13, 1818, the case was closed when the marquesa signed a receipt confirming that she had received 1,000 pesos "in ordinary Mexican currency" from her sister.[66] When La Güera made her will the next year, she did not mention the dispute among the long list of outstanding matters.

The bitterness of the lawsuit was in part due to the financial crisis caused by the revolutionary struggle. La Güera had moved from her sister's elegant mansion and sublet it to reduce her expenses and was juggling her affairs to stay afloat. The widowed Josefa's situation was also difficult. She had lost 60,000 pesos when royal troops occupied the Uluapa haciendas in the province of Veracruz and had not collected rent on the *casa grande* in the capital during the two years of litigation. Even after receiving the 1,000 pesos from her sister, she had trouble paying her lawyer 296 pesos for his services.[67]

Yet the tensions between the two sisters appear to have begun much earlier. When María Ignacia complained in 1811 because Josefa had raised the rent by a third over what she had been charging the previous tenant, Josefa testily replied that "María Ignacia has ample funds and can easily pay the 1,200 pesos."[68] And Josefa may have suspected that her father favored her sister, since she claimed (incorrectly) that he had given her the money to buy La Patera.[69] Josefa also blamed María Ignacia for letting Gerónimo violate their father's wishes that when his grandson succeed him as *regidor*, he should use his salary to support his grandmother— which even if true would have been a short-lived situation because she died on April 30, 1818, soon after he took the post.[70] Indeed, Josefa may have resented that their father chose Gerónimo rather than her own son, Alejandro, to inherit the position.

The bad blood between the sisters persisted, even after the case was settled. In 1819 the marquesa, as her mother's executrix, had yet to give María Ignacia the more than 7,000-peso inheritance from her maternal *legítima*.[71] To be sure, it was not unusual for it to take years to sort out estates and make distributions among a person's heirs, but Josefa apparently continued to hold back her sister's portion until La Güera's third husband arranged a settlement whereby he gave Josefa 5,000 pesos "simply to avoid arguments in the family."[72] And when Josefa died in 1839, she provided for her sister Vicenta in her will but left nothing to María Ignacia.[73] The friction between the sisters shows that family ties were not always harmonious, especially where money was concerned. It also reflects the high stakes involved in disputes over inheritances that were key to securing women's livelihoods.

When La Güera dictated her last will and testament on April 1, 1819, peace had returned to most of the countryside and the three lawsuits she was battling had been satisfactorily resolved. But the economy had failed to recover as expected. The decline of her fortune can be illustrated by comparing her situation in 1820 to that of 1810. When she reached her agreement with the Briones siblings in October 1811, all parties were satisfied with the plan to pay off the debt with the revenues from San Isidro and Santa María; but by 1820 that solution had proved unworkable because those revenues had vanished and the debt had reaching alarming proportions. When she provided her daughter Antonia with a dowry in June 1812, she was able to put together enough cash to give her 6,000 silver pesos; in contrast, when Paz married in 1820 that was no longer possible, and La Güera instead gave her the equivalent of 6,000 pesos in jewelry, silver, and clothing. That year she also stopped paying the *rayas* (wages) of the workers on the Hacienda de San Isidro, a situation that lasted until she disposed of the property in 1828 and the new owners agreed to cover the back wages.[74] In addition, in 1820 she borrowed 10,000 pesos from the Archicofradía del Rosario. Still confident about the future, she promised to repay the loan in five years. Instead, she would extend it several times as financial problems continued to plague her.[75] She was thus still trying to maintain a vestige of her former lifestyle, even if it meant shortchanging the workers on her distant hacienda and incurring additional debt.

CONCLUSION

Although twentieth-century narrators have depicted La Güera Rodríguez as leading a carefree and charmed life, that is not the picture that emerges from the existing records. These support views of her as a conventional lady of high society, social climber, reluctant entrepreneur, solitary widow, and devoted mother, to name just a few of her possible identities. At times she even appears as frivolous, haughty—and mischievous, as during the 1809 political intrigue. Above all, the documents reveal that she was a resilient survivor.

Doña María Ignacia Rodríguez faced many vicissitudes during her second widowhood and confronted them with self-confidence and

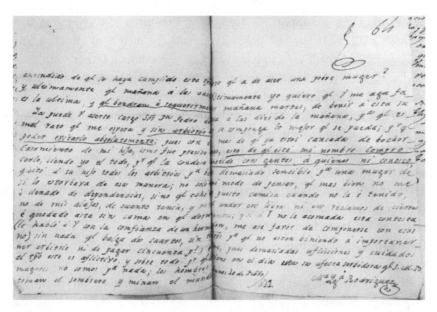

Figure 9. Two pages of a letter written by María Ignacia Rodríguez to don Pedro Gutiérrez de Salcedo on February 10, 1812, inserted in the files of a lawsuit brought against her by a local merchant. The messiness and incorrect year, which she clumsily corrected, may reflect La Güera's distress at being sued by a creditor. "El Teniente don Juan Manuel Lama de esta vecindad y comercio con doña María Ignacia Rodríguez sobre pesos," Archivo General de la Nación, Civil, vol. 473, exp. 2 (1816), ff. 92v-93.

determination. After she was banished to Querétaro, she obtained the necessary doctors' certificate to support her petition to return to Mexico City. She struggled to preserve her family's wealth in the midst of an economic crisis. She defended herself in two complicated lawsuits brought by relatives and a third brought by a local merchant. She repeatedly dealt with sickness and death. And she raised her four surviving children on her own, preparing her daughters for advantageous marriages and her son for a prestigious career. Of course, La Güera was not only highly resourceful but also extraordinarily lucky.

That is not, however, how she portrayed herself in the few instances where we have her unmediated voice. In her 1810 petitions to the viceroy she presented herself in a manner that highlighted her weakness and gender: a "poor defenseless widow" and a "wretched mother" who is "utterly alone" and the sole support of "five innocent children who are young and without a father." In the 1811–1812 letters to the merchant Lama's agent she described herself as "a solitary woman, . . . without a father, without a husband, without a brother or anyone to look after for me" while I am "burdened with children and illnesses." And she complained that she was "beside myself and very distressed" by the "many sorrows that have come together . . . to overwhelm me in the extreme."

These self-portrayals should be taken with a grain of salt, since they were meant to elicit pity and convince the viceroy to lift her banishment in 1810 and to avoid paying a debt in 1811–1812. In addition to emphasizing her own helplessness, she used the rhetoric of female inferiority strategically. In the letter of February 10, 1812, she bemoaned that "these times are distressing, especially for women who are not good for anything: men put on their hats and take on the world, but what is a poor woman to do?" In the letter of March 1812, she rebuked the merchant for "putting a lady full of obligations in such a difficult position" and reminded him that "you are a man and have other options."

Although some might interpret these statements as showing a kind of early feminist consciousness about the unjust limitations on women's actions, the next sentences suggest that she was merely using these arguments to gain the protection of powerful men. In February 1812 she continued, "Finally, I would like you to do me the favor tomorrow, Tuesday, of coming to my house at ten in the morning so that we can fix this problem; because in addition to being tired of this mess, my good name is compromised with people I don't even know, which is disconcerting for a woman like me, who has preferred not to wear a shirt if I didn't have one." In March she added, "Please arrange for these people to stop pestering me." Her approach worked: in the first instance, the viceroy quickly lifted her punishment, and in the second, she successfully put off her creditors until 1818, when her debt was canceled. If nothing else, these documents show that— in addition to having good connections and good lawyers—La Güera was a master of persuasion who knew how to craft an argument to get her way. They also reveal her facility with metaphor, perhaps one of the reasons her contemporaries considered her such an entertaining conversationalist.

This portrait of the many sides of doña María Ignacia Rodríguez is necessarily incomplete, however, because there are so many silences in the primary sources. The thirteenth clause of her 1819 will reminds us that there are many things we cannot know. It was clear that she was hiding something, for she directed her attorney, Capitán don Domingo Malo, to take 6,000 pesos from the disposable fifth of her estate and give them "to the person I shall name to him" in "secret instructions." She added that Malo should never be forced to reveal the recipient's identity to anyone, and that person should never be obliged to declare the origin of the bequest. This mystery reappeared in her 1850 will, where the twenty-first clause directed her executor to give 3,000 pesos "to the person I have designated, whom he must keep secret, and no one should know any of the particulars." Given that the beneficiary was still alive in 1850, he or she was probably younger than La Güera (unless it was that person's child). Since the written record only reveals what people were willing to put to paper, the recipient's identity is forever hidden.[76] Another mystery is how María Ignacia Rodríguez may have been involved in the independence movement, the subject of the next chapter.

3 Independence Heroine?

In the twenty-first century some writers have called doña María Ignacia Rodríguez the "Mother of the Patria" for supposedly playing a central role in Mexico's struggle for independence and being the essential link between the movements of Hidalgo and Iturbide. The available documentation does not support this interpretation. Although she was likely interested in current affairs, that hardly set her apart from many other women of her day for, as Fanny Calderón de la Barca noted, "Politics is a subject on which almost all Mexican women are well informed."[1] We do not know whether La Güera was a committed political activist or only a woman who lived through interesting times and tried to navigate a difficult situation in which the best course of action was far from obvious.

She certainly appears to have been a key player in the 1809 plot that resulted in her brief banishment from Mexico City, one of the many conspiracies that are often considered precursors of the independence struggle. After that she was at least tangentially involved in several potentially subversive activities: she was brought to the attention of the authorities for aiding the rebels on two occasions during the first phase of the insurgency, in 1810 and 1814; and she appears to have supported the final phase led by Agustín de Iturbide in 1820–1821, as well as his Mexican

Empire in 1821–1823. Because she was never tried as an insurgent, there are no judicial records to shed light on her motivations. Indeed, it is likely that she attempted to get along with all sides and protect the interests of her family above all. Even if she supported the rebellion, her contributions to national emancipation were far from pivotal.

FIRST PHASE OF THE INDEPENDENCE MOVEMENT, 1810–1814

Surviving documents shed very little light on La Güera's political convictions. When she denounced the alleged plot to poison the viceroy in October 1809, she claimed that she was only trying to protect him. It is thus unclear whether her accusation against Oidor Aguirre was meant to strengthen the hand of the *criollos* who supported home rule for New Spain while the Spanish king was in French captivity, or whether she saw this as the first step in a larger process toward independence; or whether— as the inquisitor Prado concluded—the intrigue was merely based on personal resentments and intended to get back at those who had ousted her friend Viceroy Iturrigaray in the Yermo coup of 1808.

After that her political positions continue to remain uncertain. Her exile in Querétaro during March and April 1810 put her in the heart of the nascent independence movement that began with the Grito de Dolores on September 16, 1810. Three days before it broke out, the drum major Juan Garrido denounced the Hidalgo conspiracy and claimed that doña Ignacia Rodríguez "provided money for the revolution."[2] His statement is plausible, if impossible to corroborate. Even though she had only been in Querétaro for two months the previous spring, she could have been part of an informal network of people who advocated rebellion and had already recruited Father Miguel Hidalgo and other disaffected *criollos* by March of 1810, just as La Güera was arriving in that city.[3] Indeed, she may very well have known Father Hidalgo because one of her son's entailed properties, the Hacienda de la Soledad, was in the vicinity of his parish in the town of Dolores. Thus, in carrying out the routine tasks of administering Gerónimo's *mayorazgo*, she could have been in contact with Hidalgo and other future insurgents who lived in the area—among them the Lieutenant

Mariano Abasolo, whose father had once leased that hacienda.[4] And she undoubtedly wanted to stay in their good graces to insure that the property did not suffer any damage during the revolution.

It is nonetheless curious that La Güera was not prosecuted after Garrido's denunciation and that she was permitted to return to Mexico City. Viceroy Francisco Javier Venegas must not have believed Garrido's charges against her or must not have given them much weight. Yet he took the uprising very seriously and immediately imprisoned several people for their involvement, among them doña Josefa Ortiz de Domínguez, the famous *corregidora* of Querétaro. Besides, La Güera's grave illness during this period—which she claimed she spent "continuously dying" in one bed while her daughter was dying in another—would have made it difficult for her to be deeply involved in the conspiracy.

Moreover, even if it were true that she supported Hidalgo in the summer of 1810, that does not necessarily mean that she favored a full separation from Spain at that point. Hidalgo's goals were not well defined when he initiated his rebellion, and many of his early backers thought that he wanted some sort of temporary home rule to prevent New Spain from being ruled by the French.

Indeed, there is some evidence that La Güera no longer sided with the insurgents after they became radicalized, for the letter that she sent to a creditor on December 11, 1811, referred to the rebels who occupied her properties in Guanajuato as "the enemy." She even claimed to have asked the viceroy to send troops to oust them from her haciendas.[5] To be sure, after Hidalgo's execution in July 1811, it would have been dangerous for her to proclaim her support for his movement openly. Yet her condemnation of the insurrection in private correspondence seems harsher than necessary to hide any clandestine sympathies—she could, after all, have referred to them as "the insurgents" or "the rebels" rather than "the enemy." Whether or not this statement reflected her true convictions, there is no proof that La Güera played a decisive role in the first phase of the independence struggle in 1810 and 1811.

Her links with the rebels again came to the attention of authorities in 1814, long after the insurgents had formally proclaimed independence from Spain as their goal. On June 22 the captured insurgent leader Atilano García testified "that doña María Ignacia Rodríguez, widow of the

Mayorazgo Villamil, . . . and other individuals maintained communications with the rebels and provided them with arms, money, and other aid."[6] On July 19, when the rebel priest Francisco Lorenzo de Velasco was detained, he was asked to declare "what he knows about certain acts attributed to Da. María Ignacia Rodríguez that appear to make her the protector or protected of the insurgents." Specifically, he was asked whether he had given her "receipts authorized by the insurgents . . . so that the rebels would not damage her properties, and if she gave him five hundred pesos, and how many bolts of cloth to dress the troops, . . . how much paper for their use, and other things."[7]

Although his answer has not survived, an undated letter intercepted by the authorities indicates that she did in fact give money and goods to the fighters. Written in the first person by "María, . . . who was the wife of the *mayorazgo* Villamil," it has come down to us because it was part of the Spanish government's *Prontuario de los insurgentes* preserved and annotated by Carlos María de Bustamante.[8] She may have written it as early as 1812 because she referred to the rebel occupation of her estates as occurring at "the beginning of last year," and we know from the December 1811 letter to her creditor that the insurgents had already taken the properties in Tierra Adentro by February 1811. In any case, because it provided the basis for questioning the rebel priest, her letter to insurgent officer Rafael Vega was certainly written before July 1814.

La Güera began by excusing herself for having missed a meeting with Vega because "I waited for you until one o'clock, but had to retire because I am caring for a daughter who is dying." She informed him that although she and her uncle had fallen behind in paying "the sum assigned to me by don Atilano" (Vega's commander), they would try to pay the monthly installments of 100 pesos; that she had already sent 200 pesos toward the promised 1,000; and that she would try to contribute 250 a month until the payment was completed. She closed by reminding Vega of the many sacrifices she had made for the cause:

> My two haciendas in Tierra Adentro, worth 280,000 pesos, are as if ceded to the nation, because they have been in possession of the *señores* Verduzco and Liceaga since the beginning of last year. In return, when I was with the canon Velasco, he gave me assurances that my properties would be protected and that I would not be required to make additional contributions. I nonetheless

gave the *señor* Velasco, during this year, 500 pesos, bolts of cloth to dress the troops, paper, and other things, as his secretary can inform you. . . . I did not keep the letters and receipts so they would not be discovered by the European government that forgives nothing; but I have already written said canon and the *señora* Vicario . . . for further instructions. When we meet I will tell you about all my contributions and services, and if these are not enough for the nation to look after my subsistence, I don't know what I shall do in the future, for it diminishes the nation that a solitary and helpless woman who has risked so much and served more than the men would not receive some relief and compensation for her efforts.

This letter indicates that La Güera not only contributed to the war effort, but also received visits from rebel officers and maintained a correspondence with insurgent leaders, including the famed Leona Vicaro, a member of the secret society of the Guadalupes that operated in Mexico City from 1811 to 1814. Yet we do not know whether she was part of this group or simply used her contact with Vicario as a conduit to send payments to the distant rebels. María Ignacia Rodríguez does not appear among those whom historian Ernesto de la Torre Villar identified as members of the Guadalupes, though a don José Rodríguez, possibly her uncle, was among them. Of course, because it was a secret society, there are no definitive lists of its participants. And she may have had additional ties to the rebels because the administrator of her uncle's Hacienda de la Escalera, adjacent to her Hacienda de la Patera, was a known insurgent sympathizer, "Betancourt, *confidente* of the insurgents."[9]

We also do not know whether La Güera made her contributions out of genuine support for the independence movement or merely to protect her estates while they were in rebel hands, as suggested by the letter. Nor do we know if her contributions were coerced ("assigned," as she put it) or voluntary. It is difficult to gauge the depth of her commitment to the cause from this letter because it was written to obtain relief from rebel exactions in the present and compensation in the future. And the damage to her family's livelihood—likely the sacrifices to which she referred—was indeed significant.

Rumors of her ties to the insurgents reappeared on September 18, 1817, when an informant in an Inquisition jail reported a conversation that he had overheard between two political prisoners, Fray Servando Teresa de

Mier and a certain Padre Luna. Speaking of Father Ramón Cardeña, "el cura bonito," who by then opposed colonial rule, they mentioned that when he returned to Mexico, he "became entangled with the Güera Rodríguez."[10] Yet this "entanglement" does not prove that she shared his ideas. The two had been friends for decades. He was one of the visitors to her Tacuba home who so enraged her first husband in 1802; she had given him her power of attorney in 1809 to represent her in Spain; and he owed her a great deal of money: 25,000 pesos that he had failed to repay as of 1819. It is therefore just as likely that when Cardeña visited her in 1817 they discussed the loan rather than (or in addition to) the political situation.

Perhaps La Güera was hedging her bets because, on the other side of the political spectrum, she remained close to staunch opponents of independence as well. One was the canon José Mariano Beristáin who, although he supported the early proposal for home rule, later decried Hidalgo's violent rebellion. Beristáin officiated at her two daughters' weddings in 1812, at the same time that he was preaching against the insurgents from the pulpit.[11] Her new son-in-law, Pedro Romero de Terreros, served the Crown as captain of the Escuadrón Urbano de Patriotas de Fernando VII, founded in 1810 to combat the rebels. For his loyalty he was rewarded with a knighthood in the Order of Carlos III. In 1817 he was named *Gentilhombre de la Cámara de su Majestad con entrada* (Gentleman of the Royal Bedchamber, with entry), and in 1818 as captain of the Alabarderos de la Guardia del Virrey (the viceroy's personal guard).[12] Her future son-in-law, Paz's husband Lieutenant José María Rincón Gallardo, was likewise a *patriota de Fernando VII,* and a knight of the Orden de Isabel la Católica, founded in 1815 to honor Americans who demonstrated exemplary fealty to Spain.[13]

La Güera also remained in touch with the royalist officer Agustín de Iturbide, who remained faithful to the mother country until quite late in the game. Indeed, while she was making payments to the rebels, he was brutally combating them. Yet this did nothing to dampen their long-standing friendship or business dealings. Iturbide apparently continued to visit her, especially during the period between April 1816, when he was relieved of his command for alleged abuse of power, and January 1817, when his wife joined him in Mexico City.[14] In September 1817 he signed on as the guarantor for his cousin Domingo Malo's rental of her son's

Molino Prieto, and he undoubtedly knew that Malo was managing some of her other properties and serving as her attorney as well.

It is therefore risky to read too much into La Güera's relationships with either insurgents or royalists. She was part of a small, tight-knit group of Mexican elites that included people with differing opinions about the future of New Spain. And the responsibilities of protecting her rural properties—and those of her son—necessarily put her in contact with the rebels. Indeed, given how difficult it must have been to determine what position to take in those circumstances, the most prudent course of action was to get along with everyone and try to safeguard her wealth. That may explain why she changed her tune depending on the recipient of her letters, at one time condemning the rebels as "the enemy" and at another boasting about her sacrifices to the cause despite risking the ire of "the European government that forgives nothing."

The only conclusion that can be drawn with certainty is that whatever aid La Güera gave the insurgents was so discreet—and of such minor importance—that she did not suffer any repercussions despite being denounced to the authorities for helping the rebels in 1810 and 1814, and for being in contact with Cardeña in 1817. This was not just because she was a woman or had good connections, because other women of her social class who likewise had influential friends—such as Leona Vicario, Josefa Ortiz de Domínguez, and Mariana Rodríguez del Toro de Lazarín— were severely punished for their subversive activities.

AGAIN IN THE PUBLIC EYE, 1821–1823

If La Güera's role in the first phase of the revolutionary struggle is hard to decipher, her support for the final phase, which culminated in independence in 1821, is far more certain. Again, we have no record of her opinions, but we know that by the time that General Iturbide—appointed to lead the Army of the South against insurgent Vicente Guerrero—decided instead to craft a compromise that united disparate factions behind an independent constitutional monarchy, most Mexicans supported the project. It is thus quite likely that his Plan de Iguala, proclaimed on February 24, 1821, had her full backing.

Figure 10. Momentous meeting of the Spanish officials Juan O'Donojú and Francisco Novella with the leader of the Army of the Three Guarantees, Agustín de Iturbide, to negotiate the final details of Mexican independence at the Hacienda de la Patera, owned by La Güera Rodríguez, September 13, 1821. Anonymous oil painting, 1822, Museo Nacional de Historia, Mexico City. Reproduction authorized by the Instituto Nacional de Antropología e Historia.

Given her friendship with Iturbide, La Güera was close to the seat of power. In fact, on September 13, 1821, Iturbide met Field Marshall Francisco Novella and Captain General Juan O'Donojú to negotiate the final terms of independence on her Hacienda de la Patera.[15] We do not know, however, whether Iturbide was enjoying her hospitality or simply chose that location because his cousin Domingo Malo was managing the estate. Nor do we know whether she was aware in advance that the momentous meeting would take place on her property. It is nonetheless possible that Iturbide informed her of his plans, because he corresponded with her during the period. In March 1821, when viceregal authorities detained a messenger tasked with delivering letters to various people in Mexico City, he testified that he had been instructed to give one missive "with the utmost discretion . . . to a lady known in this capital as La Güera Rodríguez," and that he was told that it "only concerned family matters without any relevance to those of the State." Moved by curiosity, the messenger had read it but said that he did not understand its contents and could only report that Iturbide signed it "Damiana" (the feminine form of one of his middle names).[16] Although the authorities destroyed that letter before La Güera received it, there may have been others.

La Güera's family was closely allied with the new Mexican regime both during the Regency, when Mexicans waited in vain for a Spanish monarch to take over, and after Iturbide was proclaimed emperor of the Mexican Empire on May 19, 1822. On September 28, 1821, two of her sons-in-law, the husbands of Josefa (the Conde de Regla) and of Antonia (the Marqués de San Miguel de Aguayo), and her nephew José Manuel Velázquez de la Cadena (the future Marqués de la Cadena) signed the Act of Independence and served on the Provisional Junta that governed the new nation until a congress was installed in February 1822.[17] Three months later, when Iturbide was proclaimed Emperor Agustín I and rewarded his supporters with prestigious positions in the imperial court, her family—but not La Güera herself—was well-represented among his courtiers. Her son served the emperor as a *mayordomo de semana* and *coronel de caballería;* her three daughters and one granddaughter (Antonia's daughter Concepción) served the empress as *damas honorarias;* and her three sons-in-law held important honorific posts: Josefa's husband received the *Gran Cruz* of the new Order of Guadalupe and was the *caballerizo mayor* of the court; Antonia's husband was a knight of Guadalupe and the *mayordomo mayor;* and Paz's husband was also a knight of Guadalupe and a *gentilhombre de cámara.*[18] In his *Cuadro histórico,* Carlos María de Bustamante described how Iturbide received daily visits with his noble courtiers by his side: these included the Conde de Regla and Marqués de Aguayo (La Güera's sons-in-law), the Marqueses de Uluapa and de la Cadena (her nephews), and the *mayorazgo* de Villamil (her son Gerónimo).[19]

Her family was so close to Iturbide that historian Virginia Guedea has described La Güera's salon as an extension of his court.[20] This scenario is entirely plausible because, as the oldest of the three sisters, she became the family matriarch after her parents died and would have received regular visits from her relatives. Moreover, since her house was across the street from Iturbide's residence on the street of San Francisco and four blocks from the National Palace, it would have been convenient for them to gather there (see map in chapter 1).

Although La Güera herself did not serve in the imperial court, she was very much in the public eye during Iturbide's regime. Indeed, in 1822 a few of his enemies circulated the rumor that he acted under the influence of a woman who bore a great resemblance to doña María Ignacia Rodríguez, and it was even insinuated that they may have had an affair.

Shortly before Iturbide was proclaimed emperor in May 1822, the Spanish soldier Modesto de la Torre recorded rumors of her political influence in his unpublished diary.[21] Describing an evening at the theater, Torre wrote that he saw "la famosa Huera Rodríguez" occupying the box across from Iturbide's:

> The famous Huera Rodríguez is a woman of history, mischief, and ancient beauty, who despite being a bit passé, still attracts the attention of the dazzled populace and also . . . commands the respect of the well-to-do. Those who are in the know about the current revolution in Mexico see in her the regulator of Iturbide's conduct and the gentle hand that moves the keys that play from time to time in this tumultuous orchestra.
> The *zaragates* or *léperos* (two terms used here for the plebes) shouted out during the intermission and sometimes even during the performance, asking for Iturbide to be crowned and proclaimed as Agustín the First. La Huera . . . didn't seem surprised by this novelty; on the contrary, she encouraged the enthusiasm of the raucous crowd and offered approving smiles, interrupted only by expressive looks between herself and Iturbide.

Crediting "those in the know," Torre portrayed her not only as an enthusiastic supporter of Iturbide's coronation, but also as a person who gave him advice—perhaps even the power behind the throne in newly independent Mexico. Still, despite mentioning their close friendship, he did not suggest that they were romantically involved. Indeed, he couldn't resist noting that, at forty-four years of age, she was already "a bit passé."

An anonymous broadside that appeared in the Mexican capital at about the same time did hint at an illicit relationship. Raising eight "doubts" about Iturbide, it began with the question of whether "La Güera Rodríguez because of her *unión carnipostática* with Mr. Iturbide" would have an honored position in the new government.[22] Of course *carnipostática* was an invented word, one that implied a carnal union, apostasy, and, indeed, ecstasy, without any of these being plainly stated.

Vicente Rocafuerte, the future president of Ecuador, who spent time in Mexico and participated in the fight against the emperor, went further by explicitly claiming that Iturbide had an affair with a beautiful lady who, although he did not name her, appeared to be La Güera. His *Bosquejo ligerísimo de la revolución de Mégico,* a thinly veiled piece of propaganda published under a pseudonym in Philadelphia in 1822, attacked Iturbide in vitriolic prose for betraying Latin American republicanism.[23] As an example of Iturbide's depravity, Rocafuerte charged that he "had an illicit affair with one of the principal ladies of Mexico whose life, because of her reputation as a lovely blonde of seductive beauty, full of charm and talent, bewitching, and endowed with a great genius for intrigue and mischief, will enter the scandalous chronicles of Anáhuac."

According to Rocafuerte, this "bewitching" lady was also Iturbide's advisor. Discussing the general's shift from royalist to patriot, Rocafuerte explained that Iturbide "decided in his perverse heart to deceive both the Spaniards and the Americans" in order to further his career. Since he couldn't think for himself, however, he consulted with his *rubia* Aspasia (a reference to the learned Greek woman who was said to be Pericles's lover and who impressed Plato with her intelligence and wit). And it was she who convinced him to modify the "servile" Plan de la Profesa to create the Plan de Iguala that ushered in Mexican independence:

> He consulted on this matter with his fair Aspasia, of whom we have spoken. She advised him that under no circumstances should he proclaim the plan as it was written in la Profesa, but that he should instead change everything that had to do with reestablishing the Inquisition and the absolute system of government that existed in the year 1808. Her reasoning was accurate, since the *criollos* and the liberal Spaniards, she told him, would never agree to a plan that represented the ideas of the servile subjects. Because it was necessary to accommodate both the former and the latter, the plan should neither openly offend the liberals nor remove all hope from the servile. Convinced by this reflection, Iturbide asked Lic. Zozaya to revise the plan in keeping with these ideas. Zozaya, because of his innate dissipation, mostly in gambling, postponed the task that had been given him, so that the exasperated Iturbide proposed the same project to Lic. D. Juan José Espinosa de los Monteros, who in effect modified it to read as we know it today, and it was proclaimed in Iguala.

Rocafuerte thus portrayed the unnamed lady not only as Iturbide's lover but also as an astute strategist who understood the complexities of the Mexican political situation and knew how to manipulate the man she loved to promote her political agenda. Indeed, Rocafuerte came close to saying that one of the foundational documents of Mexican history, the Plan de Iguala, was conceived of by a woman—a statement that when he wrote it, in 1822, would have been considered a slur.

This account of the origin of the Plan de Iguala was repeated in 1830 by the Spaniard Mariano Torrente in his *Historia de la Revolución hispano-americana*. Published in Madrid, the three-volume work was paid for by the Spanish government in an effort to discredit the men who led the Latin American countries to independence.[24] Although Torrente declined to name the fair lady "out of decency," he provided a clue in a footnote: despite "still preserving her fresh beauty," she was over fifty years old (La Güera's age when he wrote his text). His description of the enchanting dame added a few novel details:

> The first person to whom Iturbide confided the secret plan of la Profesa was one of the principal ladies of Mexico, whom nature had bestowed with so many favors that she was a model of perfection. Her elegant figure, rosy complexion, almond-shaped eyes, fine features, and the most interesting set of charms competed with the amiability of her character, the sweetness of her voice, and her subtle mind, perspicacity, vision, and rare understanding of the world. It is no wonder, then, that a woman adorned with such seductive attractiveness could win the confidence of the man well known for his fondness for burning incense on the profane altars of love.
>
> This new Ninette L'Enclos endeavored from that moment to acquire fame in the revolutionary temple by encouraging the ambition of the man who was inclined to follow his impulses and strengthening in him the idea of proclaiming independence so that he could put the supreme power in his hands.

Torrente's version is far from reliable. He had never set foot in Mexico. Because he met Iturbide when the latter was exiled in Europe in 1823, Iturbide may have been the source for some of the new details about the lady's attributes. Yet Torrente's explanation in the next paragraph about how she convinced Iturbide to modify the Plan de la Profesa was taken almost verbatim from Rocafuerte's text. Thus, in all likelihood, the

Bosquejo ligerísimo—elaborated upon by Torrente's imagination—was the source for the entire narrative.

It is notable that Torrente did not allege that the lady had an affair with Iturbide, only that she used her "seductive attractiveness" to gain the trust of the perennial skirt chaser, who was irresistibly drawn to beautiful women. To be sure, he compared her to the French courtesan Ninon de l'Enclos, who was known for her wit and beauty as well as her irreverent ideas and multiple love affairs. Yet if the fair lady's sexuality was always present, it was her political influence over the spineless soldier that formed the central piece of his argument. And he presented her motivation in encouraging Iturbide to proclaim independence not as stemming from love, but rather from her ambition "to acquire fame in the revolutionary temple."

It is impossible to determine the veracity of these rumors. Despite the innuendo in the broadside and in Torrente's text, only Rocafuerte unequivo-cally claimed that the woman who guided Iturbide was also his lover. Most readers have assumed that the unnamed lady was La Güera Rodríguez. Yet it may be that Iturbide's affair—if it existed at all—was with her daughter Antonia, who was also reputed to be beautiful and talented and who as the Marquesa de Aguayo likewise qualified as "one of the principal ladies of Mexico."

A diary kept by the Spanish functionary Miguel de Beruete in 1822 contained two entries referring to an illicit relationship between Antonia and Iturbide. On August 5, he noted that "the Empress surprised La Güera's daughter with the Emperor." On October 13 he wrote that "it is said that the newspapers of Havana and North America write shamelessly about the conduct of this government, and even include detailed anecdotes about the amorous adventures of the emperor with Antonia, daughter of La Güera."[25] Of course, we have no way of knowing whether there was any truth to these allegations. Beruete was hardly an impartial observer: he never accepted Mexico's independence and considered Iturbide to be a traitor to the Spanish empire. Yet it is noteworthy that even as he repeated gossip that compromised the emperor, Beruete was careful to distinguish the mother from the daughter, as many later texts did not.

Another reason to question the stories about La Güera and Iturbide is that most chroniclers of the independence movement did not repeat them. The only exception was Bustamante, who, after reading Torrente, copied his two paragraphs about the unnamed lady who allegedly influenced Iturbide into his 1838 *Suplemento a la historia*. In a footnote crediting Torrente for the new information, Bustamante added that the lady "was indeed beautiful and had great influence on the plan." And in his unpublished diary he identified her by name: "the so-called güera Velasco . . . who was instrumental in convincing Iturbide to form the Plan de Iguala." But Bustamante only noted her political influence and did not include a hint of scandal. In fact, he admitted to being surprised when Torrente compared her to "Ninetta L'Enclos."[26]

In contrast, other lengthy accounts of the struggle—including those by men who were no friends of Iturbide, such as Lucas Alamán, Lorenzo Zavala, and Anastasio Zerecero—presented him as very much his own man and did not link him to La Güera in the sections where they discussed the origins of the Plan de Iguala. Two Spanish historians subsequently insisted that it was Iturbide's mother's relatives (not La Güera) who persuaded him to switch from the royalist to the patriot side.[27] Most twentieth-century historians have simply ignored Rocafuerte's and Torrente's charges and credited Iturbide with developing the plan on his own.

In truth, few nineteenth-century Mexicans were familiar with the accounts by Iturbide's enemies. Rocafuerte's text was largely unknown until the twentieth century. Although Alamán had seen it, he dismissed it by explaining that "written with the sole object of making Iturbide odious, to topple him from the throne, it is a confused compilation of everything that could excite his enemies."[28] Torrente's account was buried in his long work that covered all of Spanish America; when the Mexican sections were published as a separate volume in 1918, the editors warned that the content "sometimes comes close to libel."[29] Even Bustamante, who cited Torrente several times, admitted that the author "sacrificed the truth and the exactitude of the facts" in order to defend his anti-American views.[30] And Beruete's and Torre's unpublished diaries were not discovered until the twentieth century.[31]

Sometime after moving to Mexico in 1831, the French Count Mathieu de Fossey may have heard some rumor connecting La Güera with Iturbide because his travel account mentioned, without elaborating, "They say that . . . in 1822 Emperor Iturbide was . . . susceptible to her charms."[32] Yet this statement may simply have been based on something Fossey had read, for he did not publish his *Le Mexique* until 1857, decades after the appearance of Rocafuerte's and Torrente's texts.

If other people in La Güera's social circle knew about these stories, they evidently assigned them little importance. Two years after the fall of Iturbide's empire in March 1823, she was married for a third time, to the highly respectable don Juan Manuel de Elizalde. By 1822, nearly three years before their wedding on September 5, 1825, they were such close friends that he helped her buy the Hacienda de la Escalera adjacent to her Hacienda de la Patera. The opportunity to buy her uncle's property, apparently in his bankruptcy proceedings, was too good to pass up. Because his hacienda served as collateral for the 30,000 pesos that he owed her, the purchase was also a way for her to try to recover that substantial debt. Elizalde later declared that he had given his future wife 16,870 pesos toward the transaction: the first installment of 11,502 pesos for the down payment on December 22, 1822; 878 pesos to pay its workers on March 6, 1823; and then 4,500 pesos to pay the sales tax.[33] Thus, during the time when Rocafuerte claimed that she (or perhaps another fair lady) was romantically involved with the emperor, La Güera seems to have been falling in love with her third husband.

TRANSITION TO REPUBLICAN RULE, 1823–1824

As the tide turned against Iturbide at the end of 1822, La Güera's relatives evidently distanced themselves from him. Despite their prominence in his court, they were neither among his vocal defenders nor close enough to the imperial project to suffer persecution after he abdicated on March 19, 1823. Indeed, in the fall of 1822 when Joel Poinsett, the special U.S. envoy to Mexico, visited the young Counts of Regla, he reported that he "spent some time in conversation with the Countess" (La Güera's daughter Josefa) and found her to be not only "beautiful and amiable," but also "very intelligent, and decidedly opposed to the present order of things, which she assures me is contrary to the wishes of the nation, and in opposition to all that is virtuous and enlightened in the country."[34]

La Güera's family seemingly made a smooth transition to republican rule. To be sure, they had to trade the elegant trappings of the imperial court for simpler republican fashions, and those who enjoyed titles of nobility had to give them up when these were abolished in 1826 (although Mexican aristocrats often referred to themselves later as *ex-marquesa* or *ex-conde*). According to Bustamante, La Güera's sister Josefa at first had a hard time adjusting to her new status and dreamed of moving to Spain, where she could recover her noble privileges.[35] Yet she eventually adapted and remained in Mexico City for the rest of her life, unlike some other Mexican aristocrats, who left for the continent—including one of La Güera's grandsons, Juan Nepomuceno Romero de Terreros y Villar Villamil, who had an illustrious career in the Spanish court, where he obtained the title of Duke of Regla, along with other honors.[36]

La Güera's family maintained its leading position in Mexico City's social life as well as a place in the halls of government. For example, both her sister the Marquesa de Uluapa and her daughter the Condesa de Regla contributed to the Independence Day celebrations in 1825. The countess decorated the balconies of her house with rich curtains, mirrors, and candles to add a touch of splendor to the civic festivities; and on the day itself (September 16), several orphans that she and her husband adopted for the occasion took part in the ceremonies as well. The marquesa outfitted a troop of "Cuban negresses dressed in white tunics . . . and yellow bonnets" who marched in the festive procession—and who were perhaps among the slaves liberated that day amidst great rejoicing. She watched from a place of honor, "all gussied up," seated next to Bustamante on the balcony of the National Palace.[37]

La Güera's daughter Josefa was also involved in republican politics. On August 16, 1824, Bustamante noted in his diary that the young countess, who was "as enlightened as she is beautiful," regularly observed the sessions of congress from the new ladies' gallery. She was later rumored to have been a confidante of the first president of republican Mexico, Guadalupe Victoria, and to have been involved in a plot to change cabinet officers.[38] Her close friend Henry G. Ward, the British chargé d'affaires from 1825 to 1827, described her as an influential "fair favorite" of President Victoria and admitted that because of her influence, he had himself employed this favorite to carry out his purposes.[39] Josefa thus appears to have been as interested in politics and intrigue as her mother had been.

The men in the family served republican governments in various capacities. La Güera's son Gerónimo was a colonel in the Mexican army and a deputy in the Chamber of Representatives.[40] Her son-in-law Pedro Romero de Terreros was a *general de brigada* in the Army, *ministro suplente* of the Supreme Court of Justice, and later an honorary minister of the Corte Marcial.[41] Her grandson Manuel Romero de Terreros was at various times governor of the Federal District, secretary of the State of Mexico, deputy to its legislature, and senator in the Mexican congress. He was, in addition, such a committed liberal that during Maximilian's Second Empire, before going into exile, he is said to have painted the front of his house black to mourn the death of the republic. He and his brothers were also active philanthropists: Manuel served as a member of various charity boards before leaving Mexico; Pedro served as director of the family's charitable foundation, the Monte de Piedad; and Ramón María was a strong supporter of the Philharmonic Society and the Mexican Conservatory of Music.[42] La Güera's other grandson Manuel, Gerónimo's son, followed in his father's footsteps by serving as *regidor* in the city council and deputy to the Congreso de la Unión.[43]

Despite successfully navigating the tumultuous politics of the time, the family's livelihood was adversely affected when Iturbide went into exile, effectively voiding his guarantee of his cousin Domingo Malo's lease of the Hacienda del Molino Prieto. Although the contract was not set to expire until September 22, 1824, he stopped paying rent two years earlier. By June 1822 he was 2,300 pesos in arrears. When "*el señor arrendatario* left with *el señor Iturbide*" (presumably in March 1823), he also stopped paying the workers their weekly wages, a sum that had grown to 1,150 pesos by June 12. On that date Gerónimo—by then authorized to manage his properties— sued Malo to recover the debt and asked him to provide a new guarantee for the "one that was left vacant by the absence of his Excellency Señor don Agustín de Iturbide." He also noted that Malo owed 2,000 pesos to the Marqués de Guadalupe Gallardo (Paz's husband), and at least 260 pesos to the Padres Carmelitas del Desierto, both loans secured on the Molino Prieto. When Malo responded that he did not have "the cash to fulfill this obligation ... nor the possibility of finding another guarantor," Gerónimo petitioned for the contract to be abrogated. He was unable to recuperate the funds, however, and by 1838 Malo's debt had grown to 7,054 pesos.[44]

Moreover, Malo had stopped serving as La Güera's attorney by April 1822, presumably because of his governmental responsibilities. On April 29, 1822, she therefore named a new attorney, don José María Guridi y Alcocer, another well-connected gentleman who was at the time the secretary of Mexico City's *ayuntamiento*.[45]

La Güera's financial and legal relationship with Iturbide's cousin had thus ended, but it had not ended happily. In addition to abandoning the rental contract on her son's Molino Prieto, Malo had failed to keep up the mortgage payments on her Hacienda de la Patera while he managed it. By December 1822, when they were more than two years in arrears, the administrator of the Obras Pías fund that held the mortgage wrote Malo requesting an overdue payment of nearly 1,000 pesos; upon learning that Malo no longer represented her, he sent a letter directly to La Güera instead. She must have forwarded it to the emperor, who still served as his cousin's guarantor, because it later turned up among Iturbide's papers (much to the surprise of future scholars, who did not know of this financial relationship).[46] But the appeal to Iturbide fell on deaf ears, for he was too distracted by the disintegration of his government to pay attention to his cousin's problems—or, it seems, to worry about his old friend doña María Ignacia Rodríguez.

CONCLUSION

Given the many gaps in the historical record, it is difficult to assess La Güera's contributions to Mexico's independence struggle. Like many of her *criollo* friends and relatives, she likely backed the early movement for temporary home rule that began in 1808, when Fernando VII was imprisoned by the French. And she was at the very least involved in a creole plot to undermine the peninsular faction in the fall of 1809, even suffering a brief banishment from Mexico City for her role in the affair. After that, she avoided any action that could result in another punishment.

Although she eventually favored a full separation from Spain, the timing of this shift is unclear. As late as June 1809 she petitioned the Spanish Crown for favors, still claiming to be a loyal subject. In the months prior to September 16, 1810, she may have provided some funding for Hidalgo's conspiracy, but at that point he had not yet declared independence as his

goal and instead pronounced his Grito de Dolores in support of the cap-
tive Spanish king. We have no information about whether she continued
backing the movement after it became violently destructive and advocated
for a complete break with the mother country. We only know that her
December 1811 letter to a creditor referred to the insurgents as "the
enemy" and claimed that she had asked the viceroy to send troops to
remove them from her properties.

Her alleged repudiation of the rebels—even if genuine—does not mean
that she preferred colonial domination. Many members of the *criollo* elite
favored a third option at that time: making New Spain a permanently self-
governing region within the Spanish empire. By supporting (indeed helping
to craft) the 1812 Constitution of Cádiz, they hoped to put the Latin
American and Spanish provinces on an equal footing within a representative system. Although this plan was not the same as full independence,
it was an important step in that direction because it could have given
Mexico a status similar to that of Canada or Australia within the British
Commonwealth. Whether this was also her position at this stage unfortunately remains a mystery.

After a long silence, La Güera reappeared in the historical record
because of her contacts with the rebels who were occupying her valuable
haciendas in the state of Guanajuato. She evidently gave them some
money and supplies and was also in contact with Leona Vicario, a leading
figure in the secret society of the Guadalupes, which worked from Mexico
City to help the insurgents. We will never know, however, whether the
"contributions and services" she referred to in her letter to Officer Vega
were provided because she sincerely believed in the cause or because she
wanted to protect her properties—and not just her own haciendas in
Tierra Adentro, but also her son's holdings in Monterrey and the pueblo of
Dolores, which were likewise in rebel hands—or whether she was an active
member of the Guadalupes or was merely in touch with them to facilitate
her "assigned" payments.

Whatever help La Güera may have given the insurgents during the first
phase of the independence movement was thus not only discreet but also
far less than that provided by other women. Many of her peers—including
several in her social class, such as Leona Vicario, Josefa Ortiz de Domínguez,
and Mariana Rodríguez del Toro de Lazarín—were imprisoned for their

contributions to the struggle. And some women without their status and connections were considered so dangerous that they were executed for their activities. Doña María Ignacia was in another category altogether.[47]

Neither does she appear to have played a central role in the final phase of the independence movement in 1820–1821. By then she undoubtedly supported a rupture with the mother country, as did most Mexicans after enduring a decade of warfare. Her old friendship with Iturbide placed her in the midst of momentous events. Several of her close relatives signed the Act of Mexican Independence, held positions in its first provisional government, joined the court of Iturbide's short-lived empire, and then served in republican governments. We do not know, however, whether she promoted his Plan de Iguala or whether she preferred a monarchy or republic, or whether, during some informal conversation, this "mischievous" lady said something to Iturbide or to other well-placed friends that shaped their political views and affected the course of events. This scenario can neither be discarded nor confirmed. It was not unusual for women to discuss politics with men at their *tertulias*, at the dinner table, or on other social occasions. Because public and private spheres were much less separate than they would later become, women had considerable opportunity to influence public affairs. Indeed, doña Mariana Rodríguez del Toro de Lazarín was said to have hatched the plot that resulted in her decade-long imprisonment from the privacy of her salon.

Yet it is striking that after independence was won, La Güera's contemporaries did not give her credit for contributing to the struggle, even as they praised other women as heroines. In 1825 the "Mexican Thinker," José Joaquín Fernández de Lizardi, published an almanac "dedicated to the *señoritas americanas*, especially to the patriots." In addition to short chapters describing the brave actions of Leona Vicario, Mariana Rodríguez de Lazarín, María Fermina Rivera, and Manuela Herrera, it briefly mentioned another seven Mexican women who helped fight Spanish despotism. In his *Cuadro histórico*, published in a revised edition in 1843, Carlos María de Bustamante singled out Leona Vicario and Josefa Ortiz de Domínguez. As the bright star in this constellation, Vicario was honored during her lifetime: in 1823 she was compensated by the republican congress for her financial sacrifices, and in 1827 the town of Saltillo changed its name to Leona Vicario. After her death in 1842 she was given a state funeral as well as a glowing obituary in the capital's leading newspaper.[48] La Güera received no such recognition.

It is also remarkable that in her 1843 *Life in Mexico*, Fanny Calderón de la Barca failed to connect La Güera with Iturbide or with Mexican independence. The absence of such references suggests that doña María Ignacia Rodríguez did not tell her friend any stories about participating in the revolution. This silence cannot be attributed to modesty, for the first time they met in 1840, La Güera made sure that Fanny immediately learned of her close friendship with the famous Humboldt—and she wasn't too shy to say that he had pronounced her the most beautiful woman he had met in all his travels. At a time when independence was being celebrated and when some women were lauded for their part in bringing it about, one would have expected La Güera to have proudly boasted of her own contributions if they had been worth boasting about. And Fanny would no doubt have included such details to spice up her text.

We are therefore left with many questions about the role of doña María Ignacia Rodríguez in the independence struggle. The available evidence shows that she had some contact with the rebels and apparently gave them money on at least two occasions. Whether she did so out of convenience or conviction is unclear, however. And despite her close friendship with Iturbide, we do not know whether he ever turned to her for advice on political matters. In any case, there is nothing in the historical record to suggest that she played a major part in the dramatic events of the day—let alone, as one enthusiastic blogger wrote in 2010, that she was "the principal heroine of Mexican independence, far more important than doña Josefa Ortiz de Domínguez or doña Leona Vicario."[49]

4 An Aristocratic Lady, 1825–1850

Writing long after Mexico achieved its independence about the intrigue crafted by doña María Ignacia Rodríguez in 1809, Lucas Alamán referred to her as "a lady from a distinguished family, celebrated at the time for her beauty," and Carlos María de Bustamante described the conspirator as a "lady . . . who because of her loveliness has attained a place among our fabled beauties." Yet her glory was not all in the past, for two foreigners who visited Mexico during the 1830s and 1840s found the "famous" and "aristocratic" Güera Rodríguez still spirited and charming, and a "singular figure" worthy of inclusion in their accounts of life in the Mexican capital. And Bustamante mentioned her many times in his unpublished diary, which recounted notable events of the early republic.

The last quarter century of La Güera's life coincided with the years of her third marriage. From the time she wed in 1825 until she died in 1850 at the age of seventy-one, the couple led a quiet—or at least scandal-free— existence. Although they were not involved in the kind of litigation that provided so much detail for earlier years, numerous references in public records as well as several first-hand accounts round out her biography. Far from confirming the modern view that she spent the last years of her life as a pious recluse, these sources indicate that she kept up social visits, evenings at the theater, dance parties, civic ceremonies, family gatherings, and excursions to the countryside. In the words of the editors of *Life in Mexico*, she was "enjoying the world and its vanities" well into her sixties.[1] In addition, she was involved in philanthropic activities until shortly before her death. Thus—contrary to the deeply rooted stereotype of women in past times—her world did not revolve entirely around family, church, and home.

THIRD MARRIAGE

On September 5, 1825, at the age of forty-six, doña María Ignacia Rodríguez married Licenciado don Juan Manuel de Elizalde y Martinicorena, a Chilean gentleman who was twelve years her junior. The simple ceremony took place at 7:30 in the evening in the meeting room of the Ilustre Archicofradía of the San Miguel Arcángel parish. The witnesses were her attorney, don José María Guridi y Alcocer, and her friend don Martín de Michelena. It seems that the couple was in a rush to marry, since the priest waived the customary publication of the marriage banns. Perhaps it was owing to the grave illness La Güera suffered during that time, for in June she had given up her private box at the Coliseo theater because she was too sick to attend the perform-ances (though by April 1826 she had recovered sufficiently to sue the impre-sario for its return).[2]

Although in a society with high mortality it was not unusual for a woman to marry three husbands, it was unusual for a woman to marry a man so much younger than herself. Indeed, because of their age differ-ence, La Güera shaved four years off her age on the marriage register: the bride was listed as forty-two (instead of forty-six) and the groom as thirty-four (despite being two months shy of that age). The couple amplified this fiction in later documents: the municipal census of 1842 listed her age as fifty-eight instead of her true sixty-three, and the 1848 census listed her as two years younger than her spouse.[3] These deliberate distortions serve as a warning that even primary sources are not always to be believed.

Elizalde held important positions in the colonial and then Mexican governments. Trained in both civil and canon law, he began a successful career at an early age. In 1814, when he was twenty-two years old, he was already the secretary of the *ayuntamiento* of his native Santiago; and in 1815 was a legal advisor to its merchant guild. In the spring of 1814 he was one of two Chilean deputies who traveled to Madrid to congratulate Fernando VII on his return to Spain and to inform him of local conditions. Apparently independently wealthy, he donated his salary to outfit soldiers for the royal cause and then served, again without salary, as a professor of canon law at the University of Santiago de Chile. On April 4, 1818, he was named *oidor* of the *audiencia* of Manila and set out to make the arduous journey to the Far East. Yet he never made it past Mexico City because of poor health. From there he solicited the king to name him to a position in New Spain and was still awaiting a new appointment when Mexico became independent. His services to the Crown were so notable that he was inducted into the Orden de Isabel la Católica, which honored loyal subjects.[4]

Despite his early fealty to Spain, Elizalde made a seamless transition to serving the Mexican nation. By October 23, 1821, he had sworn allegiance to the Plan de Iguala, the Treaty of Córdoba, and national sovereignty. He was an acting judge in the first national *audiencia* and was appointed as plenipotentiary minister to the United States, although Iturbide's government fell before he could leave for Washington.[5] He then served several republican governments: as first magistrate (*primer alcalde*) of the Mexico City *ayuntamiento* in 1826, governor of the Federal District in 1826–1827, and elected deputy to the Chamber of Deputies from at least 1830 until 1837. He distinguished himself in that body as its secretary in 1832 and president at various times between 1835 and 1837. After leaving government service he worked as a lawyer and *hacendado* (administering his wife's haciendas, since he had none of his own),[6] and from 1848 to 1857 he represented Chile as its general consul in Mexico.[7] In 1828 he also served on the Poor House charity board, the Junta de Caridad, along with top members of the Mexican elite—including La Güera's sister Josefa, the Marquesa de Uluapa, who served concurrently on the short-lived ladies' board.[8] By the 1830s Elizalde had joined the Archicofradía del Santísimo Sacramento y Caridad, the most prestigious lay association in Mexico, which he served as *rector*. In addition, he was a *ministro hermano mayor* of the Venerable Third Order of San Francisco, another lay group that carried immense prestige in this society.[9]

Because Elizalde thus traveled in the same circles as La Güera and her family, they would have had many opportunities to meet and socialize. They had, in fact, been neighbors for years: she had lived on the first block of San Francisco street since 1812, and in 1822 he moved into a house on the third block of that street (see map in chapter 1).[10] It is indeed possible that Elizalde, along with other luminaries of Iturbide's regime, attended *tertulias* at La Güera's house. And when, in December 1822, the opportunity arose for her to buy her uncle's Hacienda de la Escalera on favorable terms, he was ready to pitch in by giving her 16,870 pesos, a sign of their already close friendship nearly three years before they decided to tie the knot.

FINANCIAL MATTERS

In her 1850 will, La Güera praised Elizalde as a man of great "religiosity and total honesty" who had helped her clean up her papers, which "were a mess" when she married him.[11] This was a long-term project, however, because—despite owning three valuable rural estates—she had so many debts, mortgages, and outstanding loans that it took years to sort them out.

When she married Elizalde in 1825 she was heavily in debt and experiencing cash flow problems. Although a distant relative in Querétaro, José Manuel Septién, owed her 4,000 pesos, and the Salazar family owed her another unspecified amount, on balance she was in the red.[12] She still owed some 34,000 pesos on the mortgage of La Patera and 137,000 on La Escalera; owed don Martín Michelena 3,348 pesos that he had loaned her for personal expenses as well as for paying the wages of the workers on the Hacienda de la Escalera; owed another 15,204 pesos to don Luis Sulzer; owed at least 8,000 pesos to the Archicofradía del Rosario; and owed 3,809 pesos to the Padres Carmelitas del Desierto for back rent on the house where she lived before marrying Elizalde. She also owed her son Gerónimo 9,500 pesos that she had borrowed from the Villamil entail long ago; and she had not yet finished paying off her obligation to Briones's relatives. In addition, her sisters claimed that she owed them money from the division of their uncle's estate.[13] Her debts therefore totaled somewhere on the order of 250,000 pesos.

On the other side of the ledger, her net worth was quite substantial. Her three haciendas together were worth approximately 460,000 pesos, at least on paper: San Isidro was assessed at some 245,000 pesos when she inherited it in 1808,[14] and La Patera and La Escalera at 70,000 and 140,000 when she bought them in 1809 and 1822. There were, of course, costs to keeping up these properties, since the workers and mortgages had to be paid. (In 1846 Bustamante mentioned in passing that the *rayas* of La Patera alone were 500 pesos, though he did not specify for how many months and only included the detail as part of a story about how La Güera's servant was robbed and murdered on the road from Mexico City to La Patera carrying that sum, part of his lament about the insecurity and crime that were rampant at the time.)[15] But La Patera and La Escalera were again providing income because the basic staples they produced—wheat, corn, beans, and barley—were always in demand.[16] Because of these assets, as well as her good connections, La Güera's creditors allowed her to delay repaying the principal as long as she kept up with the interest.

Over the next quarter century Elizalde helped his wife liquidate as well as collect on her debts and arranged amicable settlements with the Briones family as well as with her two sisters "to avoid family discord."[17] Although the intricacies of these affairs are dizzying, the general outlines are clear. In 1827 the couple convinced Briones's surviving brother, José, and his niece, Dolores Gil Briones, "widow of Gadea," to take the Hacienda de San Isidro in lieu of the remaining 55,000 pesos "that because of the penury of the times she could not satisfy by any other means." They also convinced them to lower the interest owed from the original 5 to 2 percent, with the reduction retroactive to April 8, 1811. When the transaction was finalized in 1828, the Brioneses agreed to pay the workers' wages that had been accruing since 1820 and, because the properties were worth considerably more than the quantity owed, to give La Güera the difference in install- ments.[18] In 1833 the Elizaldes obtained an extension on her debt to the Archicofradía de Nuestra Señora del Rosario.[19] In 1835 they negotiated for another extension from the Colegio de San Gregorio for her mortgage on La Patera, explaining that she "could not currently redeem it without grave prejudice" but would do so when she received an expected inherit- ance.[20] In 1836 they consolidated various obligations and arranged for doña Dolores Gil (by then Briones's sole surviving heir) to take them on, giving San Isidro as collateral.[21] In 1840 they obtained a nine-year extension on the now 19,177 pesos due on La Patera and the 23,000 due on La Escalera. Although the interest was consistently paid "despite the state of the Republic," as late as 1848 the couple applied for yet another extension on the principal of 42,177 pesos.[22] And they had paid off many of the smaller debts, such as the 3,348 pesos to Michelena's estate.[23]

They also settled accounts with La Güera's son and her two sisters. In 1831 Elizalde gave Josefa 5,000 pesos and Vicenta 6,603 to end their claims on the Hacienda de la Escalera. (La Güera specified in her 1850 will that part of this sum should be returned to Elizalde "so that he is not prejudiced by an act of generosity and good family harmony.")[24] In 1829 she began to repay her son Gerónimo the amount she had borrowed from his *mayorazgo*. Because of her perennial shortage of cash, she gave him 5,400 pesos' worth of jewelry encrusted with pearls and diamonds, 311 pesos' worth of clothing, and only 500 pesos in cash. In 1838 she paid off the rest of the 9,500 pesos and also reimbursed him for Domingo Malo's outstanding debt of 7,054 pesos on the rental of the Molino Prieto, apparently because she felt responsible for having arranged the ill-fated contract. Meanwhile, she continued trying to collect the money from the deceased captain's estate.[25]

Each time she signed off on a transaction, doña María Ignacia Rodríguez declared (as required for married women) that she, "legitimate wife of the Licenciado don Juan Manuel de Elizalde, with his marital license as allowed by law . . . has not been pressured . . . nor intimidated or forced, directly or indirectly, by the named *Señor* her husband or by any other person in his name, and on the contrary acts of her free and spontaneous will."[26]

María Ignacia's financial problems were complicated by the continuing economic crisis, particularly by the deflation of property values. In 1826, she tried to sell the Hacienda de San Isidro but eventually gave up because no buyer offered more than 100,000 pesos for the property, which had been valued at some 245,000 before the independence war. In 1828, when doña Dolores Gil accepted it in lieu of payment, it was assessed at only 135,000 pesos. Afterward its price continued to fall: in 1837 doña Dolores requested that the assessment be reduced to an even 100,000 and that the difference she owed be adjusted accordingly. La Güera agreed to the new terms, insisting that she had never tried to profit from the transaction, but

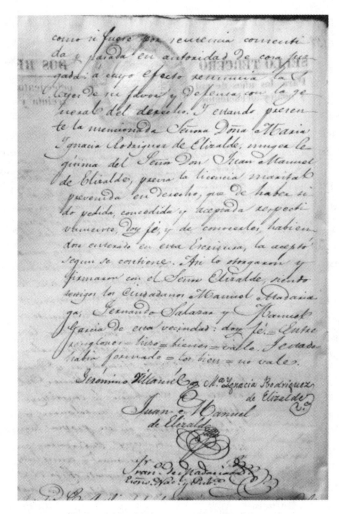

Figure 11. Receipt signed by María Ignacia Rodríguez, her husband Juan Manuel de Elizalde, and her son Gerónimo Villamil, in which she declares that she has her husband's permission for the transaction. Their elegant signatures reflect their fine educations. AHN, Francisco de Madariaga #426, vol. 2855, November 2, 1838 (1838, tomo II), f. 1208v. Reproduction authorized by the Archivo Histórico del Archivo General de Notarías, Gobierno de la Ciudad de México.

only wanted "to compensate her in some way for the prejudices and scarcity she had suffered since 1811, and the generosity with which she and her uncles had endured the lack of interest payments on the 64,000 pesos due to them" during the long years of the insurrection.[27]

Elizalde explained the causes of this dramatic deflation in an 1837 document in which he recounted the history of his wife's investments. After independence, property values "dropped considerably, especially after 1829, because of the Law of Expulsion of Spaniards [who took their capital out of Mexico when they left], the continuous revolutions that followed, as well as the scarcity of specie and the low price of produce."[28] Thus, economic factors combined with political instability to create "the calamity of these times," as her son Gerónimo put it in describing his own financial difficulties in 1838.[29]

The war with the United States caused even more hardship, as Elizalde lamented on May 16, 1848, when applying for a new extension on the mortgages of La Patera and La Escalera. For one thing, the couple had to make "copious contributions" to help the Mexican war effort. For another, their properties suffered from "destruction in the fields and enormous expenses to maintain our troops stationed on these haciendas, which miraculously have not caused our ruin."[30]

Although La Güera's rural properties did not turn out to be the excellent investment she had originally anticipated, she was nonetheless able to use San Isidro in faraway Guanajuato to reduce her debts closer to home, and La Patera and La Escalera provided a steady income. These properties also gave the couple country homes that they visited regularly. Indeed, La Güera was at her Hacienda de la Patera when she signed her last will and testament in August 1850, perhaps escaping the cholera epidemic then ravaging the Mexican capital. She and Elizalde appear to have maintained strong patron-client relationships with the workers on the estates close to Mexico City. Although she had stopped paying the workers in San Isidro when things got tight, she had borrowed money to continue paying those at La Patera and La Escalera. In 1842 the coachman who worked for the couple in Mexico City had come from the Hacienda de la Escalera along with his wife and children.[31] And don Pablo Cortés, who administered both these adjoining properties, liked his *patrones* enough to include them among his heirs when he made his will in 1830.[32]

If La Güera was not as rich as some modern authors have believed, she and her husband lived quite comfortably with the revenues from her estates and the income he earned as a lawyer and government servant. The municipal censuses of 1842 and 1848 provide a glimpse of their life-style. They lived in the same house that Elizalde had rented from the cathedral since 1822: number 6 on the north side of the third block of the street of San Francisco. Although it was not a grand mansion like the one La Güera briefly rented from her sister in 1811, the annual rent was much more reasonable: 528 pesos, compared with the 1,200 pesos she had paid Josefa, although part of the difference was due to deflation, since Elizalde's rent was also a third less than the 808 pesos the same unit had cost in 1813.[33] The reduction in rental prices indicates that the recession of the early republic had a silver lining: prices for basic necessities also declined.

The three-story building must have been a solid colonial structure. In an arrangement that was common even among the capital's elites, the Elizaldes occupied the *altos* (top floor) of the building while the *entresuelo* (second floor) was occupied by a British watchmaker, don Tomás Phillips, who ran his business out of a shop at street level. La Güera and her husband were attended to by five live-in servants in 1842: a coachman, chambermaid, cook, laundrywoman, and seamstress. Their home was big enough to house the coachman's wife and four children as well. In 1848 they only had three live-in servants: two women and a man with his wife and two young children.[34] Perhaps they had reduced their staff to try to save money, or perhaps the servants were temporarily in flux the day the census taker knocked on the door. Either way, the couple does not appear to have been too badly affected by her financial predicaments.

Moreover, the Elizalde residence had an excellent location only two blocks from the central *zócalo* (plaza) that was the heart of the city. From their balconies they could see the world pass by. Unless they fled to the safety of the countryside, they would have heard the gunfire of military coups that periodically punctuated the peace, observed the rioters who in 1828 rushed to the Parián market and left bearing looted goods, and watched General Winfield Scott's victorious army march in to occupy the Mexican capital in 1847. (We do not know, however, if La Güera was one of the ladies who threw flowerpots down on the Yankee soldiers as an act of resistance.) The sumptuous cathedral and the beautiful churches of La

PUBLIC SQUARE GUARDIOLA.
Corner of the convent of San Francisco.

LA PLAZUELA DE GUARDIOLA.
Esquina del convento de San Francisco.

LA PETITE PLACE DE GUARDIOLA.
L'ensignure du couvent de Saint François.

Figure 12. The busy street of San Francisco, where La Güera lived during most of her life, with a view of the Convent of San Francisco on the right and the home of the Marqués de Guardiola on the left. *La plazuela de Guardiola,* in Castro, *México y sus alrededores.* Harvard Library.

Profesa and San Francisco were a short walk from their door, as was the National Palace, where civic festivities were held (see map in chapter 1). From this vantage point María Ignacia Rodríguez continued to partake of the capital's social whirl.

DAILY LIFE

La Güera was among the members of high society who welcomed foreign dignitaries to Mexico City. Travelers who met her during this period were impressed with her beauty and charm, as well as her enormous pearls. The Englishman Henry Ward, who met "Madame Velasco" and two of her daughters between 1825 and 1827, noted about the mother only that her

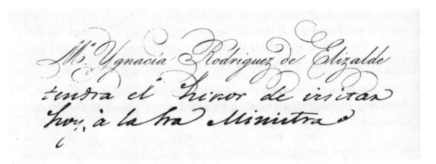

Figure 13. Calling card that María Ignacia Rodríguez sent to Fanny Calderón de la Barca on the morning of February 1, 1840, announcing her visit to the "Lady Minister." Reproduced in Calderón de la Barca, *Life in Mexico*, 142.

pearls "are all remarkable for their size."[35] (The fact that later observers did not mention her jewels indicates that she had given these away to pay some of her debts, just as she later claimed in her last will and testament.)

A month after arriving in Mexico City, Fanny Calderón de la Barca received her first visit from María Ignacia Rodríguez. The letter she wrote a relative that same day, February 1, 1840, shows that the Spanish minister's wife was immediately fascinated by this "very remarkable character." She marveled at how the sixty-one-year-old lady still conserved her liveliness and much of her good looks: "La Güera retains a profusion of fair curls without one gray hair, a set of beautiful white teeth, very fine eyes. . . . She must have been more pretty than beautiful—lovely hair, complexion, and figure." Fanny couldn't resist adding that she also had "plenty of rouge and wrinkles. Even her lips are painted red," but omitted that unflattering comment when she published the letter as part of *Life in Mexico*. Instead, she emphasized her vivacious personality: "I found La Güera very agreeable, a great talker, and a perfect living chronicle, . . . and very gay and witty."[36]

The two women saw each other often. As Fanny related in a June 5 letter to a friend in Boston, the historian William H. Prescott (which was not included in her published volume), La Güera "has taken up a serious affection for me." Repeating her initial description, Fanny now added that La Güera's hair consisted of "natural blonde ringlets." In this retelling of their conversation, Humboldt allegedly said she was "the most charming person he ever met," rather than the most beautiful, an example of how stories could change over time, even in the short span of four months that separated the two letters. Fanny also mentioned that La Güera was "married to her fourth husband," one of the many mistakes that crept into her letters.[37] Other inaccuracies were already present in her letter of February 1, for María Ignacia was twenty-four, not eighteen, when she met Humboldt; she had four children in 1803, not three as Fanny reported; and Humboldt was not a baron.[38]

Later entries in *Life in Mexico* expanded the portrait of La Güera. This "singular" lady told wonderful "original" stories about Mexican people, places, and history. Not only were they entertaining, they helped orient the newcomer to the background of the people she met. For example, on July 24, 1841 she told Fanny the story of General Manuel Barrera's ascent from rags to riches, enabled by a shrewd marriage to a wealthy woman who soon died, thereby leaving him free to marry a "pretty" but "vulgar" seamstress. (Her willingness to spread this unkind gossip suggests that she still held a grudge against the general, who was the impresario she had sued in 1826 for the return of her box at the theater.) The two women also went together on excursions outside the capital, such as—two years in a row—to the fiesta at San Agustín de las Cuevas (today Tlalpan). On most of these expeditions, Fanny and La Güera shared a carriage, usually with their husbands and, on one trip, with one of La Güera's granddaughters.

Fanny's account of their first visit to San Agustín, on June 20, 1840, provides a notable description of the good life enjoyed by the people in her milieu. The group left Mexico City around eight in the morning, and upon arriving at their host's immense hacienda,

> we found a large party assembled, and at about twelve o'clock sat down to a most magnificent breakfast of about sixty persons. Everything was solid silver, even the plates. . . . The ladies in general were dressed in white embroidered muslins, over white or coloured satin, and one or two Paris dresses shone conspicuous. . . .
>
> After breakfast we had music, dancing, walking, and billiard playing. Some boleros were very gracefully danced by a daughter of the *marquesa*, and they also showed us some dances of the country. The fête terminated with the most beautiful supper I almost ever saw. A great hall was lighted with colored lamps, the walls entirely lined with green branches, and hung with fresh garlands of flowers most tastefully arranged. There was a great deal of gaiety and cordiality, of magnificence without ceremony, and riches without pretension.

Figure 14. Portrait of Frances Erskine Inglis Calderón de la Barca, ca. 1840.
Befriending La Güera during her residence in Mexico in 1840 and 1841, her lively
travel account was instrumental in keeping La Güera's memory alive for future
generations. Anonymous oil painting, MS. Eng 1763 (57), Houghton Library,
Harvard University.

At midnight the group returned home in a convoy of seven carriages. The trip was memorable because, as they traveled the ten miles over rough roads, they encountered an "awful" thunderstorm that overturned one of the carriages. Fortunately, they "arrived in Mexico towards morning, very tired but with neither broken bones nor bruises."

Another memorable excursion was to the pueblo of Santiago to celebrate the fiesta of Spain's patron saint on July 25, 1841. On their return trip, La Güera "was all the time lamenting the state of the times and giving us a lively description of what this fête used to be in former days."

Fanny also included one of La Güera's stories in her letter of February 1, 1840. It is worth repeating at length because it is a rare example of La Güera's renowned storytelling, and perhaps even some of her voice, albeit filtered through Fanny's delightful prose:

> One of La Güera's stories is too original to be lost. A lady of high rank having died in Mexico, her relatives undertook to commit her to her last resting place, habited according to the then prevailing fashion in her most magnificent dress, the dress in fact which had been bought for her wedding. This dress was a wonder of luxury, even in Mexico. It was entirely composed of the finest lace, and the flounces were made of a species of point which cost fifty dollars a *vara* (the Mexican yard). Its equal was unknown. It was also ornamented and looped up at certain intervals with bows of ribbon very richly embroidered in gold. In this dress the Condesa de _____ was laid in her coffin, thousands of dear friends crowding to view her beautiful *costume de mort*, and at length she was placed in her tomb, the key of which was entrusted to the sacristan.
>
> From the tomb to the opera is a very abrupt transition; nevertheless, both have a share in this story. There was in Mexico a company of French dancers, a twentieth-rate ballet, and the chief danseuse was a little French damsel, remarkable for the shortness of her robes, her coquetry, and her astonishing pirouettes. On the night of a favorite ballet, Mademoiselle Estelle made her entrée in a succession of pirouettes and, poising on her toe, looked round for approbation, when a sudden thrill of horror accompanied by a murmur of indignation, ran round the assembly. Mademoiselle Estelle was equipped in the very dress in which the defunct countess had been buried! Lace, point flounces, gold ribbons; there was no mistaking it! Imagine the feelings of the relatives. Hardly had the curtain dropped immediately after the opera when the little danseuse found herself surrounded by certain competent authorities, questioning her very severely as to where and how she had obtained her dress. She replied that she knew nothing of it, but that she had bought it at an extravagant price from a French modiste in the city! She had rifled no tomb,

but honestly paid down golden ounces in exchange for her lawful property. To the modiste's went the officers of justice. She also pleaded innocent. She had bought it of a man who had brought it to her for sale and had paid him much more than *à poids d'or*, as indeed it was worth. By dint of further investigation and inquiry, this man was identified. It was the sacristan of San ____. Shortsighted sacristan! He was arrested and thrown into prison, and one benefit resulted from his cupidity since, in order to avoid throwing temptation in the way of future sacristans, it became the custom, after the body had lain in state for some time in magnificent robes, to substitute a plain dress before putting the coffin into the vault. A poor vanity after all.

This anecdote offers an intriguing glimpse of La Güera's mind. Her sense of humor was irreverent, but not anti-clerical. The story, in fact, served to explain the Mexican custom of being buried in a simple shroud, something that a foreigner might not understand. Her careful descriptions of the luxurious details of the dress also suggest her interest in fashion. And the story provides insight into the world of the opera, modistes, and the rage for everything French.

Finally, Fanny noted that as she and her husband prepared to leave the Mexican capital on January 2, 1842, her dear friend was among those who came to bid adieu. The others who visited on that last day included the former president Manuel Gómez Pedraza and his wife, along with the Echeverrías, Fagoagas, Cortinas, Escandóns, and Casa Flores—a who's who of Mexican high society and political power as well as an indication of La Güera's social circle.

Another foreigner, the French count Mathieu de Fossey, met "la blonde Rodriguez" at a party around 1832, soon after his arrival in Mexico. He devoted a page to her in *Le Mexique*, which appeared decades later in Paris.[39] Although he did not know La Güera as well as Fanny did, he was equally impressed:

> The most aristocratic woman I met in Mexico was the elderly Mrs. Elizalde, better known by the name of the Güera Rodríguez. When she spoke about republican mores and mimicked the airs of the nouveau riche, she made everyone die laughing. She was the life of the party, drawing a merry crowd to her corner.
>
> The Güera Rodríguez was the Ninon de Lenclos of her time. She was charming and retained her beauty for many years. Before she contracted cholera in 1833, I saw her be quite seductive in the evenings, although she

was already close to fifty; she had started her career as an enchantress at fourteen years. They say that in 1804 she hitched a learned voyager to her carriage, and that in 1822 Emperor Iturbide was also susceptible to her charms.

This description, published a quarter century after the fact, deserves to be evaluated with care. Fossey did not mention her in an earlier, shorter version of his travel account, *Viage a México*, printed in Mexico in 1844. By the time he wrote *Le Mexique*, he had evidently read the texts by Mariano Torrente and Fanny Calderón de la Barca. His brief reference to La Güera's friendship with Iturbide was likely based on Torrente's 1830 *Historia de la Revolución*, which similarly compares her to Ninon de l'Enclos. The reference to her flirtatious relationship with Humboldt (the "learned voyager" she "hitched . . . to her carriage" in 1804) was likely based on Calderón de la Barca's 1843 *Life in Mexico*. Indeed, Fossey's short paragraph on La Güera's children, which follows the two paragraphs cited above, bears a striking resemblance to Fanny's text, for, like her, he only mentioned La Güera's daughters and appeared to have been unaware of the existence of her son (even though Gerónimo was a deputy to congress while Fossey resided in Mexico, with a high enough profile that Bustamante commented on two of his legislative proposals in his diary).[40] Echoing Fanny, Fossey only noted that "La Güera Rodríguez had three daughters, who were married, one to the Count of Regla, the other to the Marquis of Guadalupe, and the third to the Marquis d'Aguayo. The first two were as beautiful as angels; they died in the prime of their lives."

Even if Fossey was incorporating second-hand information into his narrative, however, the first paragraph may reflect his personal experience. It is the only text that claims that La Güera contracted cholera in 1833—a statement that cannot be confirmed, though it is plausible given the severity of the epidemic that devastated the Mexican capital. And his vivid description of her entertaining a rapt audience at an evening soirée confirms other portrayals of La Güera as unusually *simpática*, the life of the party, and great fun to be around.

Carlos María de Bustamante provided many additional details about María Ignacia Rodríguez in his private diary, for he knew her entire family well.[41] Because Bustamante ran into her on several important occasions, we can surmise that she regularly participated in both the civic and religious life of the capital. For example, on Friday October 26, 1838, he saw "the so-called güera Velasco" among the multitude of people at the National Palace during the solemn ceremony marking the transferral of Iturbide's bones to the cathedral. On Saturday September 10, 1836, at seven o'clock in the evening, she was among those who witnessed the relocation of the Indian nuns of La Enseñanza from their ancient and rundown convent of San Juan de Dios to the Betlemitas Convent. Bustamante noted that "it has been exceedingly difficult to arrange this relief" for the "unfortunate" women who had been "living in the mud." The event was attended by the Ministro de Relaciones, the vicar of the nunnery, "and respectable people of both sexes who sponsored them, among them the famous *quondam* [former] Güera Rodríguez de Velasco, who has become quite pious." Another entry of Sunday May 16, 1830, similarly noted her religiosity: "Doctor Santiago preached a fervent sermon on this holy day, whose fiesta was paid for by the famous Güera Rodríguez de Velasco, who has put herself on the path to salvation, which is a good thing."

Bustamante also recounted one of La Güera's pithy sayings, thereby giving us an example of her well-known way with words. On September 4, 1846, in preparation for Santa Anna's return to the city, a triumphal arch was erected for the general to process through on the corner of her street. "The famous güera Rodríguez" asked what it was, and on being told that it was an arch, "she cleverly remarked, 'Oh, I thought it was an *horca* [noose], not an *arco* [arch].'" According to Bustamante, "this witticism has been much celebrated."

Although Bustamante praised La Güera's cleverness and religious devotion, it seems that he did not much like her. In three separate entries he revealed his misogynistic disdain for old women by describing María Ignacia and her sister María Josefa as worn-out "mummies" and "old gossips" who played a "sorry role . . . in the world."[42] And he took her daughter's side in a scandalous marital dispute that rocked the Mexican capital and inevitably embroiled the mother. Indeed, Bustamante labeled La Güera "immoral" because she allegedly supported Josefa's husband against her own daughter.[43] (In all fairness, however, Bustamante was also quite uncharitable to many of the men in his diary, probably because he did not expect his comments to see the light of day.)

Figure 15. Carlos María de Bustamante, family friend of La Güera Rodríguez, who mentions her several times in his private diary, which noted interesting events in the life of Mexico City between 1822 and 1848. From *Album mexicano* (ca. 1840). Harvard Library.

The scandal that was the talk of the town was Josefa's separation from her husband, Pedro Romero de Terreros, in 1826. Despite the early passion that led them to wed against his mother's wishes, the union of the young counts of Regla proved to be so unhappy that they sought an ecclesiastical divorce after thirteen years of marriage. La Güera, who had once been involved in divorce proceedings, apparently counseled her daughter against it, perhaps because she herself had endured so much—including physical violence—without seeking a separation. It seems that she was also quite fond of her son-in-law, even naming him the guardian of her minor daughter Paz in her 1819 will. And, although Bustamante did not give any details, he referred to an earlier falling-out between the two women that had left the mother "upset because her daughter had not let her in her house for four years."

According to Bustamante, the couple's discord had begun long before—in part, he claimed, because Josefa was much more intelligent than Pedro. Josefa worried about her children's future because she felt that her husband was mismanaging the family fortune by spending extravagantly, selling off properties, and taking out huge loans. (Indeed, Edith Couturier, historian of the Regla family, suspected that he was addicted to gambling.)[44] The straw that apparently broke the camel's back was a dispute over their children's schooling. Wanting to give them the best possible education, Josefa arranged to send them to study in England with the family of her close friend, H. G. Ward. Although Pedro had initially backed the plan, he changed his mind—allegedly influenced by "some fanatical clerics" as well as by his mother-in-law, who considered her grandchildren too young to be sent abroad.

After what must have been a bitter fight, on February 14, 1826, Pedro kicked Josefa out of the house and even managed to have her briefly "imprisoned" in the Convent of Belén. Bustamante noted that "for three days she was held incommunicado by order of her husband, who has behaved like her sultan," but afterward she received visits "every day at all hours . . . from people of all classes" who wanted to show their "compassion." Pedro also spread the rumor that she was having an affair, which Bustamante insisted was false. The couple quickly obtained an ecclesiastical divorce. Pedro agreed to pay his estranged wife a stipend of 6,000 pesos a year and she moved into her own house on the Ribera de San Cosme. In June 1826 she petitioned for a *tutor* and *curador* to be named for her children to remove the guardianship from their supposedly "stupid and prodigal" father. Pedro retaliated by sending her abroad, leaving the children behind.[45]

Pressured by her mother as well as by her husband, according to Bustamante, Josefa embarked on a grand tour of the continent. On her way back she stopped in Brooklyn, where she met an untimely death. On June 7, 1828, the thirty-two-year-old ex-countess succumbed to a bout of dysentery, surrounded by her Mexican friends the Fagoagas and the Marqués de Vivanco, who happened to be visiting New York. She was buried in St. Patrick's Cathedral, where she rested until her son Manuel repatriated her remains decades later. Soon after the news of her death reached Mexico, a solemn funeral mass was held in the Church of La Profesa in Mexico City, on August 8, 1828. "This new Dido," lamented Bustamante (comparing her to the strong and independent Queen of Carthage, who likewise met an untimely death), "abandoned by her husband and rivaled by her own mother the celebrated Güera Rodríguez, harpy of our soil, deserves our compassion. . . . She was extraordinarily beautiful, . . . an excellent conversationalist, enlightened and talented, cheerful, a constant friend and good patriot. . . . Her mother and husband will have to live with the continuous guilt of having oppressed this victim by forcing her . . . to abandon her homeland and die many leagues from her tender children."[46]

Bustamante speculated that Josefa "was returning to Mexico to reunite with her husband, and that he was prepared to receive her." Yet this interpretation is unconvincing, since Bustamante also noted that when Pedro heard about his wife's death, he exclaimed: "So now I won't have to send her 500 pesos a month!"—a sign, according to the diarist, of "how little love he had for her. . . . Such is the degree of demoralization to which we have sunk!"[47]

Whatever La Güera's role may have been in her daughter's travails, Josefa's death must have been a bitter pill for the mother to swallow. That year was particularly difficult because her youngest daughter, Paz, died in childbirth on September 15, at the age of twenty-three. La Güera thus lost two daughters within three months of each other. Bustamante noted that "just like that, these two beauties disappeared, leaving much material for gossip among those who have known the secrets of this tragicomic family."[48] They also left many children: Paz left three youngsters ranging from three to five years of age; and Josefa left six ranging from four to thirteen (see appendix B).

Even though both her daughters' widowers remarried, La Güera must have borne much of the responsibility for raising her orphaned grandchildren. Her extensive social contacts would have served them well. Indeed,

Fanny Calderón noted how in June 1841 La Güera took Paz's eighteen-year-old daughter María Guadalupe to San Agustín de las Cuevas to introduce her in high society, an indication that she took her grandmotherly duties seriously. Those who married made excellent matches and maintained their upper-class status for generations. La Güera undoubtedly attended—and may well have helped organize—their weddings, as well as the ceremony where Antonia's daughter, Guadalupe, professed as a nun in the convent of Santa Teresa la Antigua. In 1836 La Güera received her first great grandchild, and she welcomed six more during the 1840s. She was particularly close to her grandson Manuel Romero de Terreros, whom she named as one of the executors of her estate in 1850.

Joyful family occasions alternated with sorrowful ones, and La Güera was also busy attending funerals. Her son-in-law, the ex-marqués de San Miguel de Aguayo, died in 1836, as did her thirty-one-year-old nephew Alejandro. Her sister Josefa—whom Fanny described as "also a woman of great talent and extraordinary conversational powers"—left the world three years after her son, in 1839.[49] One grandchild, Antonia's daughter María del Carmen, died at the age of eight in 1838, and two others died at the age of twenty: one of Josefa's daughters in 1840 and one of Paz's sons in 1844.

In addition, La Güera was likely embroiled in some unpleasant family dramas that involved her Regla grandchildren: first, setting up a guardianship for Josefa's oldest son, Pedro, who was mentally handicapped; second, supporting two of the other Regla sons when, around 1835, they took the highly unusual step of removing part of their future inheritance from their allegedly incompetent father a full decade before his death; and third, after he died in 1846, removing their stepmother and half-brother from the ancestral home on San Felipe Neri street so that it could be sold.[50]

La Güera appears to have been close to her two surviving children. On January 8, 1835, Bustamante noted that the Deputy Villamil "was known as Geronimito, for that is what his mother, the famous Güera Rodríguez de Velasco, calls him." On April 2, 1832, he recounted "an anecdote worthy of memory," which he may have heard from the lips of La Güera herself. The incident occurred when she visited one of Gerónimo's country houses close to Mexico City: "He had invited his mother so that she could enjoy its beautiful view and extraordinary fertility and abundance. . . .

Upon her arrival, she and her son went out on the balcony to take in the sight, but at that very moment appeared a dark cloud that instead of releasing water, discharged a rain of hail of uncommon size that within minutes made the crops disappear. This incident would not have been noteworthy except that it befell a person of such renown as said lady." She would also have spent time with her son in Mexico City, for he lived only six blocks away, on the second block of Mesones street, with his wife and young son.[51] And they were further united by the fact that Gerónimo served in the Chamber of Deputies at the same time as Elizalde.

La Güera likewise enjoyed the company of her daughter Antonia, known in the family as "Tonchita."[52] The "ex-marquesa" lived two blocks away on the first block of San Francisco street with two daughters.[53] There Fanny Calderón found her in 1840, "now a handsome widow, to be seen every day in the Calle de San Francisco, standing smiling in her balcony—fat and fair."[54] An announcement in the newspaper *El Monitor Republicano* on December 25, 1846, shows that mother and daughter collaborated in charitable activities. In the midst of the Mexican-American War, doña Ignacia Rodríguez de Elizalde joined her daughter Antonia and twelve other distinguished ladies to form a junta supporting the field hospitals (*hospitales de sangre*) for injured soldiers of the Victoria Battalion that defended Mexico. Inspired by "true charity" and "social fraternity," the group invited the public to a special fundraising concert to be held on the evening of December 26 in the Gran Teatro Nacional, which they had decorated for the occasion.

This effort is not only an example of La Güera's volunteerism, but also of her sociability and patriotism. And the names of her collaborators indicate some of the members of her social circle: in addition to her daughter, they were (in the order listed in the newspaper) Josefa Cardeño de Salas, Paula Rivas de Gómez de la Cortina, Dolores Rubio de Rubio, Antonia González de Agüero, Loreto Vivanco de Morán, Cruz Noriega de Drusina, Manuela Rangel de Flores, Rosario Almanza de Echeverría, Juana Castilla de Gorostiza, Ana Bringas de Fuente Pérez, Margarita Parra de Gargollo, and Ana Noriega de O'Gorman.[55]

Gerónimo and Antonia also appear to have had a good relationship with their stepfather, Juan Manuel de Elizalde, for both relied on him for help with legal matters. After Antonia's husband died in 1836, Elizalde

Figure 16. Interior of the Gran Teatro Nacional, inaugurated in 1844 (later renamed the Teatro Iturbide), where La Güera helped organize an evening gala on December 26, 1846, to raise funds for Mexican troops fighting the United States. *Interior del Teatro Iturbide*, in Castro, *México y sus alrededores*. Harvard Library.

helped her settle the estate with "paternal affection" and represented her in several transactions, not only as her attorney but also as guarantor for her rental on the street of San Francisco. He also represented Gerónimo and his minor son Manuel at various times.[56]

La Güera thus benefited from a rich family life. Owing to her longevity and fertility—as well as to her good fortune—she became the matriarch of a large family. This situation distinguished her from her two sisters. Josefa died alone; her three daughters had perished as infants, she never remarried after losing her husband when she was thirty-one, and her only son preceded her in death, still single and without any descendants. Vicenta fared somewhat better. Although she also lost several children in infancy and died a widow, she was survived by two daughters and met six grandchildren before her death in 1845 (see appendix B). Their lives were therefore quite different from their older sister's, for María Ignacia was accompanied until her last days by a devoted husband as well as two children and more than a dozen grandchildren and great-grandchildren.

DEATH

Toward the end of her life La Güera may have become crippled: when she dictated her last will and testament on August 16, 1850, she was already suffering from her final illness, and her death certificate, dated November 1, 1850, described her as "paralytic."[57] She apparently wanted a simple burial. The first clause of her will merely specified that she "wished to be shrouded and buried with the habit and in the manner that I have communicated to my husband." Perhaps her instructions were like those she had detailed in the will she made during a previous illness, in 1819, when she asked to be "shrouded with the habit of the religious of San Diego and buried in the churchyard of my parish, to which my body shall be carried by four men, without any pomp, memorial service, or honors." The capital's newspapers did not note her passing (though to be fair, obituaries were uncommon for any but the most famous at the time).

Her will detailed her various properties and debts. She declared that her only belongings were the haciendas of La Patera and La Escalera, and that she left no jewels because she had given them all away during her lifetime. Following Hispanic inheritance rules, her husband, children, and grandchildren were the mandatory heirs of four-fifths of the estate, so she could only dispose freely of the remaining fifth. She directed her executor (her husband, or in his stead her surviving children Gerónimo and Antonia and her grandson Manuel Terreros) to use that portion to pay for her funeral and masses for her soul, to give 3,000 to an unnamed person she had secretly designated to her husband, and to give whatever remained to her second husband's niece, Dolores Gil Briones de Gadea (spelled Guedea in this document, reflecting the inconsistent spellings that characterized the era).

On November 1, 1850, celebrated as All Saints' Day in Mexico, doña María Ignacia Rodríguez was laid to rest in the churchyard of San Francisco, on the same street where she had lived most of her long life. She joined her father, mother, second husband, and several relatives who

Figure 17. The Church of San Francisco, in whose churchyard La Güera Rodríguez was buried in 1850. Her parents, second husband, and other relatives were also buried there. *Atrio del Convento de San Francisco,* in Castro, *México y sus alrededores.* Harvard Library.

were also buried there.[58] After her death the grieving Elizalde—that man of great "religiosity and total honesty"—entered the priesthood, taking vows in the Oratorio de San Felipe Neri; he died at age seventy-nine in 1870.[59] Her son Gerónimo died in 1861 at the age of sixty-three and her daughter Antonia in 1864 at the age of sixty-seven. La Güera had outlived her parents and sisters, two husbands, five of her seven children, and several grandchildren.

CONCLUSION: REFLECTIONS ON AN EXTRAORDINARY LIFE

María Ignacia Rodríguez de Velasco left few material possessions behind. In 1949 Artemio de Valle-Arizpe claimed to have seen five items that once belonged to her: a wooden box inlaid with tortoiseshell and gold and decorated with her miniature portrait; several bundles of letters that she had written her son and grandson Manuel, long missives penned in her fine hand; a silk shawl woven with gold and silver threads that depicted scenes of aristocratic life; another shawl embroidered with several figures, so worn that only the shields of Spain and of the Mexican Empire, as well as the figure of her friend Iturbide, were still visible; and her wide cedar bed, painted with pastoral scenes against an olive-green background.[60] Unfortunately, if it is true that these articles existed when Valle-Arizpe wrote his book, they may since have disappeared, for I have not been able to locate them despite diligent efforts. I have not even found her grave for, according to an elderly spokesman for the Church of San Francisco, a descendant came several decades ago and moved her remains to an unknown location.[61]

There is much that we will never know about La Güera Rodríguez, for we cannot know what was not written down. Without her personal papers, we cannot divine her intimate thoughts, nor the identity of the mystery person to whom she bequeathed a secret legacy, nor whether she had any lovers besides her three husbands. Nor can we be certain about her political convictions or confirm whether she ever said anything to Iturbide that influenced his ideas about the future of Mexico. Nor can we know if she was happy, though it is safe to assume that her third husband was very much in love with her to marry a woman twelve years older than himself.

There is nonetheless much that we can learn from the written record. In our times, La Güera Rodríguez has been portrayed as an extraordinary woman, an exceptional figure who broke the rules that bound women in her day. It is certainly true that she made enough of a mark on her society that her nickname was well known. She stood out because of her unusual beauty as well as her intelligence and charm. She attracted attention as a great conversationalist, life of the party, and occasional subject of gossip. She demonstrated remarkable resilience in confronting personal vicissitudes and adjusting to difficult political and economic times. She did not, however, appear to have challenged the social conventions of her time, place, gender, and elevated social class. Her aristocratic circle was very sociable and hospitable with foreigners. Many women became widows and remarried; had numerous children, of whom several died; headed their own households; administered their property and that of their minor

children; defended themselves in court; and took advantage of their connections to improve their family's position. In a society where religion was
deeply woven into the fabric of daily life, most people attended church
regularly and celebrated religious holidays with varying degrees of sincerity. It was also routine for women to be interested in public affairs and to
take part in political discussions and intrigues. Indeed, the control of
information through "gossip"—evidently one of La Güera's strengths—was
an essential survival skill and a source of female power. It was, in fact, the
way that she participated in the *criollo* conspiracy of 1809. Yet nothing in
the historical record suggests that she was the glamorous vixen or defiant
rebel who would become an icon of Mexican history.

PART TWO The Afterlife

5   The First Hundred Years
    after Her Death

La Güera Rodríguez's true life story is quite different from that of the semi-fictitious figure who gained fame at the end of the twentieth century. That persona was not born overnight, however. During the first hundred years of what we might call her posthumous journey, her steps toward celebrity were slow and halting and left her with a long way yet to traverse.

After her death, doña María Ignacia Rodríguez receded from public view until the early twentieth century. Her reappearance began slowly, with short passages in erudite books that reached a limited audience, in particular Guillermo Prieto's *Memorias de mis tiempos* and three books written by her great-great-grandson, the Marqués de San Francisco Manuel Romero de Terreros y Vinent (grandson of her beloved grandson Manuel Romero de Terreros Villar Villamil). By focusing the attention of historians on the independence period, the centennials of the Grito de Dolores in 1910 and of emancipation from Spain in 1921 contributed to La Güera's resurrection. So did new editions of nineteenth-century works, notably the publication of an abridged version of Mariano Torrente's *Historia* in 1918, the first Spanish-language edition of Fanny Calderón de la Barca's *Life in Mexico* in 1920, and the rediscovery and attribution of Vicente Rocafuerte's *Bosquejo ligerísimo*. These texts provided the foundation for the gradual construction of her legend. And she was more visible in the new works than in those published during her lifetime because she was openly identified by her name or nickname rather than mysteriously referred to as a "distinguished" or "principal" lady.

Yet if La Güera had already embarked on her grand odyssey into the land of legend, she was not yet a household name. The tales told about her during the first half of the twentieth century deserve to be carefully scrutinized. Although some can be corroborated with historical documentation, others are either totally false or unreliable because they built on old unsubstantiated rumors or appeared for the first time—without any supporting evidence—more than fifty years after her death. As various authors copied each other, their stories became ever more fanciful, her image became ever more glamorous, and her alleged political influence grew ever stronger. Still, in this first incarnation she was represented as a Grand Aristocratic Lady who, though witty and patriotic, was not yet the promiscuous rebel or major heroine that she would later become.

LA GÜERA DISAPPEARS FROM THE SCENE, 1850–1900

The contrast between La Güera's invisibility during the second half of the nineteenth century and her extraordinary fame in the twenty-first is astonishing. It is not that women were completely omitted from nineteenth-century histories, for they were from the start included in the pantheon of heroes constructed for the new nation. As early as 1825, José Joaquín Fernández de Lizardi had published an almanac praising eleven women for their contributions to Mexican independence. In the next few decades a handful of women, especially Leona Vicario, Josefa Ortiz de Domínguez (La Corregidora), and Mariana Rodríguez del Toro de Lazarín, were regularly singled out for their roles in fighting Spanish despotism.[1] But María Ignacia Rodríguez was conspicuously absent from the early accounts glorifying the national heroines.

Toward the end of the century a new genre emerged: collections of biographical sketches of important historical personages. In 1884 Francisco Sosa published his mammoth *Biografías de mexicanos distinguidos*, which contained short vignettes about some three hundred distinguished

Mexicans. Ten women were among their number, including the by then obligatory Josefa Ortiz de Domínguez and Leona Vicario, as well as Malinche (the Indian interpreter who helped Cortés conquer New Spain), several writers, and the founder of a charitable institution. Yet La Güera did not appear, even in the relatively long entry devoted to Iturbide. Nor was she included in Antonio García Cubas's five-volume *Diccionario geográfico, histórico y biográfico,* published between 1888 and 1891.

Neither did she figure in compilations that focused entirely on women. Beginning in 1887, the early feminist Laureana Wright de Kleinhans featured biographical sketches of women in her journal *Violetas de Anáhuac* to prove that the fair sex had contributed to Mexican history. A hundred of these profiles were collected in her *Mujeres notables mexicanas,* published posthumously in 1910 as part of the Porfirian government's effort to integrate women's history into the centennial of the Grito de Dolores. (Indeed, the Ministry of Public Instruction sent copies to all Mexican primary schools as a way to encourage girls' education.)[2] The "notable women" ranged from indigenous royalty and colonial nuns to nineteenth-century writers, singers, actresses, teachers, philanthropists, and the first female doctor in Mexico. A dozen independence heroines were included, but not La Güera. Nor was she among the dozen heroines profiled by the celebrated chronicler of Mexico City, Luis González Obregón, in his 1895 *México viejo.*[3]

The centennial of 1910 saw a veritable explosion of interest in heroines of the independence period, especially Leona Vicario and La Corregidora. They were lauded in civic ceremonies and monuments, depicted on commemorative stamps, and had schools named after them.[4] The renowned historian Genaro García honored Vicario with a scholarly book-length biography. And they were not the only ones: a two-volume collection recounting noted episodes of the independence wars included three chapters on some two dozen women.[5] Still, La Güera was missing from these books, as well as from the patriotic celebrations.

Her absence from the historical memory of the time shows that she was not yet considered a central actor in Mexican history. This silence also reflects the decreased importance assigned to the early intrigues of the viceregal court. For La Güera's contemporaries Alamán and Bustamante, her denunciation of the *oidor* Aguirre in the fall of 1809 was significant enough to merit a brief mention in their narratives. But that incident—the only one in which we can document that she played a key role—was no longer of interest to historians by the end of the nineteenth century. Instead, they emphasized the events unleashed by the Grito de Dolores in 1810, in which La Güera barely figured.

HER RESURRECTION, 1900–1949

The resurrection of La Güera Rodríguez began in 1906 with the publication of Guillermo Prieto's *Memorias* of life in Mexico from 1828 to 1853.[6] The famed writer and statesman mentioned her twice in his gossipy work. First, in a brief sentence, he described a group of "dirty old men" exchanging the latest rumors and savoring "the pithy sayings of La Güera Rodríguez." Then, in a longer passage, he wrote:

> Squarely in front of la Profesa spent her last days, married to don Juan Manuel Elizalde, La Güera Rodríguez, dubbed the Mexican Venus because of her extraordinary beauty, praised by the baron von Humboldt in his work.
>
> La Güera was not only notable for her beauty, but also for her cleverness and for the position she occupied in high society, becoming related to the count of Regla and the marquis of Guadalupe.
>
> The friendship Iturbide had with her, it is said, exerted a great influence on Independence.
>
> This influence was such, her contemporaries maintained, that even though it had been formally determined that the entrance of the Ejército Trigarante should be through Tacuba street, the route was changed to process through San Francisco and La Profesa, because that was the desire of the lady favored by the caudillo of the Three Guarantees.
>
> La Güera's daughters were very pretty; one of them (Pepita, wife of the count of Regla) died in the United States, and the other was the mother of Joaquín Rincón Gallardo, Guadalupe, and Rosa.
>
> The beauty of the señora de Rincón can be seen in the lovely image of the Virgen de los Dolores in La Profesa, whose visage I know to be her portrait.

In these few lines Prieto not only depicted La Güera as a well-known personage in Mexico City, famed for her entertaining conversation, but also revived the rumor of her relationship with Iturbide. Moreover, he introduced the first reference in print of the story that has since been repeated many times: that Iturbide changed the route of his triumphal procession of September 27, 1821, in order to pass by her balcony on the street of San Francisco.

It is difficult to know if there is any truth to this tale. It did not appear in the many earlier descriptions of Iturbide's entrance into Mexico City. Alamán, for example, described how the Army of the Three Guarantees marched down the Paseo Nuevo and turned onto San Francisco, where a triumphal arch had been erected at the beginning of the street and the city councilmen waited to give Iturbide the keys to the city. After the ceremony they continued straight to the National Palace in the *zócalo,* a route that would have taken Iturbide directly by La Güera's house in any case.[7] And Prieto's page on the Mexican beauty contained at least one obvious error: she was not, in fact, "praised by the baron von Humboldt in his work." We only know of his admiration for her through Fanny Calderón's text—an indication of the pivotal role of *Life in Mexico* in keeping alive the memory of María Ignacia Rodríguez.

Moreover, Prieto was not an eyewitness observer. Despite the implication in the title that his work was a memoir, his portrayal of La Güera was second hand. Since Prieto was born in 1818, he might have met her in the 1830s or 1840s, but he never claimed to have done so; and the entrance of Iturbide's army took place when he was but three years old. Although Prieto cited "her contemporaries" as the source of his information, by the time he wrote his book—sometime between 1886 and his death in 1897[8]—most of her contemporaries were long gone. So he was relying on his memory of their memories, perhaps not the most reliable source, but evidence that La Güera had not been entirely forgotten.

Even though some of Prieto's details may have been apocryphal, his text reminded readers that there was once in Mexico an unusually beautiful and charming lady. It put La Güera in the middle of an important historical event, cemented the story of her close friendship with Iturbide—and even hinted at a possible romantic involvement for those who so wished to interpret the statement that she was "the lady favored by the caudillo." It also suggests that by the late nineteenth century she was referred to as "the Mexican Venus," a moniker that would be taken up by later works and contribute to her near-mythical status, since Venus was the Roman goddess of beauty, love, sex, and fertility.

La Güera's second step on the road to fame came with three books published by her descendant Manuel Romero de Terreros between 1909 and 1921. This eminent scholar of Mexican art and architecture was also one of the country's first social historians. His generation (which also included Luis González Obregón) reacted against the political histories of the nineteenth century by narrating stories of daily life. Focusing on interesting individuals as well as local customs and manners, their *costumbrista* narratives returned to the colonial period and affirmed that it was a legitimate part of the nation's history. Doña María Ignacia Rodríguez was a particularly attractive figure for this author because she also permitted him to exalt his illustrious ancestors.

Romero de Terreros introduced La Güera in his 1909 *Los condes de Regla,* a history of the Regla family that contained four sentences about her because she was the mother of Josefa, the third Countess of Regla.[9] Repeating what he had read in Fanny Calderón's letter of February 1, 1840 (which he reproduced in the original English in a long footnote), he affirmed that

> at the beginning of the nineteenth century doña María Ignacia Rodríguez de Velasco y Ossorio Barba was one of the most celebrated ladies of the viceroyalty, not only because of her sharp wit, but also because of her beauty, which must have been very great because Humboldt considered her the most beautiful woman he had met. Because of the profusion of blonde curls, which adorned her head according to the fashion of the times, she was known to all by the nickname la "Güera," and her house became the center of spirited *tertulias* attended by the most select members of society.

He then proceeded to list the titles and offices of her first husband as well as to introduce her children, "one son and three daughters, who inherited all the beauty of their mother, such that they were called 'Venus and the three Graces.'" The book also included the miniature portrait of La Güera—the only picture we have of her—that was in the possession of her descendants (see fig. 1). Surprisingly, the image fails to support the tale of her extraordinary beauty, in part because of the poor quality of its black-and-white reproduction.

If his first short representation of La Güera was fairly straightforward, the next one was less so. His 1919 *Ex-antiquis: Bocetos de la vida social en la Nueva España* included a full chapter on "Venus and the Three Graces." Besides recounting the history of the mother and her three beautiful daughters (mostly emphasizing whom they married, how many children they had, and what titles they held), it also contained what his "most esteemed friend," Luis González Obregón, in the foreword called "delicious . . . picaresque details and whispered gossip elicited by their words and deeds." Because *Ex-antiquis* was a more popular work than *Los condes de Regla* (and was indeed reprinted with a simpler title in 1944), these "delicious" and "picaresque" stories about María Ignacia Rodríguez brought her to the attention of a wider reading public.[10]

Romero de Terreros warned his readers that "innumerable are the stories and anecdotes told about the 'Güera,' and though some may be authentic, there is no doubt that the majority lack substance and present doña Ignacia as having much less virtue than was likely for a grand lady of the viceregal court." Despite this disclaimer, he nonetheless added a few tales of his own. It is unclear whether they came from family lore, whether they were based on something he had read, or whether they too "lacked substance." Besides, any stories that had been passed down through the family would have been third or fourth hand, since he never met his grandfather, Manuel, who had been close to La Güera, because he died two years before the author was born.

Some tales are entirely false—for example, that she bequeathed her splendid jewels to dress an image of the virgin in the church of La Profesa, when La Güera's last will and testament clearly stated that she had disposed of all her jewelry during her lifetime, giving it to her children and creditors, not to the Church. Several of the names and dates are also wrong, notably the name of her second husband (Juan Ignacio, not Mariano) and the year of her death (1850, not 1851). These mistakes have since been copied many times. (Indeed, after finding several errors in the work, Valle-Arizpe deleted a statement praising the marquis as an excellent researcher from a revised edition of his book *La Güera Rodríguez*.)[11] Thus Romero de Terreros, despite being La Güera's great-great-grandson, is not always a reliable source for her biography.

Some of his stories nonetheless have a grain of truth in them, and they were certainly entertaining and remained part of her legend. For example, he claimed that Viceroy Revillagigedo had forced La Güera to marry her first husband because he found them flirting outside the barracks of the Granaderos, a regiment housed by the *zócalo* whose officers "were the richest and best-looking youth of the nobility." Walking by the barracks every afternoon, she and her sister Josefa established courtships with two of the soldiers that "scandalized some neighbors and served as a diversion for others." One day "they were surprised by the viceroy in person." Revillagigedo was furious because "if such conduct is reproachable in our day, think of how much more it would have been in those times when ladies only ventured into the street accompanied by their fathers, husbands, or chaperones." The viceroy called in the girls' father to ask what he did every afternoon. When the *regidor* explained that he went to the Sagrario to pray the rosary, Revillagigedo admonished him: "You should instead pray in your house and watch over the honor of your daughters." The two men then decided that the girls should marry their beaus "to silence wicked tongues." Because the boys' parents opposed the matches, the viceroy intervened to facilitate the sisters' unions with their future husbands.[12]

It is true that Villamil's father—but apparently not the father of Cosío, Josefa's intended—opposed the marriage. His opposition revealed the difficult relationship between father and son. Yet the father did not mention any dishonorable conduct on the part of "la niña" or refer to being pressured by the viceroy. Instead, he objected because his son did not seek his permission before becoming engaged and because he lacked sufficient funds to maintain a family. And even if it were true that the viceroy had encouraged the two sisters' marriages, it is doubtful that La Güera married against her will—not only because the Catholic Church insisted on freedom of marriage and could invalidate marriages entered into under duress, but also because the senior Villamil's opposition to the union would have given her a way to get out of the engagement if she had so desired. Nor was the alleged incident brought up later during the couple's ecclesiastical divorce case, where it could have strengthened the argument for a separation. On the contrary, a witness in the 1802 proceedings referred to the love-struck Villamil's courtship of his future bride, and his attorney insisted that Villamil had "broken the closest ties" with his father due to "his tender, blind, and intense love for her."[13] Moreover, there was no need for the couple to marry quickly because María Ignacia was quite young (at fifteen, well below the median age of marriage for noblewomen, which was nineteen)[14] and she was not pregnant (her first child was born ten months after the wedding). Indeed, her sister waited another two years to marry, despite the alleged pressure from the viceroy.

Another unsubstantiated anecdote added a new twist to the story of how, after her second husband died, La Güera won the battle with his family over his estate. According to Romero de Terreros, because the Briones siblings accused her of feigning pregnancy, she "decided that the birth of her child should be in the presence of witnesses. . . . But because the event occurred sooner than expected, she was forced to call to her bedroom some gentlemen who were at that moment walking down the street, so that they could corroborate the authenticity of the birth." Thus exonerated, La Güera named her child Victoria because she represented a victory in the lawsuit.

It is indeed true that the Briones family sued her over the estate and that after the child's birth they requested that a priest in Mexico City certify that she had been pregnant. It is also true that when Victoria died, La Güera inherited the entire estate and, to end the lawsuit, gave her husband's relatives a fifth of the legacy. But there is no evidence to confirm— or deny—the rest of the story. In any case, the new details not only portrayed her as an audacious woman who summoned perfect strangers into her bed chamber, but also recalled the European queens who called in witnesses to authenticate the birth of a royal heir.

In his narration of the episode in which La Güera was banished from Mexico City, Romero de Terreros also went beyond what can be verified in the historical record. Elaborating on the few sentences in the histories by Alamán and Bustamante about the punishment of a "distinguished lady" for being involved in a conspiracy, he gave them a new meaning, claiming that her punishment followed a trial before a panel of inquisitors in 1810 for advocating independence. According to his narrative, "It so happened that the judges of that feared institution were well known to her as friends and, after a trial that bordered on the ridiculous, the Archbishop Viceroy . . . only imposed the penalty of a short exile to the city of Querétaro, a punishment she gladly accepted." He concluded that "she was definitely a supporter of Independence . . . and never abandoned the cause."

Again, this story has some basis in fact but also contains some inaccuracies. Although the viceroy called her in for a meeting in October 1809 (not

1810), there is no evidence that she ever faced a tribunal of judges. She was not banished for advocating independence, but for plotting to undermine the leader of a rival political faction during the colony's early struggle for self-government within the Spanish empire. Finally, her three petitions to return to Mexico City show that she did not accept her penalty lightheartedly. Yet in his retelling of the incident, Romero de Terreros succeeded both in bringing La Güera's political activities to the attention of his readers and in linking her to the later Hidalgo Revolt, to which her denunciation of the *oidor* Aguirre had no connection. This new falsehood would become a key in constructing the myth of La Güera as an independence heroine.

By then having read Prieto's *Memorias* (cited in his bibliography), Romero de Terreros also repeated the story of how Iturbide changed the route of his triumphal procession to honor his "great friendship" with La Güera. And he added a new flourish: that as Iturbide passed in front of her house, "the future Emperor of Mexico stopped the march for a moment and, taking a feather from his hat, which displayed plumes of three colors"—symbolizing the Three Guarantees embedded in the Plan de Iguala—"had one of his assistants send it up to the beautiful 'Güera.'" Although the addition of this chivalrous gesture highlighted their special relationship,[15] the marquis of San Francisco denied any romantic liaison between his great-great-grandmother and the Liberator of Mexico.

Ex-antiquis also revived the story of her friendship with Humboldt by incorporating the passage from Fanny Calderón's letter of February 1, 1840, into the text. This time the long citation was not just relegated to a footnote, as in his earlier book. And because the author translated Fanny's passage into Spanish, he made it easily accessible to Mexican readers who until that point could only read *Life in Mexico* in the original English-language version.[16]

In addition, Romero de Terreros added new details about La Güera's old age by claiming that she "spent the last years of her life dedicated to spiritual exercises, having entered the Third Order of San Francisco," a lay association whose members devoted themselves to prayer and were buried in the drab habit of the order. I have been unable to confirm this statement. In 1921 González Obregón professed to having heard a similar rumor from an elderly gentleman who had met La Güera in his childhood.[17] But all we can say with certainty is that her third husband was a member of that group and that the first clause of La Güera's 1850 will stated that she wished to be "shrouded and buried in the habit and place I have indicated to my husband." Yet the custom of using the coarse shroud of a favorite order was so widespread in her social class that it did not necessarily signify deep piety or membership in a particular devotional association.[18] Indeed, well before she married the deeply religious Elizalde she had asked, in her 1819 will, to be buried in the habit of San Diego. And her 1802 divorce case shows that she participated in many religious rites and spent considerable time in the company of priests. Moreover, even though Bustamante in 1830 described her as having "put herself on the path to salvation," that does not mean that her life revolved around mass and spiritual exercises. Fanny Calderón's description of La Güera when she was in her early sixties, as well as her participation some years later in organizing the gala fundraiser for the Victoria Battalion, suggest that she was far from a recluse who stuck close to home and church.

Whether or not they were true, Romero de Terreros's choice of anecdotes reminds us that the purpose of his books was to glorify his ancestors. It is no surprise that he described doña María Ignacia as "the most prominent figure of Mexican society in the eighteenth and nineteenth centuries."[19] His account emphasized her ties to the noble, rich, famous, and powerful. Indeed, he not only portrayed her as imitating European royalty by calling in witnesses to Victoria's birth, but claimed that news of her beauty reached the king of Spain, who requested a painting of "Venus and the Three Graces" so that he could admire them. Although Romero de Terreros wrote that the painting was "stored with many others in a warehouse of the Royal Palace of Madrid," it may never have existed, since it has disappeared without a trace.[20] His invention of the gift of her jewelry to La Profesa likewise highlighted her wealth, piety, and charity. But it is worth noting what the author omitted: he did not air the family's dirty laundry (for example, that both she and her daughter Josefa had been involved in divorce proceedings) and skipped over the mundane aspects of La Güera's life, such as dealing with debt and sickness or bearing seven children and watching five die during her lifetime. Instead, he emphasized the more glamorous parts of her life that fit the story he wanted to tell about his lineage.

Marking the 1921 centennial of Mexican independence with another book, *La corte de Agustín I, Emperador de México,* Romero de Terreros found a new opportunity to defend his great-great-grandmother's virtue. By then having seen Rocafuerte's screed against Iturbide, he felt the need to refute his accusations squarely. A section devoted to "Supposed Relations between Iturbide and the Güera Rodríguez" reproduced Rocafuerte's diatribe at length and also repeated Prieto's story of how Iturbide changed the route of his triumphal procession to pass by the house of his "favored" lady. Romero de Terreros questioned the veracity of both narratives: "Although in reality there was no reliable proof for these assertions, throughout the nation the rumor spread that the leader of the Three Guarantees maintained amorous relations with the famous 'Güera Rodríguez,' and some even claimed that she was a major influence on Independence." The Marquis insisted that neither story was true; that although she supported independence and was a great friend of Iturbide's, they did not have an affair and she did not influence the course of historical events. For lack of better evidence, he asked, "If La Güera Rodríguez had so much influence over Iturbide, . . . why wasn't this lady appointed to any position in the new empire's court?"[21]

Of course, by including long citations from the works of Rocafuerte and Prieto, Romero de Terreros mainly succeeded in spreading them further. The effect of his book was thus the opposite of what he intended. Although he portrayed his ancestor as a Proper Patriotic Lady, many readers would only remember the claim in the chapter's subtitle of "supposed relations between Iturbide and La Güera Rodríguez," rather than the refutation, and those who had not read Rocafuerte or Prieto now had their words inscribed in their memories. Although some historians who subsequently used these sources were careful to emphasize that the stories were only rumors (for example, Rafael Heliodoro Valle in his 1922 book *Cómo era Iturbide,* who briefly mentioned her alleged political influence on Iturbide without insinuating that they had a romantic relationship),[22] many others would not be as circumspect.

Until this point, references to La Güera Rodríguez had appeared in short passages embedded in longer works known mainly to students of history. That situation began to change with the centennial edition of *Excelsior,* the capital's principal newspaper, which reached a large audience. On September 27, 1921, the hundredth anniversary of Iturbide's triumphant march into Mexico City, it printed a long article with the

LA BELLA "GÜERA" RODRIGUEZ

Un Episodio Romántico de la Agitada Vida del Libertador de Nuestro País, el Generalísimo Don Agustín de Iturbide

Por JOSE MIGUEL DE LA PEZA

Figure 18. Striking full-page illustration that accompanied the article "La Bella 'Güera' Rodríguez" by José Miguel de la Peza, published in a special centennial edition of *Excelsior*, September 27, 1921 (fifth section, p. 6). Digital reproduction by the Acervo Micrográfico de la Hemeroteca Nacional de México.

arresting title "The Beautiful Güera Rodríguez: A Romantic Episode in the Agitated Life of the Liberator of our Country, Generalísimo Don Agustín de Iturbide."[23] Accompanying it was a striking drawing of a ravishing María Ignacia Rodríguez coiffed in the flapper style of the day—an image that made her look much more attractive than the rather plain woman in the portrait reproduced by Romero de Terreros. The headline was misleading, however. Though it hinted at romance, the piece did not follow through with that promise. Its depiction of La Güera was nonetheless memorable and immediately boosted her fame.

The author of the article, José Miguel de la Peza, wrote that when he visited Luis González Obregón and asked him to share some anecdote about a woman of the independence period for the special centennial issue, the eminent chronicler recounted several stories about María Ignacia Rodríguez that he attributed to conversations with elderly friends who had known her long ago. First, he described her "exquisite beauty": when she entered a room, people stopped in their tracks to gaze upon her "as though they had seen a virgin, radiant with beauty." Next he praised her appealing personality as "a woman ahead of her time, because of her sincerity and the joy that she spread around her" as she "talked with each and every one of her innumerable admirers," though without leading any of them on.

In a variant of Fanny's narrative, Peza wrote that one day in 1803 the wise Baron Humboldt met her at a party at the viceregal palace and was so dazzled that he could not leave her side. They became "inseparable" companions, which led to much gossip "although no one could ever prove that they were anything more than good friends." Accompanying him to the unveiling of the equestrian statue of Charles IV known as *El caballito* (an event that did in fact take place on December 9, 1803), she gave proof of her irreverence: when the baron lauded its excellence, she pointed out "with her characteristic liberty" that it had a defect "known to all"—a veiled reference to an alleged mistake in the horse's anatomy. Although this story is impossible to prove or disprove, it contradicts contemporary accounts of the statue's great perfection.[24]

Peza went on to enumerate La Güera's three marriages, beginning with the first one where the viceroy, rather than pressuring the couple to marry, as in Romero de Terreros's version, instead served as the *padrino*, or sponsor, of the wedding—an unlikely story, given that Revillagigedo had already left Mexico by then and the marriage certificate listed her parents as the *padrinos*. Peza also added a detail about her old age that González Obregón claimed to have heard from a certain Señor Agreda (possibly the son of schoolteacher Manuel de Agreda): "that, in the 1840s, when as a child accompanying his father they met a very *simpática* old lady leaving the Profesa church, his father greeted her with the utmost respect and affection, and in answer to some question, the *viejecita*, lifting her skirt, revealed the habit of the Third Order of San Francisco, which she was wearing as if already in a shroud." It is difficult to know if this memory was accurate. The elderly gentleman's recollection may in fact have been influenced by reading Romero de Terreros's story about La Güera's old age.

In any case, the meat of the article was about La Güera's contribution to Mexico's independence. First, Peza lauded her perspicacity in "ardently" promoting the call for an autonomous government under Viceroy Iturrigaray in 1808 by "taking advantage of the influence she had among both royalists and *criollos* who, attracted by her beauty, surrounded and followed her." According to Peza, had the plan not been undermined by the coup led by Yermo and his peninsular allies, Mexico could have been part of a larger Spanish Commonwealth—something like Canada in the British Commonwealth—and avoided "the spilling of so much blood" that has led to the "discord and misfortunes we still suffer from today."

Skipping over the Hidalgo revolt, Peza then took up the story in 1821 and portrayed La Güera as "collaborating, if in an indirect way, with the consummation of Independence." Because she lived close to the Profesa church, she allegedly joined the meetings known as the Juntas de la Profesa presided over by canon Matías Monteagudo. Peza credited her not with conceiving of the Plan de Iguala (as Rocafuerte alleged), but only with recommending the appointment of her friend Iturbide as the potential military leader of the independence movement. This new detail would become another key element in constructing her legend.

Peza denied that there was any love between La Güera and the future hero: "It was said that wherever La Güera went, she was involved in some amorous liaison, but this was only because her beauty gave rise to envious murmurings." Repeating Romero de Terreros's version of the story that the Army of the Three Guarantees changed the route of its procession to march by La Güera's balcony so that Iturbide could stop to give her some feathers from his hat, Peza explained that it was simply because the Liberator "wanted to honor the beautiful woman who had put him on the path to glory."

Emphasizing her profound Mexicanness, Peza concluded that "La 'Güera' Rodríguez de Velasco, the most beautiful woman of her day, . . . was a consistent supporter of the cause of Independence and its assiduous collaborator, and thus for many reasons deserves to be remembered by posterity . . . by our beloved *Patria*, which like her has been turbulent and calumnied, and like her envied for her enchanting beauty." Peza was the first of many narrators to use La Güera as a symbol for the nation, in this case because both were beautiful, restless, and misunderstood. Yet in his representation, she was still a Proper Patriotic Lady, though highly spirited and irreverent.

Just as La Güera was becoming ever more tightly bound to Iturbide in the public eye, the stories of her relationship to Humboldt were also reemerging and becoming more titillating. A pivotal step in this process was the 1910 publication of a collection of essays marking the German government's donation of a statue of Humboldt to celebrate Mexico's centennial. Writing about his Teutonic countryman's stay in Mexico, Arnold Krumm-Heller asserted that Humboldt felt a "deep passion" for the young beauty that "distracted him from his studies." To be sure, it was the "chaste love . . . of a learned scholar," but it was such a "profound" emotion—the strongest he had ever felt for a woman—that he could not forget her after he returned to Europe.[25] Krumm-Heller produced no new information to back his claims; his only "proof" was the well-worn passage from Fanny Calderón's letter.

Even that narrative should be scrutinized, because it was entirely based on what María Ignacia Rodríguez herself told Fanny nearly four decades after Humboldt's visit. No one apparently considered the possibility that La Güera might have exaggerated how much time she spent with the famous scientist—even though, as a reputedly talented storyteller, she was fully capable of choosing how to present herself. Indeed, it is plausible that in their first meeting she would have boasted of her close relationship with the revered foreign visitor in order to impress the Spanish ambassador's wife. In any case, La Güera provided no hint of a romantic relationship with Humboldt; on the contrary, she portrayed their friendship as one of companionship and shared intellectual curiosity. It was Fanny who added the suggestion that he was "under the influence of her fascinations" and indulged in a "slight *stratum* of flirtation." These comments can be seen as an attempt to spice up her narrative for the reader, for she was already thinking ahead to publishing her letters in the form of a travelogue. The last line of her first entry on La Güera—"so I have caught him—it is a comfort to think that 'sometimes even the great Humboldt nods'"— also permitted Fanny to show off her erudition, for she was paraphrasing a line in Horace's *Ars Poetica*.[26] It was thus Fanny who introduced the myth of the irresistably seductive Güera.

It is nonetheless a huge step from the flirtatious friendship described by Fanny to the deep—though platonic—passion asserted by Krumm-Heller. But after he made this leap, others would follow. The tale of their love captivated the famed writer Alfonso Reyes, for example, who wrote of Humboldt's *amores* with La Güera in his essay "Rumbo a Goethe," published in the Argentine literary journal *Sur* in 1932. Thus, even though Humboldt's biographer, Vito Alessio Robles, in 1941 insisted that there was no evidence for such a story, the legend had already begun to enter the Mexican imaginary.[27]

While these tales about La Güera were mostly recycling—and embellishing—nineteenth-century narratives, some new information was also emerging. Evidently having seen her divorce case during his perusal of Mexican archives, González Obregón hinted that the priest Mariano Beristáin might have been her suitor. His 1922 *Calles de México: Vida y costumbres de otros tiempos* included a sentence about La Güera: "This lady, doña María Ignacia Rodríguez de Velasco, was the famous Güera Rodríguez, who figured prominently in the romantic chronicles of those times because she had her dillying and dallying with the canon Beristáin and with Iturbide, was married three times, and was celebrated for her talent and beauty by Baron von Humboldt when he visited Mexico in 1803."[28] Because González Obregón's book was immensely popular, already having appeared in a sixth edition by 1944, the name of a potential new paramour became part of her legend.

Newly discovered records also linked La Güera more closely with Hidalgo's insurrection. In preparation for the centennial of Mexican independence, Genaro García combed archival repositories for documents on that movement. His monumental *Documentos históricos mexicanos,* published in 1910, devoted the entire fifth volume to insurgent women. Although La Güera was not one of the main heroines featured, she appeared in a brief entry that reproduced the 1814 document asking Señor Velasco to declare what he knew about her contributions to the rebels.[29] It would have been easy to overlook this reference, however, because it took up but one page of a very long work and García identified her only as María Ignacia Rodríguez, without pointing out that she was better known as La Güera Rodríguez. Another tidbit came in a 1932 issue of the *Boletín* of the National Archives. Reproducing the document referring to her "entanglement" in 1817 with the priest Ramón Cardeña—her old friend and by then a known opponent of colonial rule—it thereby suggested her continued involvement with the rebels. And this time she was referred to by her nickname.[30]

Elías Amador added another previously unknown detail in his 1946 *Noticias biográficas de insurgentes apodados.* His list of known conspirators included a short entry on "Güera, La; Ignacia Rodríguez" that cited the September 1810 denunciation of Hidalgo's conspiracy by the drum major Juan Garrido, who alleged that doña Ignacia Rodríguez provided money for the revolution. According to Amador, Garrido's allegation was proof that she was "strongly committed to supporting the cause of Independence." Then, paraphrasing González Obregón's *Calles de México,* Amador added that "many stories are told about the Güera Rodríguez, rumored to be a restless woman in whose romantic adventures worthy of a novel figured the canon don Mariano Beristáin and other important people of the metropolitan capital."[31] Yet it is noteworthy that Amador did not include Iturbide among La Güera's possible lovers, a sign that he did not take this rumor seriously.

It would take a while for the new material about her political activities to enter the broader literature. In 1948 Luis Castillo Ledón incorporated Garrido's testimony into his biography of Hidalgo when he affirmed that "la Güera Rodríguez, a lady descended from old noble families, famous in Mexico City for her extraordinary beauty, gave money for the revolution."[32] But neither the books on *mujeres célebres* nor the biographical dictionaries of the time mentioned her.[33] She was as yet unknown to the Mexican painters whose magnificent murals graced the walls of public buildings in the 1930s and 1940s, constructing a pictorial iconography of hundreds of historical figures that included Leona Vicario, Josefa Ortiz de Domínguez, and Gertrudis Bocanegra. And in 1948, when the names of four independence heroines were inscribed in gold on the wall of honor of the Chamber of Deputies, she was not one of them. (They were Josefa Ortiz de Domínguez, Leona Vicario, Mariana Rodríguez del Toro de Lazarín, and Antonia "La Generala" Nava.)[34]

Although the stories about her support for the first insurgency were not yet widely known, La Güera's fame as the brains behind the Plan de Iguala was spreading thanks to two articles by General Rubén García in *Todo*, a popular magazine that circulated widely.[35] Part of a longer series on Iturbide, the installments of December 30, 1948, and January 6, 1949, revived the old rumors of their illicit affair and of her influence on Mexican independence. By then the favorable opinion of Iturbide had shifted: in an age that fetishized democracy, the Liberator was no longer the hero celebrated in the 1921 texts commemorating Mexico's emancipation. Instead, García viewed him as a corrupt and immoral leader who ultimately betrayed his people by putting a crown on his head; and he repeated the accusations Rocafuerte had made in his 1822 *Bosquejo ligerísimo*.[36] While earlier authors had questioned the veracity of that text, García insisted that "Rocafuerte's statements are absolutely true" having been authenticated by the historian Lucas Alamán. Of course, Alamán had done no such thing, having on the contrary dismissed Rocafuerte's book as "a confused compilation" of lies designed to "excite Iturbide's enemies."[37]

In developing his story of how "the lovely Güera Rodríguez shaped Mexico's destiny," General García quoted the *Bosquejo ligerísimo* at length. Then he added his own flourishes: that when "la rubia Aspasia" had an affair with Iturbide, "he was thirty-five years old and she was close to forty, which explains the power she had over him, as did her sagacity and love of Independence." In his version, she influenced the Profesa plotters, not by attending their meetings as Peza had claimed, but by inviting them to her "magnificent mansion" to share information over cups of chocolate. At a sumptuous dinner at her table—where she was supposedly the only woman in attendance—she persuaded Viceroy Apodaca to appoint Iturbide as the commander of the southern army. García then reverted to Rocafuerte's narrative about how she advised the Profesa conspirators to revise their plan, thereby producing the historic Plan de Iguala. During their amorous trysts she also convinced "her boorish but passionate colonel" to abandon the royalist cause and support Mexican independence which she, a true "patriot," had long wanted.

It is worth noting the differences between the perspectives of General García and Rocafuerte. Both affirmed that La Güera used her beauty, charm, and intelligence to manipulate the great men of the hour. But Rocafuerte considered this a stain on both Iturbide and doña María Ignacia. In contrast, far from judging her harshly, García praised her for using her special gifts in the service of the nation. His articles consequently enhanced her image as a heroine, if a slightly naughty one. They also show how views of women's political activities had changed since the nineteenth century.

La Güera's status as a central figure in republican society was further reinforced by Leopoldo Zamora Plowes's 1945 *Quince Uñas y Casanova aventureros: Novela histórica picaresca.*[38] The title of this "Mexican comedy" referred to Santa Anna as "Quince Uñas" because, having lost a leg, he only had fifteen nails on his fingers and toes. At a thousand-plus pages, the novel was not exactly a popular work (although it was subsequently reprinted several times, including in a condensed edition).[39] Yet La Güera stood out because she occupied four pages close to the beginning of the first chapter as one of the many historical figures who peppered the text. With great imagination and colorful prose, Zamora expanded on what he had read in various works.[40] In an invented (but plausible) scene, he placed his protagonist, Casanova, at the theater one evening in 1841, where he met "la señora de Rodríguez" sharing a box with Fanny Calderón. Smoking cigarettes and fanning herself coyly, the bejeweled elderly Güera regaled him with stories of her friendships with Humboldt and Iturbide, her visit to Paris, where she was known as the Mexican Venus, and the latest gossip about the people in her social circle. Many of the details, such as her travels abroad, were completely fictitious (she never left the country). So was the dialogue, which Zamora used as a vehicle to satirize the pretentiousness of the Mexican elites and to express his disillusionment with corrupt politicians. By putting some of these sentiments on La Güera's tongue, he enhanced her reputation as an astute observer as well as an engaged participant in the world around her.

CONCLUSION

This account of La Güera's journey during the first half of the twentieth century traces the gradual process by which she entered historical memory. Her fame grew slowly at first. After vanishing from the public eye for the half century after her death, she returned, initially in brief references hidden inside long works with limited circulation, and then in periodicals with a wider readership—although, in an era without the internet, those who didn't read the paper that day would have missed them. By the 1940s the references to her were multiplying, and her presence in a historical novel shows that she was beginning to capture the imagination of novelists as well as historians and chroniclers. Yet while the memories of her life and deeds were being recovered, they were also distorted by the introduction of false details and apocryphal stories—a reminder that the categories of history and fiction are not as separate as we would like to believe.

Despite her increasing presence in Mexican letters, a hundred years after her death doña María Ignacia Rodríguez did not yet enjoy celebrity status, nor was she considered a major independence heroine. Neither had the rumors of her affairs with various men gained much traction. This situation was about to change, however, because the gifted writer Artemio de Valle-Arizpe was about to pull these disparate strands together and weave them into the beautiful tapestry that made her an icon of Mexican history.

6 The Legend Crystallized in Valle-Arizpe's *La Güera Rodríguez*, 1949

Although by the 1940s doña María Ignacia Rodríguez de Velasco was beginning to be known to the reading public, it was Artemio de Valle-Arizpe's *La Güera Rodríguez* that catapulted her into the limelight. Published in 1949 and revised several times before the author's death in 1961, the book is still being read in a 2011 edition that added the subtitle "true tales about a surprising and entertaining personage in Mexican history."[1] And that is exactly how most readers understood the text: as true tales about an interesting historical figure.

The work was an immediate sensation that made generations of Mexicans fall in love with La Güera. Valle-Arizpe's captivating prose is a delight to read. He brought his characters to life with vivid dialogue as well as masterful descriptions that evoked the sights, sounds, and smells of bygone times. He sprinkled the text with allusions to classical literature, verses from Golden Age poetry, and popular proverbs. He provided the historical context that served as the backdrop to a life that spanned the transition from colony to independence. His decision to use her catchy nickname as the book's title also made her unforgettable. And the drawing that illustrated his title page became the iconic image with which she has since been associated.

ARTEMIO DE VALLE - ARIZPE

LA GÜERA RODRIGUEZ

LIBRERIA DE MANUEL PORRUA

5 DE MAYO 49-6   MEXICO. D. F.

1950

Figure 19. Title page of the biographical novel *La Güera Rodríguez* by Artemio de Valle-Arizpe, with the illustration that became her iconic image. The first edition of 1949 depicted her as a Greek goddess, but it was this image from the second edition of 1950, modified in later editions, that helped attract a wide reading public.

Like other prominent figures of his generation, Valle-Arizpe (1888–1961) was a true renaissance man: a lawyer, diplomat, chronicler, and prolific writer who authored dozens of books on historical topics as well as fourteen works of pure fiction.[2] *La Güera Rodríguez* came relatively late in his career. After collecting fascinating tidbits about her for many years, he let his imagination fly. Although he was not a professional historian, his narrative is thoroughly grounded in his knowledge of Mexican history. He had studied archival materials about colonial New Spain in the Archivo de Indias when he was posted to Madrid in the early 1920s, found more information in Mexican archives when he returned to his homeland, and read widely in the published literature. Because he included a short bibliography and occasional footnotes as well as long citations from original documents, most readers have assumed that the book is an accurate biography. However, although loosely based on her life, it should be classified as a historical novel because it combines history with a heavy dose of fiction.

Valle-Arizpe was, in fact, the originator of many of the myths that have since been associated with La Güera. By including even the most outlandish stories without evaluating them, he propagated them further; and he added some completely new tales for which he provided no evidence. His inventions were not just small details that helped bring her story to life. Instead, they transformed her from the grand aristocratic lady of the early twentieth-century narratives to a highly sexualized woman who defied convention at every turn and played a crucial role in helping Mexico achieve independence.

LA GÜERA'S NEW LIFE STORY

La Güera Rodríguez opens with a chapter entitled "Weddings by Supreme Mandate," based on the story recounted by Manuel Romero de Terreros of how Viceroy Revillagigedo supposedly forced María Ignacia and her sister María Josefa to marry their beaus. In Valle-Arizpe's hands, however, the anecdote paints a very different picture than the one told by La Güera's great-great-grandson.

The first sentence sets the tone of the book: "They were two beautiful maidens, full of cheer, whose pleasure took them daily to the barracks of the Granaderos" to flirt with the "dashing" officers. Valle-Arizpe portrays the girls as "sassy" but innocent, perhaps suffering from an "excess of youth" but having done nothing wrong. In his telling, both maidens were in love with their future husbands and not only willing but eager to tie the knot. If the girls represented a breath of fresh air, the viceroy and the couple's parents represented the decadence of the colonial regime. The prudish ruler hated to see young people laughing and having fun. The girls' father was a servile subject who bent over backward to please his sovereign. Despite his long list of distinguished names and titles—which Valle-Arizpe repeats at length for comic effect—the *regidor* was a "vacuous fool. . . . It is hard to believe that such an extremely stupid man could have such extremely intelligent daughters." The young men's parents were no better, opposing their sons' marriages because the sisters had been the subject of malicious gossip. Striving above all else to keep up appearances, they were "haughty," "vain," and "captivated by pride like all imperious people." But love won out in the end and the nuptials were celebrated with great luxury and rejoicing.[3]

This short first chapter introduces several themes that Valle-Arizpe develops throughout the book. From the start he defines La Güera not only by her beauty, but also by her intelligence and readiness to break rules in pursuit of her goals. Indeed, he portrays her as far superior to the silly aristocrats who surround her. As becomes clearer as the work progresses, they represent the past, whereas she represents the future. Her quest for individual happiness for herself—and independence for the nation—made her a symbol of modernity. And no matter how scandalously his protagonist behaved, she always had the author's sympathy, for she could not help it if she had fire in her blood or if men fell for her without provocation.

This chapter also reveals how Valle-Arizpe interweaves fact with fiction. Accepting Romero de Terreros's unsubstantiated (and highly dubious) anecdote, he adds many elements that expand on the page in *Ex-antiquis.* In doing so, he puts his own spin on the old story. In particular, while the Marqués de San Francisco glorified Mexico's colonial past and was proud of his great-great-grandmother's links to the viceregal court, Valle-Arizpe uses the episode to deride the viceroy and mock the aristocracy. And while Romero de Terreros's Güera was an unimpeachably proper lady, Valle-Arizpe's was the opposite.

The proportion of falsehoods varies in subsequent chapters. Some were built on a relatively solid documentary foundation, such as those that recount the litigation with her first husband. Having unearthed the long files of the divorce case that were buried in the national archives, Valle-Arizpe quotes from them liberally. His discussion of the events is sometimes confused, perhaps because—as he readily admits—he did not finish reading the "unwieldy tomes" that "made his head spin."[4] Yet he accurately reproduces selected accusations, counteraccusations, and testimonies from the originals. And these are so dramatic that they needed no modifications to make his text entertaining (though he nonetheless couldn't resist elaborating on them).

Other parts of the narrative rely far more on his imagination. Many of Valle-Arizpe's inventions are minor details that round out her portrait. For example, he portrays her as the blue-eyed picture of "perfection." He tells us that she was petite in stature, reaching just up to men's hearts, which she regularly broke just by batting her eyelashes. She moved with such grace that when the Golden Age playwright Félix Lope de Vega penned his verses about the "hija del aire" with her "airy walk," he must have "written them just for her, guessing that there would someday exist in New Spain a woman with such elegant rhythm in her step." She was also the embodiment of kindness. "In all of Mexico there was no more outstanding and singular a lady than the Güera Rodríguez." Of course, this portrait is mostly fiction: although previous texts mentioned her beauty, blonde ringlets, and vivacity, we do not even know if her eyes were blue.[5]

Some inventions are embellishments of what previous authors had written. For example, in describing her first wedding to a man of noble lineage, he places the ceremony in the cathedral (although it in fact took place in the chapel of the Hospital de los Bethlemitas). In describing her second marriage, which Romero de Terreros only indicated was brief and left her pregnant and embroiled in a lawsuit with Briones's siblings, Valle-Arizpe suggests that the elderly Briones—whom he portrays as a full four decades older than his wife (although he was in fact only twenty-five years her senior)—died because La Güera wore him out in the marital bed.[6] Copying a mistake in Romero de Terreros's text, Valle-Arizpe also refers to her second husband as Mariano (rather than Juan Ignacio). In fleshing out Prieto's reference to her "pithy sayings," he credits La Güera with coining the adage "Fuera de México, todo es Cuautitlán" ("Outside of Mexico City, everything is Cuautitlán"), a phrase still used today by Mexico City residents to disparage everything outside the capital.[7] Valle-Arizpe provides no evidence for these claims, which had never appeared in prior accounts. Yet these stories serve the author's purposes. The first highlights the importance of her family, for the cathedral would have been the most elegant wedding venue in Mexico City. The second buttresses his view that she had a voracious sexual appetite. The third provides proof both of her clever way with words and of how her fame—and sayings—spread far beyond her social circle and lifetime.

Other fabrications are much bolder because they take her persona in new directions. Notable among them are the stories of La Güera's alleged romantic liaisons. Besides her three marriages, Valle-Arizpe writes that she "had other marriages in which God did not intervene. Gallant affairs that her soul, always thirsty for love, demanded."[8] The chapters devoted to these illicit relationships form the core of his work. Not only do they occupy twice as many pages as the chapters devoted to her marriages, but the prose in these sections takes on a new tone that imitates the steamy style of romance novels, however much refined by learned allusions. Consequently, these are the most memorable parts of the text.

The rumors of La Güera's affairs had originated with her first husband, who accused her of committing adultery with a visiting Frenchman in 1801 and with three priests in 1802. Although Villamil withdrew the first suit and was unable to prove anything in the second, Valle-Arizpe repeats them uncritically.[9]

Indeed, he goes well beyond the charges in the ecclesiastical divorce case in depicting her alleged affair with the distinguished canon José Mariano Beristáin. Whereas Villamil had accused his compadre Beristáin of taking his wife to a party on one occasion and staying overnight at their house on another, Valle-Arizpe concocts an entirely fictitious story about how Beristáin moved in for an extended stay, ostensibly to work on his famous manuscript "in tranquility." It was a good story. Questioning how Beristáin could have more peace and quiet there than in his own home, Valle-Arizpe concludes that he must have been "working happily, very happily and well, on other things with which the incomparable and beautiful lady assisted him very efficiently." What she saw in the "ugly little man" was unclear; he must have had "something lovely, a hidden treasure" that "pleased her intimately, . . . a little music box, as they say" that he shared with her in the siestas they took together every afternoon.

And Beristían was not the only one. According to Valle-Arizpe, she also "enjoyed herself" with the French doctor Luis Ceret, as well as with "two saucy ecclesiastics": Ramón Cardeña, the handsome "cura bonito" who would later run into trouble for supporting independence, and the "dissolute cleric" Juan Ramírez (whose name was actually Ignacio), for she was "addicted . . . to the chorus of the Church." In his telling, her "naughty doings" were "deliciously savored by the entire city, which buzzed with the tales of her sinful acts."[10]

Villamil does not come off well, either. Valle-Arizpe portrays him as a "silly *caballero calatravo*," a hot-headed "dimwit," "fool," and "coward." He was a noble good-for-nothing, one of those people who, "when because of his total ineptitude accomplishes little in life, boasts endlessly about what his ancestors did"—in this case, "an ancestor who killed many Indians." And it was Villamil who pushed the good-hearted Güera into other men's arms. In their early years of "marital bliss," she was "pacified, . . . and the fire in her blood was contained, which was a great feat, because she was by nature difficult to tame." Then, because of his irrational jealousy and consuming rage, he began to berate and beat her. If La Güera sought love elsewhere, it was because of the "mala vida" she endured. In presenting María Ignacia as a long-suffering wife, Valle-Arizpe takes her side. Yet he nonetheless insists that she repeatedly "broke her marriage vows," even committing "sacrilegious adultery."[11]

Valle-Arizpe also elaborates on the story of her close friendship with Humboldt, which had originated with Fanny Calderón de la Barca and had then been converted into a passionate—but chaste—relationship by Krumm-Heller. In Valle-Arizpe's narrative, the friendship became a torrid affair. La Güera "had a knack for seduction, and with only one breath could make the virtuous fall." She lifted Humboldt "from the human level of science to the divine heights of love." She was "the siren who sang to him, and he happily allowed himself to be lured." They were "almost never apart, they were two with one will, united with one body and one soul. They shared delicious times together, . . . only pursuing their appetites and desires." At her side the "arid" scholar "experienced the delight that love brings." When Humboldt left Mexico, their "goodbye ripped up their souls and broke their hearts."[12]

Valle-Arizpe enriches his tale with details that reflect his familiarity with the colonial world. Painting lovely vignettes of life in viceregal times, he describes how La Güera and the Prussian scientist were constantly together as she introduced him to people and places, took him around in her carriage, and entertained him with her witty conversation. The couple walked arm in arm through the Alameda park, attended bullfights and plays at the Coliseo, and enjoyed "magnificent" meals at her table. She serenaded him with her "mellifluous voice" as she played the guitar and clavichord, and then spent many hours in his quarters viewing his scientific specimens and absorbing the knowledge for which the great man was famous. One particularly racy incident was loosely based on Peza's (unsubstantiated) story about the unveiling of the statue of Charles IV. In Valle-Arizpe's version, La Güera shocked the gathered multitude by pointing out that the genitals on the king's horse were incorrectly depicted. Milking the tale for all it was worth, the author explains that on the subject of male anatomy, she had much "personal experience."[13]

The chapter on her passionate affair with Iturbide rests on a similarly weak foundation. Apparently unaware that Miguel de Beruete had alleged that it was her daughter Antonia who had the affair, Valle-Arizpe makes the mother Iturbide's paramour.[14] Accepting the accusations that originated with Iturbide's enemies, he includes long citations from Rocafuerte's and Torrente's diatribes against the emperor and reproduces in its entirety the 1822 broadside that suggested that Iturbide had a "carnipostalicious" union with La Güera Rodríguez. Although Valle-Arizpe had read the books that dismissed these stories as false (such as Alamán's *Historia* and Bustamante's *Suplemento a la historia*), he nonetheless insists that Rocafuerte's words were "authoritative" and Torrente's history was "documented"—though neither was anything of the sort. In his telling, once La Güera and Iturbide crossed paths (around 1816, he claims, although we know that they had in fact been friends much longer), their attraction was magnetic: "They could be seen together everywhere. They spoke sweet nothings to each other while with their eyes they exchanged their souls. They were both imprisoned and chained by their love." And this love gave La Güera the power to influence historical events because Iturbide, dazzled

by his mistress, confided his deepest thoughts to her and let her guide his actions. Even as the turbulent developments of the next few years led them apart, she always "occupied a firm and principal place in Iturbide's heart."[15]

In developing these tales, Valle-Arizpe was at least building on something he had read in previous texts, however unreliable. Other illicit relationships he concocted out of thin air. In a chapter entitled "Fire Meets Flame," he introduces the story of her dalliance with Simón Bolívar. The future Liberator of South America had indeed visited Mexico City in March 1799, when he was sixteen years old, but there is no record of his having met doña María Ignacia Rodríguez—let alone of their having had an affair.

The fable of their romance is highly improbable. According to historian Rafael Heliodoro Valle, who wrote a book on Bolívar's stay in Mexico, the young man spent only eight days in the capital and had to leave in a hurry after voicing his opinions about independence to the viceroy. He would have had little opportunity to have an affair with La Güera during his short visit because his host, the *oidor* of the *audiencia*, Guillermo Aguirre, kept him busy by shepherding him about town to meet the principal gentlemen of the realm.[16] Moreover, María Ignacia was at the time a twenty-one-year-old married lady with three small children, the youngest only six months old. Although her marriage may already have been unhappy, her jealous husband did not mention Bolívar when he accused her of adultery in 1801 or when he filed for divorce in 1802, even though the long depositions in these cases referred to several incidents as far back as 1798.

But two small details in the historical chronicles caught Valle-Arizpe's eye and set his imagination aflame. First, that Bolívar stayed at the grand house on the corner of Damas and Ortega owned by the Marquesa de Uluapa, "the beautiful sister of that famous 'güera'"; and second, that Josefa—who may in fact have met Bolívar—"was fascinated by the vivacity of the *caraqueñito*."[17] As a result, Valle-Arizpe assumed that La Güera had also met him and, in his view, any man who met La Güera immediately fell in love with her. What the author did not know, however, is that the marquesa did not live in that house because she had rented it to the *audiencia* judge, and that by that date María Ignacia Rodríguez was probably living in Tacuba rather than in Mexico City.

In contrast to many of the other chapters, the one that deals with her alleged fling with Bolívar is devoid of source references, another sign that the story is entirely fictitious. Yet Valle-Arizpe's descriptions of their affair are so vivid that they seem just as real as the incidents for which there is some historical documentation. The future hero, "instead of exploring the city with the meek *oidor* Aguirre y Viana, preferred to go out with the resplendent Güera." Her explanations of what they were seeing were much more interesting than the old man's "solemn, . . . erudite and, by the same token, boring" words. "In flesh as well as spirit they were conjoined," united by "fire and flame." But their "happy hours" together—extended by Valle-Arizpe to several weeks instead of the maximum possible eight days—came to an end when Bolívar spoke his mind and had to quit Mexico abruptly. Indeed, his meeting with the viceroy takes up nearly half the seven-page chapter. When La Güera heard what had happened, she "laughed and laughed interminably," imagining how the viceroy's retinue must have suffered, for "she knew them to be timid, indecisive cowards . . . Bolívar was similarly overtaken by mirth; his eyes almost popped out of his head laughing." The young couple thus literally had the last laugh, making fun of the highest authorities of the land. Yet their joy was short-lived. After he departed, La Güera was left with "delicious memories . . . planted forever in the depth of her heart, like flowers bathing her in their delicate scent for the rest of her life."[18]

Even though the relationship Valle-Arizpe depicts was rather tame, it served several purposes in his narrative. It positioned his protagonist as a woman who flouted public opinion and was open to romantic entanglements. It allowed him to belittle the colonial authorities, who represented a regime whose star was fading. It provided the first building block for constructing La Güera as a prescient national heroine, one who as early as 1799 was a critic of the viceregal government (which she most likely was not, especially given her friendship with several viceroys and her attempt to obtain honors from the Spanish king as late as June 1809). And it allowed the author to include another important historical figure in his story.

The purpose of La Güera's other affairs is not as obvious, for the famous Bolívar, Humboldt, and Iturbide were not the only men who supposedly succumbed to her irresistible charms. Without any pretense of providing historical documentation, Valle-Arizpe introduces a series of additional lovers that she allegedly took after the death of her second husband, for the merry widow "didn't care what people thought, but only followed her wishes and appetites." The author does not bother to name these men—as indeed he could not have, since they never existed. Banished to Querétaro, she "filled her idle days . . . by devoting herself to seeking . . . beaus . . . and she lacked for none." (Of course, we know that during that time she was instead extremely sick and caring for a gravely ill daughter.) Upon her return to Mexico City, she "had many and good suitors" and continued to "entertain herself" with "a rich notary who fell hard for her, . . . a portly doctor with the scent of a macho goat, . . . a learned professor who satis-fied her laudable quest for knowledge, . . . a powerful attorney," and many other "handsome men, magnificent beasts with great stamina in the ways of love." But, despite this "continuous nourishment," her "thirst could not be quenched."[19]

In trying to explain these new twists on her already intriguing saga, it is worth noting that Valle-Arizpe never claimed to be telling a true story. From the start he hints that he is working in a fictional genre. His fore-word alerts the reader to the "picaresque" nature of his tale and warns that the book is much more than a biography of doña María Ignacia Rodríguez. "Its purpose," he explains, "is to explore a moment in the Mexican soul centered around one of our most brilliant figures." He signals its literary tenor by using archaic language that often sends readers scurrying to the dictionary. His decision to call his chapters *jornadas* instead of *capítulos* recalls the term for "acts" sometimes used in Golden Age dramas. Moreover, several anecdotes as well as learned references (such as his allu-sion to "the physician of his honor") show that he is thinking of well-known Spanish plays.[20] Thus, instead of trying to deceive his readers, Valle-Arizpe was indulging himself by writing an entertaining—and highly marketable—historical novel that also had didactic purposes.

DOÑA JUANA TENORIO

By making La Güera a female Don Juan, Valle-Arizpe playfully inserted himself into the canon of western writers who have rewritten that famous story. In fact, immediately following the list of her conquests quoted above, he notes that she was a "doña Juana Tenorio." This reference to José Zorrilla's 1844 work—one of the most popular plays in Spain and Mexico—

reveals the source of his inspiration for creating a false narrative about La Güera's love life.[21]

La Güera's *jornadas* have a double meaning, for as he takes us through her days (the literal meaning of the term), Valle-Arizpe is also recounting her journey (an alternate meaning) in search of happiness. Her quest leads to an ill-fated first marriage, a brief second marriage cut short by death, and numerous adventures that take her down the wrong path until she finds peace and fulfillment in the arms of her last husband, who tames the spirited traveler and brings her back to domesticity and faith. Thus, just as with don Juan Tenorio, the libertine protagonist is redeemed by love.

This reading of La Güera Rodríguez as a female don Juan Tenorio explains not only her "continuous loves" but also Valle-Arizpe's depiction of her old age—which is almost entirely fictional, since he had very little information about that period of her life. The chapter on her third marriage is titled "A Good Death Honors an Entire Life." Expanding on the tidbit in Romero de Terreros's narrative, Valle-Arizpe asserted that because she enjoyed the "glory" of a good marriage, La Güera's "former restlessness" was finally stilled. "Time deadened her libido, pacified her, and restored order in her life." She became a "misanthrope," venturing out only to attend church and pray. Elizalde thus fulfilled "the arduous . . . task"—first given by God to Iturbide, according to Valle-Arizpe—"of bringing the tempestuous Güera Rodríguez back to the righteous path."[22]

There are, to be sure, important differences between La Güera and don Juan Tenorio. Rather than setting out to wreak havoc on the world, she only wanted to satisfy her constant "yearning for something more,"[23] and she did not engage in brawling and murder. Valle-Arizpe's ending is also much sunnier than Zorrilla's. Repenting only when close to death, the play's protagonist was saved at the last minute when his beloved doña Inés returned from the grave and fetched him to accompany her to heaven. In contrast, the pacified Güera enjoyed many years of happiness with a spouse who was still alive and completely devoted to her. Despite these differences, it is nonetheless Zorrilla's romantic version—where love triumphs—that serves as Valle-Arizpe's model rather than the earlier, darker versions of the Don Juan story in which the sinner cannot be saved despite his repentance.

Many of Valle-Arizpe's inventions are thus essential to the plot. Not only does it require her multiple affairs, but also explains several references to her as manly: "she always stepped with valor," affirms the author, and "she was never cowardly or of effeminate heart."[24]

Moreover, some scenes that at first seem incongruous make sense in the context of other Spanish *comedias*. For example, early on, Valle-Arizpe tells the story of a ragged ruffian who falls madly in love with La Güera when he sees her walking on the streets of Mexico City. His obsession is such that one dark night, he conjures the devil and offers his soul in exchange for the woman he desires. Exuding sulfur and belching flames, the "hideous demon" rebuffs him by explaining that he already has his soul, and that "as for La Güera Rodríguez, I would love to have her for myself, you miserable wretch."[25] The competition between God and the devil was, of course, central to many Spanish plays and should immediately have alerted the reader to the literary rather than historical nature of the text.

INDEPENDENCE HEROINE

Valle-Arizpe also adds a second theme to La Güera's quest: her desire to see Mexico separate from Spain, a goal that supposedly began when Bolívar planted the idea of independence in her heart. His portrayal of her political activities goes far beyond the available documentation. Valle-Arizpe affirms that she was "a bold propagator of Independence from the time it was proclaimed by don Miguel Hidalgo y Costilla until it was consummated by don Agustín de Iturbide." And (contrary to what we know of the ever-discreet lady) she openly supported Hidalgo's revolt and cursed the "vile" Fernando VII for all to hear. Indeed, Valle-Arizpe paints her as a traitor to her class by repeating the old (false) stereotype that "all the rich and people of distinguished lineage were royalists by conviction" and could not understand how she could defend the "wild insurgent rabble" that pillaged, raped, and murdered.[26] She thus supposedly defied her peers and showed solidarity with the "good guys" in Mexican history who fought against Spanish tyranny.

Valle-Arizpe offers few concrete details about La Güera's support for the revolution. He claims (without any evidence) that "the subtle don Miguel Hidalgo, in his travels to the capital, visited this lady . . . and attracted her to the noble cause." Thus, even before she was exiled to

Querétaro, she was allegedly funding his movement.[27] (To be sure, she later gave the insurgents money, although probably only small sums, and possibly only to protect her estates that were in rebel hands.) His other proof is her banishment from Mexico City for subversive activities, which did, in fact, occur, though not on the date or for the reason Valle-Arizpe imagined. Building on the narrative of Romero de Terreros, Valle-Arizpe erroneously places the incident after Garrido's denunciation of the Hidalgo revolt in September of 1810. In fact, La Güera had been banished from the Mexican capital six months before the Grito de Dolores, for her part in an 1809 intrigue that had nothing to do with Hidalgo and that never led to a trial before a panel of inquisitors.

Yet one of the dramatic highlights of the book is the fictional Inquisition trial that supposedly resulted in her banishment. The "valiant" Güera was "completely unfazed" by the meeting with the stern judges, whom she knew well. Sweeping into their chamber all sweet smiles, rustling silk, and wafting perfume, she stared them straight in the eyes and, fanning herself coyly, began to enumerate their vices and peccadillos. Daring them to convict her only if they wanted the public to learn their secrets, she left them "flabbergasted and red faced." Now it was the inquisitors who were fearful: "The three imposing judges, who made most men's blood turn to ice," were terrified that their hidden misdeeds might come to light. The triumphant Güera had "felled them with the sharp sword of her tongue."[28] She was thus purportedly expelled from Mexico City not only because of her support for the rebellion, but also because she made a mockery of the Holy Office.

Valle-Arizpe offers more concrete information about the last phase of the independence movement led by Iturbide, but this part of his narrative also contains many falsehoods. As she embarked on her final adventure, La Güera supposedly freed herself from the constraints of her society at the same time that she helped free Mexico from colonial rule. Following Rocafuerte, Torrente, and Peza, Valle-Arizpe writes that it was she who convinced Iturbide to change sides, she who obtained his appointment as the new military leader, and she who conceived of the Plan de Iguala.

Valle-Arizpe adds his own flourishes to these tales. One was a concocted if plausible-sounding letter from King Fernando VII outlining the conditions under which he would support Mexican independence. Because she was allegedly so central to the intrigue, Valle-Arizpe claims that La Güera had the letter in her possession. No one ever saw it, he explains, because, once she used it to formulate her strategy, she prudently destroyed the missive.[29] (The fact that Valle-Arizpe reproduces the lost letter in its entirely is another indication that we should question the veracity of his text.) Then, elaborating on the story that originated with Guillermo Prieto, Valle-Arizpe writes that after independence was won, Iturbide not only acknowledged her by marching his victorious army past her residence on September 27, 1821, but also by putting her at his side that evening to watch the celebratory fireworks from the balcony of the National Palace.[30] Thus Valle-Arizpe goes much further than the old narratives in depicting their illicit affair and making her the true mastermind behind independence.

Valle-Arizpe also puts his own stamp on what happened after Mexico achieved its independence. Although La Güera arranged for her three daughters, son, and sons-in-law to obtain honorific posts, she "did not herself wish to occupy a position in the court" of Agustín I because "she was the fifth essence of cleverness and extremely well-informed about everything that concerned her."[31] Valle-Arizpe protects his protagonist from the taint of collaborating with an undemocratic regime by claiming that she warned Iturbide not to put a crown on his head (highly unlikely, given her family's enthusiastic participation in the imperial regime). Because he ignored her sage advice, the emperor went down in ignominy and became one of the "bad guys" in Mexican history, while La Güera remained an untarnished heroine. Besides being far more astute than he, she was also firmly committed to independence long before he came around to it—yet another interpretation with little factual basis.

A TALE FOR ITS TIME

Valle-Arizpe's representation of La Güera Rodríguez is very much a product of his time and place. Not only does it reveal his values and views of history, but it also served his lifelong project of instilling patriotism and creating a national identity. In the years that followed the extraordinarily divisive Revolution of 1910, it was particularly important to celebrate Mexico's past by creating new heroes who could serve as part of the glue holding together the imagined community of the Mexican nation. Doña María Ignacia Rodríguez was an ideal addition to the country's patriotic pantheon.

Valle-Arizpe gave Mexico a heroine who strengthened national pride in many ways. His text is peppered with superlatives.[32] Mexico had the most beautiful and brilliant woman in the Americas, an "extraordinary" and "original" figure who could hold her own against the best in the Old World—a list that included the Duchesse de Bourgogne, Madame de Maintenon, and even Venus. Mexico's Liberator was not to be outdone by South America's, either: if Bolívar had his Manuelita Saenz, then Iturbide had his Güera. Mexico also acquired its own Don Juan—albeit a much-improved version, because the protagonist was a woman with a pure heart and the story had a happy ending.[33]

La Güera Rodríguez was meant to teach the complicated history of the independence struggle to a newly expanded reading public. By weaving his narrative around the beautiful lady and relating her to three of the most famous men of the independence period, Valle-Arizpe was able to recount Mexico's path to nationhood in great detail. Because his account is so entertaining, it made the stuffy patriotic history fun to read. Indeed, in his hands La Güera became the embodiment of the nation, connected to some of the most important events of the Mexican past and a central figure in a narrative of national progress.

Although he relied on some of the stories told by Romero de Terreros at the beginning of the twentieth century, Valle-Arizpe's perspectives differed from the earlier writer's in significant ways. Despite sharing an admiration for the Hispanic heritage, Valle-Arizpe had a much more negative view of the colonial regime. He ridiculed the aristocracy and portrayed it as obstacle to progress. Thus, in supporting the separation from Spain, La Güera supposedly had to break with her social class. His portrayal of Iturbide also reflected contemporary values. Unlike the more conservative Romero de Terreros, who idealized the man who finally achieved Mexican independence, Valle-Arizpe made Hidalgo—who failed to liberate the nation—the hero, while depicting Iturbide as a traitor.

By praising La Güera's political activities, Valle-Arizpe also reflected new attitudes toward women. While in the nineteenth century Rocafuerte and Torrente disapproved of her alleged role as Iturbide's advisor, and in the early twentieth century Romero de Terreros felt the need to deny that she could have influenced historical events, Valle-Arizpe applauded—and magnified—her contributions to Mexican independence. By making her an active agent of change rather than the simple object of men's lust for sex and power, he celebrated women's competence.

His exemplary patriot was a modern woman, not a silent, subservient female in the traditional mold. Her "vital exuberance"[34] was for him a positive life force and her alleged defiance of restrictive social mores a healthy sign of the arrival of a modern world in which individuals could freely pursue happiness. To be sure, his text contained widespread stereotypes about women in the past—unsurprisingly, since he wrote a quarter century before the emergence of the field of Mexican women's history. He presented La Güera as an exceptional figure because she led an interesting life. With unusual intelligence and an unquenchable thirst for knowledge as well as love, she didn't fit into the straitjacket that supposedly constrained women at the time. Valle-Arizpe thus portrayed her as brazenly challenging convention because he imagined the society of her time as being far more repressive than we have since learned that it was. And he believed, approvingly, that she was far ahead of her time.

Yet Valle-Arizpe's novel also reveals his ambivalence about the changes in women's status during his lifetime, for he was evidently uncomfortable with the power, autonomy, and unbridled sexuality of his protagonist. His Güera achieved her influence by working behind the scenes and using her feminine charms to manipulate the men who made history, because any other kind of female power would have been illegitimate. Indeed, her politics were often an extension of her love life. If Iturbide consulted her and sent her letters, for example, it had to be because they were lovers, not simply because he valued her opinions or wanted to discuss their mutual business dealings (which was much more likely). Thus, even while he made her an important national heroine, Valle-Arizpe's portrayal of La Güera followed gendered stereotypes of women as accessories to the country's great men.

Writing squarely in the middle of the twentieth century, Valle-Arizpe was less concerned with sin than the Catholic writers of the Don Juan saga that preceded him. Yet he embedded the salacious details of her love life—which were necessary for his plot—in a parable that made them acceptable. In his tale, La Güera's fire needed to be tamed and a good marriage was the only way to contain it. She was thus under control during each of her three marriages, for it was the unattached woman who was dangerous. And Valle-Arizpe's tale had a traditional ending: her life's quest ended when the erotic and free-spirited heroine was domesticated by a man and ended her days, as a proper woman should, devoted to Home and Church. She did not therefore represent female liberation or threaten patriarchy in Valle-Arizpe's version of her life story.

CONCLUSION

Valle-Arizpe's goals in writing *La Güera Rodríguez* not only explain many of his inventions but also the omissions that keep it from being a more complete biography. While his narrative emphasizes her supposed romantic liaisons and political activities, it glosses over the other parts of her life that do not fit the plot, such as her fulfillment of the traditional roles of mother, grandmother, and daughter or her persistent financial difficulties. Yet he apparently had the information to expand on these aspects. In a chapter describing the surviving objects that had belonged to María Ignacia Rodríguez (a miniature portrait decorating a tortoiseshell box, two fine shawls, and her painted bed), Valle-Arizpe notes in passing that he had held in his hands some thick packets of letters that she wrote to her son Gerónimo and to her grandson Manuel Romero de Terreros "in her firm, small hand." He dismisses them as "simple family letters without importance, as any lady of that time would write to her close relations," only revealing her "love and tenderness," "prudence," and "great facility with the pen."[35] His lack of interest in the mundane matters contained in this correspondence reminds us that his aim was never simply to write her true history.

Valle-Arizpe's book was a watershed in La Güera Rodríguez' journey from obscurity to fame, yet the figure he created was a far cry from the woman of flesh and blood who lived long ago. Mixing fact with fantasy, he created, or in some cases, merely collected and disseminated, most of the myths that have since become part of her persona. In the process he transformed her from the enchanting but proper lady of earlier narrations into a naughty patriot finally tamed by a man. Because he presented

her as an extraordinary personage—"a woman of wonder," as he put it[36]—
Valle-Arizpe elevated her from the human level to the realm of the marvelous, a significant step in making her a legend. And, because he persuaded
his readers that he was telling her true story, nearly all future depictions of
her built on his text. The influence of his historical novel is a testament to
the enduring power of fiction.

7 La Güera after Valle-Arizpe

THE POWER OF FICTION

Once Artemio de Valle-Arizpe's fictionalized tale about María Ignacia Rodríguez entered the world of Mexican letters in 1949, it took on a life of its own. By 1955 it was already being praised as "the famous book . . . that has reached such an extraordinarily wide circulation."[1] In fact, it was such a bestseller in the 1950s that it was said to have been sitting on the desk of the Secretary of Labor (and future president) Adolfo López Mateos when a fair-skinned labor leader, Leonardo Rodríguez Alcaine, walked in; he walked out with a nickname that stayed with him forever: La Güera Rodríguez Alcaine.[2] This is but one example of the book's popularity. By the time Valle-Arizpe died in 1961, *La Güera Rodríguez* had gone through nine editions, and it was reprinted in 2006 and 2011 in the Lectorum series that made the classics of Mexican literature available to a large audience.

Valle-Arizpe's version of his protagonist spread, not only because of the diffusion of his text, but also because some readers were so taken with her figure that they wanted to retell his stories in their own works. These new representations appeared slowly at first and then proliferated as the years went by—not so much in official histories, where La Güera barely registered, as in popular works. By the turn of the twenty-first century her appearances accelerated, and her visibility increased dramatically as the bicentennial year of 2010 approached.

Very few readers questioned the veracity of Valle-Arizpe's account. In 1960 the historian Juan Ortega y Medina dismissed the "amorous legend" of her affair with Humboldt as a total fabrication and criticized Valle-Arizpe for inventing the "delicious tale" that, although it "might be necessary for his novelesque plot, is unacceptable in the exposition of a historian." Tracing the origin of that story to Krumm-Heller in 1910, Ortega y Medina explained that it was part of the "donjuanesque legend" that was "created to compensate . . . for the hero's masculine deficiency," for it was rumored that he had "a decided homosexual tendency."[3] In 2002 the writer José Joaquín Blanco offered a broader criticism: that Valle-Arizpe "confused history with gossip and rumor. . . . He rarely referenced sources or proof for his affirmations. . . . He took from history what he wanted and invented the rest. Above all he invented adventures of the bedchamber. . . . Thus our Frenchified libelist . . . converted our Güera into a local version of madams Maintenon, La Vallière, Montespan, de Pompadour, and du Barry (the latter in the childish Hollywood version of Dolores del Río)."[4] And, in a recent article, the historian Fernando Muñoz Altea criticized Valle-Arizpe for "lacking seriousness in his conclusions, mixing up dates, inventing conversations, and distorting personages to create a novelized account, without using documentary sources, and prejudicing the honor of a woman who can no longer defend herself."[5] These writers were nonetheless exceptional in doubting Valle-Arizpe's narrative.

Because most readers accepted his uncorroborated anecdotes and flat-out falsehoods as fact, those who repeated them believed that they were telling her true story. Indeed, a 1990 study of *La Güera Rodríguez* concluded that it should be classified as a "true documentary testimony" rather than as a "novelized biography" because it was so fully documented. And in 1982 portions of Valle-Arizpe's text were reproduced in a popular history textbook because the publishers believed that it was an accurate historical narrative.[6]

Principal among the tales that were endlessly reiterated and embellished were those about her love affairs, beginning with Simón Bolívar (whom she may never even have met) and including her friends Alexander von Humboldt and Agustín de Iturbide. But these were not the only invented stories. To wit: La Güera was the most beautiful woman of her day; she was unconventional, bold, and provocative; she had a voracious sexual appetite; she was the talk of the town, known for coining the adage "Fuera de México, todo es Cuautitlán"; she was forced to marry her first husband; she wore out her elderly second husband in bed; she was audacious, even calling in strangers to witness the birth of his posthumous child; she was tried by a panel of inquisitors for supporting Hidalgo's insurgency and bested the judges by threatening to reveal their dirty secrets; she arranged to have her lover Iturbide appointed supreme commander of the southern army, convinced him to change from the royalist to the patriot side, and then conceived of the Plan de Iguala; he altered the route of his triumphal procession to honor her with a feather from his hat; she was his best counselor, with far more common sense than he. In short, she was rebellious both in her personal life and political activities. Although the list could go on, these were the myths that were most often included—and thus solidified—in new portrayals of María Ignacia Rodríguez.

Even though successive authors cited Valle-Arizpe as the source of their information, their versions of La Güera Rodríguez were not an exact copy of his creation. As they interacted with his text and adapted her story to their different formats and purposes, certain aspects of her life came to the fore and others receded. In particular, the closing chapter of her life that was essential to Valle-Arizpe's plot—her alleged turn to domesticity and faith in her old age—disappeared from most later representations because that narrative held little appeal for readers at the end of the twentieth century and dawn of the twenty-first. What made her a favorite for the new era were her supposed glamour and sexual freedom, strength and independence, intelligence, and bold political activism.

In addition, new false details were introduced and, once in print, continued to shape her legend. One was that La Güera was the model used by the famed sculptor Manuel Tolsá for the Virgen de la Purísima in the Profesa church—even though both Prieto and Valle-Arizpe noted that it was her daughter Paz who served as the model and that it was for the sculpture of the Virgen de los Dolores, not la Purísima. As with the tale of her affair with Iturbide, the rumor mill conflated the mother with the daughter, and images of both sculptures were often mistakenly presented as the portrait of La Güera.[7] Another innovation was that she not only initiated the ecclesiastical divorce from her first husband (in some versions even poisoning him to obtain her freedom), but that she also obtained it. As time went one, she thus became "one of the first divorcées in Mexico."[8] This statement not only flies in the face of centuries of Church-authorized separations, but also distorts the facts of the judicial proceedings, since it was her husband who initiated the suit, and the couple abandoned the case and reunited. Yet a modern heroine has to be autonomous, and returning to an abusive husband was simply unacceptable. As time went on, her political role was also expanded to include such additional activities as spying in the viceregal court; and she eventually went beyond advocating for independence to become a feminist who challenged patriarchy.[9] One text even introduced the fiction that at the end of her life, repenting for the scandalous behavior of her youth, she entered a nunnery.[10]

Valle-Arizpe's depiction of the spirited Güera was thus but one stop on her route to stardom, for she would be transformed yet again in the hands of new narrators. Her continuing evolution can be traced in a variety of works, including newspaper and magazine articles, novels, plays, comic books, historical dictionaries and scholarly works, popular histories, an opera, and, finally, blogs, radio and television programs, and performances uploaded to YouTube. Because each of these genres targeted a different audience—from highly cultured readers to consumers of mass media—she became ever more firmly embedded in Mexican cultural memory.

VALLE-ARIZPE'S STORIES TAKE ON A LIFE OF THEIR OWN, 1950–1975

La Güera Rodríguez was itself a work in progress during the 1950s as Valle-Arizpe revised new editions of the book. Most of his changes were minor stylistic modifications or additions to the bibliography that incorporated older works he had missed the first time around (such as Torrente's *Historia* and Fossey's *Le Mexique*). He also corrected a few factual errors (such as the date of her death) and added footnotes, thereby strengthening the book's reputation as a reliable biography. Finally, he included newly discovered material brought to light by Rafael Heliodoro Valle in a series of newspaper articles on "Rediscovering Iturbide" that were published in

Excelsior in 1951. But none of these revisions modified his central story about doña María Ignacia Rodríguez. Indeed, Valle-Arizpe used the new information to strengthen his tales about her adulterous affair with Iturbide.

Doing so required reading quite a bit into Valle's material. His article of January 2, 1951, summarized the testimony of the messenger who in March 1821 turned in a letter that Iturbide had written to "a lady known in this capital as La Güera Rodríguez" and which was subsequently lost. The article of January 19 reproduced the letter sent to María Ignacia Rodríguez by the administrator of the Fondo de Obras Pías in December 1822 requesting that she pay a debt. In a prologue to the letter, Valle wrote, "I cordially regret that Lic. Artemio de Valle-Arizpe did not know of this document . . . which would have given much color to his delicious recent book *La Güera Rodríguez.* The presence of this document among Iturbide's papers is indubitable proof of the magnificent relations between them."[11]

To be sure, this material only shows the longstanding friendship and business relations between La Güera and Iturbide. The first letter could have been about anything, including the general's plan to meet the top two Spanish authorities to negotiate independence at her Hacienda de la Patera (as in effect happened on September 13, 1821). The second letter was originally sent to Iturbide's cousin Domingo Malo because he had been serving as her attorney and renting her son's Molino Prieto; it likely reached Iturbide because he was his cousin's guarantor on the rental contract. Although these documents were hardly proof of a romantic relationship, Valle's insinuations served to pique the interest of readers of the capital's leading newspaper while also publicizing Valle-Arizpe's "delicious" book, which had only been circulating for little more than a year.

One of the first who was inspired to rewrite La Güera's story was the noted playwright Federico Schroeder Inclán. His "anti-historical comedy" *Hoy invita la Güera* was performed at the Globo Theater in 1955, with the famed actress Lola Bravo playing the part of La Güera. The play received rave reviews; indeed, critics considered it the best Mexican play of the year, and it was revived at least twice more, in 1962 and 2010.[12]

Hoy invita la Güera is a humorous farce with a fictional plot set in the time of the Pastry War (1836–1838), when France invaded Mexico, ostensibly to collect the debts of a French pastry chef. La Güera is a beguiling patriot who plots with sensible politicians to try to avoid the conflict. Making the ultimate sacrifice for the nation—her honor—she seduces a visiting French prince in an attempt to convince him to cancel the debts. When her ploy fails because of Antonio López de Santa Anna, she puts a curse on him—and the general did indeed lose his leg in one of the battles of that war.

Although Schroeder acknowledges his debt to Valle-Arizpe—even referencing him in the dialogue by noting "how meticulous is our señor don Artemio de Valle"—the playwright insists that "this Güera . . . is not the 'Güera Rodríguez.' . . . This one is fundamentally theatrical and essentially extra-historical." Yet he includes some of the most salacious stories from Valle-Arizpe's text, with the dates completely scrambled, for, as his Güera puts it, "We make history our way, without worrying about dates, which are so tiresome."[13] For example, in the first act (when the real María Ignacia Rodríguez would have been sixty years old), she gives birth to a girl. Schroeder resurrects the tale of her calling in strangers to witness the birth and adds a heated competition between two gentlemen who step forward to claim paternity. The characters allude to her many lovers, including Bolívar, Humboldt, and Iturbide. And she mentions that her current husband, portrayed as an aristocratic wimp, has charged her with adultery in divorce court. Thus, despite the author's denials, his Güera was clearly derived from Valle-Arizpe's heroine. And what appealed to Schroeder about her was her sexual liberty combined with patriotism.

From the start, the reviewers understood who the play was about. Appraising the premiere, Armando de María y Campos wrote that Schroeder was "inspired by the now famous book *La Güera Rodríguez* by Artemio de Valle-Arizpe, a biographical chronicle of the life of doña María Ignacia Rodríguez de Velasco, well known for her beauty and restless life marked by passions both amorous and political."[14] Any doubt about the identity of the protagonist was dispelled in 2010, when a new production of the play changed the title to simply *La Güera Rodríguez*.[15]

Hoy invita la Güera increased La Güera's fame, at least among the capital's literati who attended theater productions. The play not only reinforced her reputation as a sexy and unconventional lady, but also as a thoroughly political animal who used her beauty and charm as instruments to further the good of the nation. The hilarity of Schroeder's tale also made her one of the most amusing—if still dignified—figures in Mexican history, a characteristic that added to her growing allure.

Four years later, in 1959, she appeared anew in two Mexican periodicals. In May, Agustín Barrios Gómez mentioned her in his popular *Ensalada Popoff* column, published every Sunday in the newspaper *Novedades*. Marking the centenary of Humboldt's death, the article reiterates the rumor that "it was said that he was in love with . . . the legendary Ignacia La Güera Rodríguez," the "most beautiful woman" he had ever seen. Although the reference is brief, the column was widely read.[16] In August, Anita Brenner's *Mexico/This Month* devoted a feature article to La Güera. The magazine reached a smaller—but also different—audience. Designed to promote good relations between the U.S. and Mexico, the English-language publication was subsidized by the Mexican government, which bought most of the copies to place in its embassies. The two-page article, "'La Güera' Rodríguez," rehashes some of Valle-Arizpe's stories and introduces new errors (such as confusing the names of her three husbands with those of her daughters' spouses). Yet the first sentence shows how her figure could be used to make Mexico enticing to a U.S. audience while at the same time emphasizing that Mexico was in no way inferior to the Northern Colossus: "Whatever your schoolbooks may have said, the most talked-of woman on the American continent during the early 19th century was not Dolly Madison" (wife of President James Madison). She was instead María Ignacia Rodríguez, "Mexico's most exciting and versatile woman."[17]

Both journalists thus used her personage to boost national pride. The fact that they chose to write about La Güera Rodríguez is further proof that Valle-Arizpe's book had caught the eye of Mexican intellectuals.

Valle-Arizpe's Güera was also disseminated in a semi-popular text aimed at university students. In 1967, Arturo Sotomayor excerpted three chapters from *La Güera Rodríguez* in his book *Don Artemio* to give his readers a taste of the long work. The chapters that he selected were three of the most titillating: those that narrated her alleged relationships with Humboldt, Hidalgo and his followers, and Iturbide.[18] Thus the rumors of her affairs as well as of her role in the independence movement continued to spread.

At the same time, she was working her way into scholarly works independent of Valle-Arizpe's text. In 1960 Carlos Olmedilla reproduced part

of a previously unknown document that highlighted her political influence. His article in the leading Mexican history journal, *Historia
Mexicana,* described the 1822 manuscript diary kept by Spanish soldier
Modesto de la Torre and copied two paragraphs asserting that "la Huera
Rodríguez" was "the regulator of Iturbide's conduct and the gentle hand
that moves the keys that play from time to time in this tumultuous orches-
tra."[19] Although the readership for this piece was limited, the passage was
later picked up by historian Manuel Calvillo in his *La República Federal
Mexicana.*[20] Published in 1974 and reprinted in 2003, the book repeated
Torre's story linking La Güera and Iturbide for readers who had missed
Olmedilla's reference—just as Valle-Arizpe's book had done for those who
missed the various works that mentioned her before his did.

For the first time, La Güera also appeared in two well-known historical
dictionaries, if only in very brief entries. The 1964 edition of the
Diccionario Porrúa de historia, biografía y geografía de México provided
details on her marriages and children and stated that she was "celebrated
for her splendorous beauty" and also "a supporter of Hidalgo and a good
friend of Iturbide."[21] The 1969 *Diccionario de insurgentes* by Josep María
Miquel i Vergés included her (along with more than one hundred other
women) in a paragraph that summarized the document published by
Genaro García in 1910 that implicated her as "the protector or protected
of the insurgents" in 1814.[22] Moreover, her miniature portrait was reproduced in two art books that presented her as a lady of high society who
was notable for her beauty, ingenuity, and "friendship with famous persons of the epoch."[23] Still, although her visibility was increasing, the myths
that were already circulating about her had not yet made much headway
in the academic literature.

In fact, La Güera Rodríguez was not yet widely considered an important
historical figure. She was not included in other collections of biographical
sketches of the period that featured several independence heroines, not
even one by Aurora Fernández that dealt exclusively with "women who
honored the nation."[24] As late as 1975, a lengthy doctoral dissertation on
insurgent women only mentioned her in passing, in a single paragraph
noting that she contributed money to the rebellion between 1810 and
1814.[25] But the pace of her journey to fame was about to speed up as she
moved into the mass media with assistance from the feminist movement.

LA GÜERA AS FEMINIST ICON, 1975–2000

The development of the feminist movement during the decade of the 1970s—highlighted by the first U.N. World Conference on Women, held in Mexico City in 1975—breathed new life into La Güera Rodríguez. Looking for examples of women who made history, a new generation went back to the historical record—and to Valle-Arizpe—where they found the "magnificent and extraordinary" María Ignacia Rodríguez, whose alleged political role and sexual freedom made her a particularly appealing figure for the women's liberation movement. I myself was part of this process of rediscovery when I published a long selection from her 1802 divorce case in my 1976 book *La mujer mexicana ante el divorcio eclesiástico,* thus helping to make her part of the emerging field of women's history.[26]

But it was mass media that made her a celebrity. A milestone in her journey from literary to popular memory came in 1977, in a sumptuously sensuous feature film made by renowned filmmaker Felipe Cazals. Starring the voluptuous actress Fanny Cano, *La Güera Rodríguez* portrayed her as a seductive beauty who was fully committed to the cause of independence.[27] Although it was not one of Cazals's most successful productions, it was shown in several of Mexico's huge movie theaters during the fall of 1977 and again in the spring of 1978, thereby reaching thousands of viewers who might not have read the periodicals and scholarly works, seen Schroeder's play, or been familiar with Valle-Arizpe's novel.[28]

The film disseminated Valle-Arizpe's stories because, according to the authors of the film script (Emilio Carballido and Julio Alejandro, best known for writing the script for *Viridiana*), it was based entirely on that text. The script had been passed around for many years until Cano's husband (and the eventual co-producer) convinced Cazals to direct it so that his wife could play the gorgeous "courtesan" who was also a national heroine. Indeed, Ms. Cano said it was "the role she had dreamed of playing all her life."[29] The movie was billed as the story of

a woman who, amid the hypocrisy of Mexico at the beginning of the last century, stood out for her character, wit, and courage: the Fair Rodríguez, who was both hated and admired for saying and doing what she felt in any situation.

> She was rebellious and irreverent both in political affairs (collaborating with the insurgents in the fight for independence against Spain) and in her amorous adventures (her love affairs with Iturbide, Bolívar, bishops, and viceroys were common gossip). Her daring necklines were the scandal of a generation. She had a smile for every moment, and her sense of humor never left her. She was always in command, a woman who loved life . . . and who made it treat her well.

The advertising slogan set the tone by affirming that "an entire epoch looked down her décolletage." By depicting her in profile, the movie poster accentuated that part of her anatomy, thus emphasizing her sexiness as a marketing strategy to attract viewers into the theater.

Besides compressing time and space to fit a 113-minute format, the film adds many new elements to Valle-Arizpe's stories. As the scriptwriters admitted in a handwritten note on the original film script, "If what we depict did not actually happen, it is the way we would have liked it to occur." For example, when La Güera's first husband fires a gun at her, it is because he finds Bolívar jumping from the balcony outside her bedroom window, although the Liberator (whom she may never even have met) had left Mexico nearly three years before the incident. In her dramatic (but invented) encounter with a panel of inquisitors, La Güera accuses them of pederasty, a detail not present in the novel. Her true love, Juan Manuel Elizalde, appears early on as a Mexican patriot, long before the Chilean gentleman had set foot in New Spain. And there are wonderful (imagined) scenes of her handing him jewels through a garden gate in the middle of the night to fund the insurgency, hiding his cache of weapons in her dressing room, and meeting with La Corregidora to discuss strategies for achieving independence. La Güera not only steers Iturbide to lead the break with Spain, but also supposedly prevents him from denouncing Hidalgo's movement in 1809, for she is (implausibly) shown as supporting it at that early date, with Iturbide already her suitor. The movie does not, however, present Iturbide as her lover, and it ends before the heroine is stained by complicity with his empire. The last scene occurs during the emperor's coronation. Instead of attending, La Güera visits the disillusioned Elizalde: as they kiss passionately, they envision a better—republican—future.

The film thus narrates the tale of Mexican independence through a romantic love story. Because she was true to Elizalde for more than a

Figure 20. Poster advertising the movie *La Güera Rodríguez,* directed by Felipe Cazals, 1977. It depicts the actress Fanny Cano as María Ignacia Rodríguez. Stanford University Special Collections, MSS Prints 0368. Reproduced with permission from Felipe Cazals.

decade, the movie's Güera was less promiscuous than Valle-Arizpe's. Yet, as film critic Julia Tuñón points out, her actions were always linked to her "unrestrained eroticism."[30] Indeed, one of the recurring images is a life-size semi-nude portrait of La Güera that the audience only sees from the back, while various men peer at it lasciviously. At the end, Elizalde declares that it is time to cover it up, presumably a sign that he has domesticated his wanton lady—and also an indication that the movie has not fully abandoned Valle-Arizpe's vision of the proper finale where the feisty dame is tamed by a good man and lives happily ever after.

Much of the film's portrayal of La Güera nonetheless reflects new perspectives about history, social justice, and gender relations. The dialogue appealed to the budding feminist and counter-cultural audience of the 1970s. La Güera affirms that "I walk where I wish and don't like to be mistreated," and "In a small and timid environment, given to pettiness, anyone who simply aspires to have fun, . . . who is irreverent and spontaneous and sincere, will cause scandals." In several scenes she stands up to the viceroy and to the men in her life. For example, when Elizalde first proclaims his love for her but says he would want to wear the pants in the family "like an old-style man," she lets him go, with tears in her eyes. In other scenes she declares "I want to be free," not only as a citizen but also as a woman. When the viceroy criticizes her behavior, she asks "How is my private life an affair of state?" After he replies that "a viceroy is like a father to each of his subjects," she shoots back: "Then first give food to all your children, the majority of whom are hungry and showing more flesh than I because they lack decent clothing. But the day will soon come when this situation will change."

The film's Güera is thus a woman ahead of her time who can serve as a role model for Mexican youth. She refuses to be boxed in by tradition and is unwavering in her political convictions. Despite being a wealthy aristocrat, she shows solidarity with the poor. She is at once beautiful, sexy, strong, brilliant, and powerful—and a patriot, of course. As a liberated woman, she is a fitting heroine for the new era. And, even more than in the case of the written texts, the film's sensational visual images remained engraved in the memory of all who saw them.

By the 1980s, interest in María Ignacia Rodríguez was on the rise. In 1982 one of Mexico's leading composers, Carlos Jiménez Mabarak, created an opera in her honor. "The only Mexican opera set in the independence period" was performed at the Palacio de Bellas Artes in September 1982 and at the Festival Internacional Cervantino in 1983, with famed Guillermina Higareda in the starring role. The title, simply *La Güera*, indicates that she was by then so well known that it was unnecessary to mention her last name.[31]

The libretto by Julio Alejandro (also one of the scriptwriters for the film) follows her life from the time she supposedly bids adieu to her lover Bolívar (in the first act), through her star-crossed first and second marriages (in the second act), until she refuses to help her lover Iturbide become emperor (in the third act)—a twist provided by Alejandro, who has his protagonist declare that once Mexico achieved its independence, her work was done. She is portrayed throughout not only as living life with gusto, but also as having a strong social conscience—even defending a slave in the first act—and playing a vital role in the independence struggle.

Although the opera received mixed reviews and reached a relatively small audience, it shows La Güera's growing appeal for Mexican artists. It also shows how her identity continued to change. She now became not only an indomitable heroine, but also a staunch republican (a stance that cannot be verified). She also believed in social equality, or at least in individual freedom (ideas that likewise cannot be verified).[32] As in the film, the opera's version of La Güera followed Valle-Arizpe in representing her as an enlightened woman who rebelled against the conventions of her social class and time period.

La Güera Rodríguez did not just appear in artistic productions, but also in texts designed to teach Mexican history to a popular audience. For example, in 1982 a small pamphlet entitled *La Güera Rodríguez* was published in the inexpensive *Cuadernos Mexicanos* series distributed in CONASUPO supermarkets.[33] The attractive issue contained lovely illustrations of historical scenes and personages, a short introduction (that repeated several errors from earlier texts), and the complete eleventh chapter of Valle-Arizpe's book that not only presented her alleged affair with Iturbide but also told the story of the final phase of the independence movement in great detail. Because it was published by the Secretariat of Public Education, it carried the government's semi-official imprimatur.

The editors evidently did not realize that much of Valle-Arizpe's account was fictional.

Neither did the authors of two historical encyclopedias that listed her as a major national figure: the 1977 *Enciclopedia de México* and the 1989 *Diccionario enciclopédico de México ilustrado*.[34] Both repeated some of Valle-Arizpe's inventions, for example, about her nonexistent Inquisition trial that now supposedly took place in 1811. The latter also mentioned the romances with Bolívar, Humboldt, and Iturbide. Because these falsehoods appeared in authoritative non-fiction texts, the line between fact and fantasy was becoming increasingly blurred.

To be sure, professional historians resisted the pull of the legend.[35] One of the first general histories of Mexican women, Julia Tuñón's 1987 *Women in Mexico: A Forgotten History*, contained a cautiously worded paragraph on doña María Ignacia Rodríguez.[36] Although she referenced some of the myths, Tuñón pointed out that they might be apocryphal. Her Güera was

> a beautiful, intelligent, ingenious woman, famous for her coquetry and amorous adventures: she had three husbands and, apparently, several lovers, including, according to tradition, Simón Bolívar, Alexander von Humboldt and Agustín de Iturbide. Her first husband ... accused her before the Divorce Tribunal of repeated adultery; she, in turn, accused him of frequent physical abuse, which was a common practice among husbands in those years. An important part of the myth represented by "La Güera" is her support for Mexico's independence. Her image expresses the limits and possibilities for a woman of talent in this period of change and continuity.

The author's caveats were nonetheless overlooked by many of her readers, who accepted the rumors as facts.

A prize-winning telenovela about the independence period, *La antorcha encendida* (1996), even presented La Güera as a royalist rather than an insurgent. She only appears three times in the 140 episodes: in brief scenes where she flirts with the young Bolívar and later with Humboldt, and in a key moment where she suggests to the viceroy that he should name Iturbide as the new general to combat the rebels. It seems that the two prominent historians who advised the producers, Jean Meyer and Carlos Herrejón Peredo, did not believe the tales about her illicit affairs or about her important role in the struggle. The popular television show nonetheless increased her stature as an interesting figure in the viceregal court and provided memorable images of La Güera, played by the beautiful and elegant Christian Bach.[37]

And some narrators of her story did not give her any political role at all. In 1984 the elderly José Fuentes Mares only represented her as a lady who was "enamored of love." His wonderfully entertaining *Las mil y una noches mexicanas,* a Mexican version of the *Arabian Nights,* was the last book written by the eminent historian.[38] Dispensing with a bibliography and footnotes, Fuentes Mares compiled his favorite stories about the Mexican past—stories that he considered just as compelling as the tales spun by Scheherazade. One of these was the saga of La Güera, the subject of his third chapter.

Despite taking his information from Valle-Arizpe's text, Fuentes Mares inevitably modified it in the process of distilling it into seven pages. His version emphasized "the intimacies and amusing dalliances of doña María Ignacia Rodríguez." The author was careful to note that many of the episodes associated with her were based on hearsay, and that even the story of Iturbide changing the route of his procession to pass by her balcony could not be proven. Yet that did not stop him from repeating it or from gleefully listing her rumored affairs. Thus, Fuentes Mares recounts that La Güera entertained many men "between her sheets": besides three husbands, her amorous conquests not only included the Liberator Agustín de Iturbide, but also illustrious "canons, soldiers, visitors of note, such as the *caraqueñito* Bolívar and the sage geographer, historian, and ethnographer Alexander von Humboldt." But he never mentions her support for Hidalgo's rebellion or her alleged authorship of the Plan de Iguala— though he credits her with being aware of the plot because "nothing ever happened without her knowledge," and with giving Iturbide excellent advice, for "women easily divine truths that men ignore."

His privileging of her love life is not just a function of the brevity of his chapter, since he found space to affirm that at the end of her life the "restless" Güera found peace in her marriage to Elizalde. Indeed, Fuentes Mares is the only late-twentieth-century writer to mention the story that she professed in the Third Order of San Francisco—and he embellishes Valle-Arizpe's narrative by alleging that "she lacerated her flesh with penitences and filled her brain with pious readings."

Instead, his omission of her alleged contributions to the independence movement reveals his historical perspectives, for he was much more conservative than Valle-Arizpe. Fuentes Mares evidently subscribed to the old-fashioned view that history is made by men, a notion that was not only being challenged by a new feminist generation but had already been questioned by Valle-Arizpe himself when he gave La Güera Rodríguez a central role in Mexico's independence struggle. Fuentes Mares also presented Iturbide as the true author of the Plan de Iguala and as the "Father of the Republic," while Valle-Arizpe had portrayed him as an ambitious traitor. Thus, by using pieces of *La Güera Rodríguez* selectively, Fuentes Mares expressed views of the Mexican past that were at odds with those of Valle-Arizpe.

Because it was so amusing, *Las mil y una noches mexicanas* was an immediate success. It had gone through four editions by 1986 and was then reprinted at least two more times, in 1997 and 2006. By disseminating some of the tales in Valle-Arizpe's long and erudite novel, it kept alive the spicy gossip about La Güera's illicit liaisons. It was also the first of a new genre of popular histories—many of them anti-feminist—that devoted a scant few pages to her story in their comedic renditions of the Mexican past. But it was tame in comparison with some of the representations that would follow.

In 1990 La Güera Rodríguez recuperated her political role and became even more visible to a mass audience as the subject of a comic book in the successful *Hombres y Héroes* series, which was designed to teach history to the working classes.[39] Comics were a fixture of popular culture at that time in Mexico, constantly in the public eye as adults bought the inexpensive *historietas* at sidewalk stands and read them on buses and subways. The 158th issue chronicled the life of "La Güera Rodríguez, beautiful Mexican conspirator." Like the movie, the comic proved that a picture is worth a thousand words. The images of a Wonder Woman–like Güera are unforgettable. The artist, José L. Echave, depicts her as a provocative sexpot—as was obligatory in this commercial genre. Yet, despite including a long list of her alleged affairs, the text emphasizes her political activities. Indeed, the authors, Rémy Bastien and Dolores Plaza, went further than any previous writer in making her an important independence heroine.

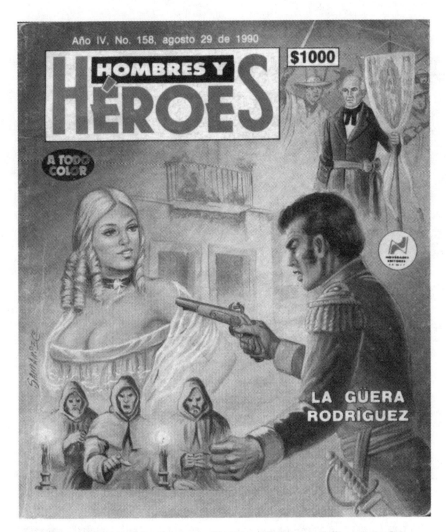

Figure 21. Cover of comic book issue on "La Güera Rodríguez: Bella conspiradora mexicana." The illustrations represent the incident where her first husband fired at her with his pistol; the three inquisitors who allegedly tried her for participating in the Hidalgo Revolt; and Father Miguel Hidalgo (upper right). Drawing by José L. Echave. *Hombres y Héroes* 158, año IV (August 29, 1990). Private collection of Silvia M. Arrom.

Although claiming to be a true history, this version of her life mixes up dates and people and introduces new falsehoods. For example, in this telling it was La Güera rather than her estranged husband who initiated the ecclesiastical divorce case, a reversal that highlights her boldness and autonomy. The text opens in 1804 with La Güera meeting three of the gentlemen whom Villamil accused of being her lovers: Luis Ceret (an incident that in reality occurred in 1801), and Mariano Beristáin and Ramón Cardeña (actually in 1802). They are here plotting independence together (improbably, since it is only 1804; the Frenchman Ceret had left the country long ago; and Beristáin would later oppose the insurgency). In this narrative Villamil's charges of adultery, which led him to fire his gun at her, are completely unfounded; she is instead involved in a political conspiracy. As a flashback shows, her political convictions are so strong that it is she who encourages the young Bolívar, during their brief romance, never to waver in his quest for independence. And she works toward this goal constantly by sending money to Hidalgo in 1810, confronting a panel of inquisitors after being denounced as a subversive, suffering banishment to Querétaro, masterminding the Plan de Iguala, and convincing Iturbide to carry it out. Although Iturbide is depicted as being madly in love with her, the comic book equivocates as to whether she reciprocated his feelings, for her motivations are represented as political rather than personal. When Iturbide is deposed—because he failed to heed her advice—she goes on to marry her third husband and lives happily until her death (incorrectly dated to 1849 instead of 1850).

The last page lauds "this marvelous lady, so outstanding for her beauty, talent, courage, and boldness," who represents "the dawn of a . . . new creole and mestizo Mexico, full of contradictions but alive and flourishing." She was thus the symbol of a vibrant nation on the path toward progress. She was also a player as important in the public sphere as many men. Yet she was still primarily a sexy dame.

La Güera's growing reputation as a national heroine was enhanced by the publication in 1995 of the *Prontuario de los insurgentes*.[40] This collection of documents intercepted by the Spanish government during the independence struggle includes two that refer to her ties with the insurgents Francisco de Velasco, Rafael Vega, and Leona Vicario in 1814 and that detail her financial support of the rebels in exchange for their protection of her estates.

Although part of the first document had been published by Genaro García in 1910, the second provides new information. Their presence in this scholarly tome focused additional attention on her political activities.

Her celebrity had grown to such an extent that in 1997 the *Encyclopedia of Mexico,* produced in English by a collective of leading scholars, chose her as the only woman of the independence period to include in the book. The entry on María Ignacia Rodríguez de Velasco y Osorio Barba, written by Virginia Guedea (the same historian who edited the *Prontuario*), shows how uncorroborated rumors and inaccurate information continued to creep into historical narratives. Guedea describes the "pro-independence socialite" as "renowned for her beauty, charm, and sharp wit, as well as for her scandalous behavior and friendship with important figures of the day . . . with whom it was said that she also had affairs." Her (probably fictional) friendships with Simón Bolívar and Miguel Hidalgo are presented as a given. Her trial and banishment are described as taking place after (rather than before) the Hidalgo revolt broke out. Yet the description of her political activities is credible:[41]

> She was firmly on the side of the insurgents, although not openly, lending them money, supporting them in other ways, and corresponding with them. Two of her estates were given to José Sixto Verduzco and José María Leceaga [sic] from 1813 onward, in return for guarantees from the rebels that her property would not be touched.
>
> As a rich property owner and society hostess, la Güera Rodríguez held a salon in Mexico City. Distinguished society figures attended her parties, both Autonomists and members of the colonial elite. Among them was Agustín de Iturbide. La Güera Rodríguez was also in contact with Los Guadalupes, whose members helped the revolutionary cause from Mexico City, and many of whom were women. When Iturbide decided to join in the race for Independence, la Güera Rodríguez knew of his plans. She also corresponded with him during his unification of the pro-Independence forces. In his brief spell as emperor, her salon formed part of his court.

Although Guedea does not exaggerate La Güera's political influence, the fact that she is the only independence heroine profiled in the two-volume *Encyclopedia* shows that by the end of the twentieth century she was considered a central figure in Mexican history. It also shows the growth of her international reputation.

LA GÜERA IN THE TWENTY-FIRST CENTURY:
HEROINE FOR A NEW AGE

La Güera's popularity skyrocketed during the first decade of the twenty-first century. Her representations could go in several directions, depending on what stories each narrator wanted to tell about the Mexican past. Although the scholarly texts normally qualified their statements, some of the others made increasingly outrageous claims, though without offering new documentary evidence. As successive authors copied each other, the false "facts" increasingly came to be accepted as true parts of her biography.

Her love life was still a favorite subject for many, especially in humorous books written by well-known journalists around the turn of the century. For example, in *Amores mexicanos* (1998), José Manuel Villalpando declares that her romance with Iturbide was "the most famous love story in the history of Mexico."[42] In *Las grandes traiciones de México* (2000), Francisco Martín Moreno devotes a short chapter to Iturbide's alleged double betrayal: first, he betrayed his wife during his affair with La Güera; then he betrayed his mistress when he made his wife the empress, thus shattering La Güera's (invented) dream of occupying the Mexican throne.[43] In *Álbum de pesadillas mexicanas* (2002), José Joaquín Blanco refers to her as a "slut" and "supposed nymphomaniac." Although he notes that her scandalous affairs with Bolívar, Humboldt, and Iturbide may never have existed, these are the parts of her legend that Blanco discusses in his essay.[44]

Her alleged sexual escapades are also analyzed in a scholarly work, Montserrat Galí Boadella's *Historias del bello sexo* (2002).[45] Galí devotes half a chapter to La Güera Rodríguez in building her argument that the bourgeois culture of republican Mexico, allegedly exemplified by Leona Vicario, was more prudish than the aristocratic culture of the Enlightenment, allegedly exemplified by María Ignacia Rodríguez. Her portrayal of La Güera as a highly educated woman who was interested in expanding her knowledge and engaging in political discussions is entirely plausible, as is her description of the sociability of daily life. So is her treatment of La Güera as representative of many women in her social class, rather than as an exception. However, her conclusion that La Güera was a "libertine" is less persuasive because, in order to support it, Galí accepts as true the charges of adultery made by her first husband, affirms that she counted Bolívar and Iturbide among her many lovers, and claims that her main goal in life was the pursuit of pleasure. These assertions go well beyond the available evidence and show how even good scholars could be taken in by Valle-Arizpe's tales.[46]

In the hands of other authors, La Güera became a sage rather than a trollop. A notable instance is the 2005 novel *El águila en la alcoba: La Güera Rodríguez en los tiempos de la independencia nacional*, written by the distinguished lawyer and history aficionado Adolfo Arrioja Vizcaíno. Despite her presence throughout the narrative, the protagonist is a man, fictional government functionary Miguel Ángel Velázquez de León. La Güera is his good fairy, offering advice about his career and love life as well as using her numerous contacts and knowledge about local affairs to smooth his way. At the same time, the novel recounts entertaining episodes of her life (mostly taken from Valle-Arizpe) in parallel with the story of how Mexico achieved its independence.

La Güera takes center stage only at the end of the novel, when Arrioja uses her to express his disappointment with the course of Mexican history. There are no heroes in his tale: Hidalgo is an incompetent leader who cannot control his bloodthirsty followers, and Iturbide is a vain dimwit who lets power go to his head. Only the wise Güera Rodríguez comes out on top. She has been working to liberate herself and her country from the start—and to bolster his case, Arrioja introduces new details that would later be copied by others, even though he never claimed to write a factual biography; on the contrary, his introduction cites the novels of Tolstoy and films of Visconti as his inspiration.

In this version of her life, María Ignacia Rodríguez initiates the ecclesiastical divorce to get rid of her stupid and violent husband. The viceroy approves it in an official-sounding decree that could never have existed because only ecclesiastical officials, not viceroys, had jurisdiction over marriage. Arrioja also claims, again incorrectly, that she gave Hidalgo strategic advice and even suggested that he use the banner of the Virgen de Guadalupe to attract adherents to his cause. Moreover, like many authors before him, Arrioja affirms that she manipulated Iturbide to get him to abandon the royalist cause and lead Mexico to independence. His contribution is to present her love affairs as strategic, designed to help her achieve her goals. Until the end, when Iturbide supposedly betrays her by putting the crown on his head—at which point she abandons him and retreats into private life—she is always in control, pulling the strings of Mexican political power.

But the men she worked through were unworthy. Everything would have been better, according to Arrioja, if she had been in charge instead of being forced to operate from behind the scenes. Mexico would have taken a different path "if Iturbide had been the woman and she the man." Without patriarchal restrictions, the prudent Güera could have been a great leader, "our Catherine of Russia." A stable government could have been consolidated. Thus, in a world with gender equality, La Güera—"the most notable woman in Mexico"—could have saved the country from its sad future.[47] In this representation, La Güera never became the heroine Mexico needed because of the sexism that constrained her.

While Arrioja portrayed her as the thwarted savior, other texts made her one of the leading heroines of the independence struggle. She plays a major role in popular histories such as Armando Fuentes Aguirre Catón's *La otra historia de México: Hidalgo e Iturbide* (2008). This two-volume work opens with a section on La Güera that recounts some of Valle-Arizpe's "delicious" stories to lighten the "solemn tome." After thus drawing in the reader, the more serious sections that follow present her as a firm supporter of Hidalgo's movement and, as Iturbide's lover, a crucial influence on the consummation of independence.[48]

La Güera is also one of the principal heroines featured in works on insurgent women such as Sebastián Alaniz's *Mujeres por la Independencia* (2009). This small volume dedicates a full chapter to each of four heroines: the "indomitable" Leona Vicario, the "tireless" Josefa Ortiz de Domínguez, the "impetuous" Gertrudis Bocanegra, and the "beautiful and intelligent" Güera Rodríguez. Perhaps because it is written for schoolchildren, Alaniz omits any reference to her love affairs, although he repeats many of Valle-Arizpe's other amusing anecdotes about her life. Instead he emphasizes La Güera's wisdom, bravery, and steadfast support of national sovereignty. And, as an incentive to his juvenile readers, he adds the (completely invented) flourish that she was a voracious reader and excelled at math.[49]

La Güera's prominence reached new heights during the 2010 bicentennial year. Schroeder Inclán's half-century-old farce was revived, with its

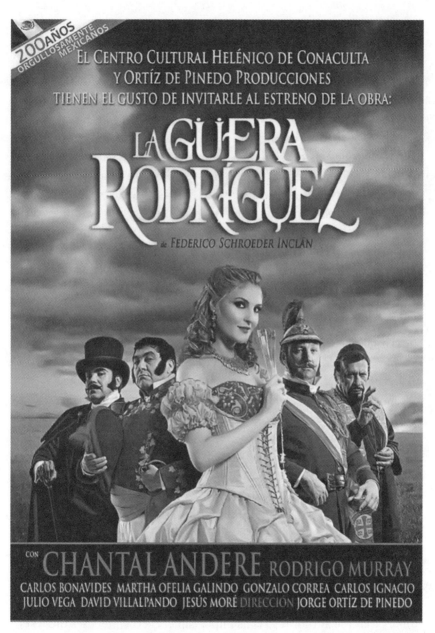

Figure 22. Poster advertising the play *La Güera Rodríguez* by Federico Schroeder Inclán (1955), presented anew during the celebrations of the bicentennial of the Grito de Dolores in 2010. Photograph by Rodrigo Cassou. Reproduced with permission from Ortíz de Pinedo Producciones.

striking TV advertisement and poster plastered all over Mexico City.[50] Jiménez Mabarak's opera was presented anew, with the original soprano's daughter, Lorena von Pastor, playing the part of María Ignacia Rodríguez.[51]

New works also abounded. La Güera appeared—along with Hidalgo and other insurgent leaders—in *Antorcha y Cenizas*, a hilarious comedy by Oscar Flores Acevedo and Eduardo Borbolla. By emphasizing their scandalous love lives, it sought to bring the great national heroes "down from their pedestals to show their human sides."[52] La Güera also starred in a solo performance that linked her to Hidalgo romantically—a new invention—in which she read an entirely fictional love letter that the priest of Dolores allegedly sent her from his prison cell while awaiting execution.[53] She was the subject of a fanciful tale in Javier Sunderland Guerrero's *Las revoltosas*, a collection of short stories about female rebels in Mexican history.[54] And the Crononautas Tijerina composed a "corrido a la Güera Rodríguez" that praised her as "an implacable woman" and "pillar of the insurgents."[55]

As use of the internet expanded, dozens of blogs and websites recounted her (largely fictitious) biography.[56] So did Celia del Palacio, in a short entry in her book on some hundred independence heroines, *Adictas a la insurgencia*.[57] La Güera was also featured in television dramas and on talk shows purporting to tell her true story and thereby restoring an allegedly forgotten figure to her rightful place in history.[58]

Perhaps the most widely read—as well as the most risible—of her representations in popular histories was by Francisco Martín Moreno, whose bestselling *Arrebatos carnales* (Carnal ecstacies) interweaves history with sensational stories about "the passions that consumed the protagonists of Mexican history."[59] The second volume of his series devotes a long chapter to La Güera Rodríguez. In descriptions that can only be characterized as soft-core porn, Martín Moreno briefly details her sexual adventures with the priests Beristáin and Cardeña, the French doctor Ceret, and the painter Francisco Rodríguez—a new addition to the list of her legendary paramours. Notably absent are her affairs with Bolívar and Hidalgo, rumors that the author rejects as implausible. He then focuses the rest of the chapter on her intimate relations with Agustín de Iturbide. In the process, the author narrates key episodes of Mexican history; claims that La Güera was crucial to Iturbide's career because of her cleverness and connections; and asserts that because of her influence on Iturbide, she was "the first woman in Mexico who, without having been elected, exercised power."

Yet Martín Moreno does not portray her as a political figure. Instead, his Güera is primarily motivated by her lust and emotions. She helps Iturbide because she loves him, and if in the end she turns against him, it is out of envy, not political convictions. In Martín Moreno's telling, she couldn't forgive the Liberator, first, for refusing to leave his wife in order to place her on the Mexican throne, and second, for having an affair with her daughter Antonia, which she belatedly discovers. "The empress who was never enthroned" (as the chapter is titled) leaves the reader with vivid memories of a sex-starved beauty who only inadvertently makes history because of her love for the man of the hour.

Moreover, the book illustrates the chapter with an elegant drawing of a beautiful woman, purportedly María Ignacia Rodríguez. The image is not her portrait, however; it is taken from Ignacio Cumplido's 1851 periodical *Presente amistoso dedicado a las señoritas mexicanas,* which reproduced a European lithograph to accompany an article about a certain "Juliana." The mistake has since been repeated many times.

La Güera also appeared in more serious works. She inspired a carefully researched undergraduate thesis by César Alejandro Martínez Núñez.[60] She was included in a scholarly work on women in Latin America, *Las mujeres en la Independencia de América Latina,* a sign of her increasing international visibility.[61] And, naturally, she acquired her own Wikipedia page, proof of the degree to which she had become an important historical figure. To be sure, it included many false details as well as real ones. And because it was illustrated with the lithograph of "Juliana" popularized by Martín Moreno, it helped disseminate that image as her quasi-official— although erroneous—portrait.[62]

By the end of the bicentennial year, La Güera Rodríguez was so well known that when a fantastical *alebrije* (a papier-mâché sculpture) with her glamorous image was paraded in a street procession commemorating the two hundred years since the Grito de Dolores, bystanders immediately recognized her as one of Mexico's beloved heroines.[63] The contrast between her absence from the 1910 centennial celebrations and her ubiquitous presence in 2010 is striking.

Figure 23. Drawing of "Juliana" mistakenly presented since 2010 as a portrait of La Güera Rodríguez. It is instead a European lithograph of an unidentified woman reproduced by Mexican publisher Ignacio Cumplido, an example of the international circulation of lithographic images during the nineteenth century. *Presente amistoso dedicado a las señoritas mexicanas* (1851), vol. 1, p. 100. Harvard Library.

Figure 24. Papier-mâché figure of La Güera Rodríguez paraded in a procession on the Paseo de la Reforma celebrating the bicentennial of the Grito de Dolores in 2010. Molly, "Alebrijes," *The Amazing Adventures of los von ZauRunyon!* (blog).

La Güera's fame continued to grow after the dust of the bicentennial festivities settled. In subsequent years she remained a darling of popular publications, of lectures and performances uploaded to YouTube, and of "authoritative" biographical sketches scattered throughout the internet. Mexican writers and artists evidently had an insatiable desire to tell her story and the public had an insatiable appetite to hear it.[64]

Her position as one of Mexico's most important heroines was firmly consolidated. Indeed, the Museo de la Mujer, a museum dedicated to Mexican women's history that opened in 2011, placed her as one of only four women in the room dedicated to "insurgent women," alongside the famous Josefa Ortiz de Domínguez, Leona Vicario, and Mariana Rodríguez del Toro de Lazarín. The image of La Güera Rodríguez (an imagined "photo-sculpture") is accompanied by a caption that identifies her as "significant not only for her support of the insurgency but also for her transgression of the social mores of her time."[65]

Figure 25. Life-size photo-sculpture of La Güera Rodríguez in the room dedicated to insurgent women in the Museo de la Mujer, Mexico City. Photograph by author, March 2015.

Some writers went much further in their claims. In September 2010 an enthusiastic blogger pronounced La Güera "the fundamental heroine of Mexican independence, much more important than Doña Josefa Ortiz de Domínguez or Doña Leona Vicario."[66] In 2011 humorist Antonio Garci dubbed her "The Mother of the Patria" because she was the alleged link between the Hidalgo revolt and the achievement of independence under Iturbide in 1821.[67] In 2012 journalist Reyna Lorena Rivera published a splashy article in *Excelsior* that declared that La Güera was not only "vital to Independence" but "the most politically powerful woman in the entire history of Mexico."[68] In 2013 blogger Ana Díaz called her the key to the country's independence because "behind every great event is a great woman. . . . It is probable that without her, Mexico's independence never would have been consummated."[69] And in 2017 blogger Carlos Urena affirmed that she was "the woman who seduced a nation and changed the history of Mexico."[70]

Thus, nearly two hundred years after independence was won, doña María Ignacia Rodríguez de Velasco finally entered the pantheon of Mexican heroes. In some accounts she even eclipsed the formerly reigning heroines of 1910.

Yet her prestige as a political actor did not erase her legend as a femme fatale. If some narrators celebrated her sexuality, others condemned it. Either way, they believed and then propagated the stories of her affairs with numerous prelates and viceregal authorities, with Bolívar, Humboldt, and Iturbide—and, very occasionally, with Hidalgo as well. She was the one "who initiated Simón Bolívar in the joys of love," "the seductress of Independence," "the sexual symbol of her epoch, the Marylin [sic] Monroe of her day," "a true *vedette* known for her loose behavior," "a sex addict," even "one of the ten most famous prostitutes in history."[71] It is thus clear that the representation of women as sexual beings was a large part of what made her attractive to many of those who narrated her story.

CONCLUSION

In the seventy years since the publication of Valle-Arizpe's *La Güera Rodríguez*, the figure he created has made her way ever deeper into the collective imaginary. As she did so, successive narrators modified her to suit the messages they wanted to convey to their audiences. La Güera thus meant different things to different people at different times: the embodiment of sexuality and scandal, a liberated and powerful woman, the victim of a patriarchal regime, an important figure in the shaping of modern Mexico, a symbol of the nation. Because so many of her depictions were based on inaccuracies, however, it became increasingly difficult to disentangle the woman from the myth, for falsehoods had become an inextricable part of her legend.

Conclusion

Doña María Ignacia Rodríguez's journey to stardom took more than a century. During her lifetime she was known as a beautiful and vivacious figure who was the occasional subject of gossip because of her disputes with her first husband and the rumors linking her to various political conspiracies. But in many respects—such as her connection to foreign visitors and leading politicians, as well as her discreet support for home rule and, eventually, independence—she did not stand out from her peers; and she was not one of the patriots like Leona Vicario who were recognized as national heroines during their lifetime. After her death in 1850, La Güera disappeared from the world of Mexican arts and letters for the rest of the nineteenth century.

How, then, can we explain her resurrection beginning in the early twentieth century? Part of the answer is that she left a paper trail, because cultural memory depends on the written word. Four texts produced by her contemporaries are largely responsible for rescuing her from oblivion: Fanny Calderón de la Barca's lively descriptions of her friend in 1840 and 1841; Vicente Rocafuerte's sensational allegations about her relations with Iturbide in 1822, some of them repeated by Mariano Torrente in 1830; and Guillermo Prieto's memories of tales he had heard during his younger days. This is only part of the explanation, because other women of the time also left interesting paper trails, but they did not have a descendant like Manuel Romero de Terreros to keep their memory alive by writing histories to exalt his ancestors. Nor were they chosen in the middle of the twentieth century to be the protagonist of a bestselling historical novel. So there was an element of luck involved in La Güera's posthumous celebrity.

Although fanciful stories about her began to circulate in the first half of the twentieth century, it was Artemio de Valle-Arizpe's *La Güera Rodríguez*, first published in 1949, that put her on the path to becoming an icon. His decision to use her as the central figure of a work about the independence period was a stroke of genius. Humanizing the great men of history—Bolívar, Humboldt, Hidalgo, and Iturbide—it made "the starchy scenes of National Independence" fun to read.[1] Valle-Arizpe's Mexican version of the don Juan Tenorio story shared the perennial attraction of the original, for it followed the time-tested plot in which a libertine rogue is redeemed after a series of scandalous escapades—in La Güera's case, through the love of her third husband. Thus, the sex-obsessed and potentially transgressive heroine who supposedly entertained a string of lovers while she defied colonial authorities is properly tamed once she completes the task of liberating her country. In addition to the satisfying story line, the book also bolstered readers' nationalism, for in Valle-Arizpe's hands Mexico acquired a marvelous new independence heroine. Not only was she an ardent patriot but also the most beautiful, brilliant, and charming woman in the Americas, a singular personage who was larger than life, the model of perfection—almost a goddess.

Valle-Arizpe's *La Güera Rodríguez* was far from an accurate biography, however. In crafting his extraordinary character, he collected various anecdotes about doña María Ignacia Rodríguez—including some that were demonstrably false or highly dubious—and added many of his own, without new documentation to support them. In fact, the nineteenth-century texts were so schematic that they left many gaps that could be filled with imagination. And that is precisely what Valle-Arizpe did when he spun tales about La Güera's numerous affairs and essential role in the independence struggle. At the same time, he paid little attention to the more mundane aspects of her life, such as the routine travails of bearing seven children, watching three die young, and helping to raise nine grand-children after the death of two adult daughters. He also overlooked her everyday tasks, such as running a household, managing property, defend-ing herself in court, and dealing with debt and sickness. Instead, he emphasized her beauty, sexiness, audacity, and political influence—the elements that helped him develop his picaresque tale. And these were the stories that captivated the Mexican public.

Valle-Arizpe's text mixed fact with fiction so skillfully that it fooled most readers into believing his fables, and it inspired many new works that repeated—and embellished—his tales. As La Güera Rodríguez appeared in a play, an opera, a feature film, comic books, novels, newspapers and mag-azines, historical dictionaries, and academic works, she became ever more widely known. By the time of the bicentennial of the Grito de Dolores, she starred in a proliferation of popular works and the image of her gorgeous face, blonde ringlets, and shapely figure was instantly recognizable. The contrast between her absence from the 1910 centennial celebrations and her ubiquitous presence in 2010 is a sign of how far she had traveled on the road from obscurity to fame.

How do we explain her continuing allure? For if Valle-Arizpe provided the principal elements of her legend, it spread because there were people who wanted to tell certain stories about her and others who wanted to believe them. For a legend to persist, each generation has to validate it anew. Part of La Güera's appeal was the way she could be manipulated for multiple purposes. By selecting different parts of Valle-Arizpe's narrative and adding their own inventions, new narrators fashioned a Güera accord-ing to their tastes, ideology, values, and agendas. As she was repeatedly transformed, she also remained relevant.

The figure of La Güera Rodríguez was open to very different interpreta-tions. She could represent a proto-feminist or a slut. She could either be the embodiment or the violation of feminine ideals, a source of the ambiv-alence that made her so interesting. As the viceroy put it in the 1977 movie, "What is this woman anyway, demon or angel?"[2] In some ways she was the perfect male fantasy: beautiful, fun to be with, and sexually avail-able. Yet she was a female fantasy as well: ambitious, resourceful, wise, autonomous, and powerful. Her story could thus be claimed by men and women, misogynists as well as feminists.

She also served as a vehicle for writers to express divergent views on the Mexican past. Some used La Güera to glorify the elegant viceregal society, others to deride it as decadent and oppressive. Some used her to enhance Iturbide's reputation, others to diminish it. Some used her to praise egalitarianism and republicanism; to denounce sexism; or to exalt the greatness of Mexico. She could also be used to highlight women's important contributions to history. Either way, her figure reflected widespread misconceptions about women's roles in the past: whether celebrating or denouncing her, most narrators assumed that she defied social conventions because they did not understand the wide range of behavior considered acceptable for women in La Güera's day.

The different versions of La Güera Rodríguez reveal the changing cultural context as well as a growing acceptance of women's political activities. Over time, her aristocratic standing, so important to Romero de Terreros, was downplayed in favor of her (improbable) solidarity with the lower classes. The closing chapter of her life that was essential to Valle-Arizpe's plot—her alleged turn to domesticity and faith in her old age—disappeared from most later texts as that view of proper gender roles became increasingly old-fashioned. Instead, it was her alleged glamour and sensuality, bravery and rebelliousness, and intelligence and political commitment that made her a heroine for a new age. Thus, over the course of the twentieth century, she was transformed from a Proper Aristocratic Lady to a Naughty Patriot Tamed by a Man, a Wise Woman, Feminist, and finally, a Fully Liberated Heroine.

Her story was increasingly tailored to fit the heroic narrative of the fight for national sovereignty. This shift in her persona was part of the process of nation building that exalted larger-than-life figures linked to the warfare that built the Mexican state. Expanding La Güera's influence on the revolutionary movement required, among other things, that the date of the intrigue that led to her banishment from Mexico City be changed from 1809 (nearly a year before the Grito de Dolores and without any relation to Father Hidalgo's insurrection) to 1810 or 1811; and that she be subjected to an (invented) formal trial like the other major heroines. It also required not only believing the malicious rumors that she controlled Iturbide, but also adding such new details as her convincing the viceroy to name Iturbide as supreme commander to combat the rebels (a detail that not even Iturbide's enemies had imagined). Her rising reputation as a political actor also reflects the rehabilitation of Iturbide as Mexicans took a less Manichean view of their history: after having been vilified for undermining republicanism, he was, by the twenty-first century, again receiving his due as the man who freed Mexico from colonial rule. As the woman who supposedly guided the Father of the Nation, she became the Mother of the Patria. She could even serve as a heroine for those who were disillusioned with the traditional masculine heroes, because in many new representations she did not share their defects.

La Güera Rodríguez had become a symbol for the nation. Coincidentally, she was born on November 20, Day of the Revolution, and died on November 1, the All Saint's Day so important to Mexican culture. She modeled the ideal patriotic virtues of being strong, opposing cowards, and fighting for the homeland. Indeed, as Julia Tuñón suggested, she and Iturbide can be seen as a new founding couple for the Mexican nation, just as Malinche and Cortés had been for the colony.[3] If the first creation story represented *mestizaje* (the mixing of races and cultures), the second represented the modernity of a country on the march toward progress.

The contrast between the two couples suggests that Mexican racism contributed to her appeal. If María Ignacia Rodríguez was in real life fair-skinned and European looking, she became even whiter—with pale blonde hair and blue eyes—beginning with Valle-Arizpe's novel. By choosing to depict the "most beautiful" woman in the Americas thus, elite writers and artists in the second half of the twentieth-century were no longer even paying lip service to the ideal of race mixture so self-consciously proclaimed by an earlier generation of intellectuals and symbolized by the Malinche-Cortés pairing. Instead, the new heroine was an aspirational figure who was not only wealthy, healthy, and accomplished, but also had the look of a Hollywood star.

Yet there are many similarities between Malinche and La Güera, for both have been depicted as not only clever but dangerously sexy, and always accompanied by a whiff of intrigue and scandal.[4] La Güera thus joins the long list of women who have been represented—and misrepresented—through gendered stereotypes. Female historical figures are often portrayed in binary categories, as either saints or witches, madonnas or whores– or in the case of María Ignacia Rodríguez, as "la puta libertadora" (the liberating whore), to quote the title of a recent text.[5] Most narratives define her first and foremost by her sexuality. They highlight her good looks. When they present her as a heroine, it is usually as an accessory to a famous man. She wields her power over him through love and physical attractiveness. Even feminist writers emphasize her alleged sexual freedom. To be sure, La Güera could just as easily have become a symbol of the long-suffering mother who sacrifices for her children, for she was the mother and grandmother to a large brood and for many years raised them on her own. Yet most narrators have chosen to remember her as a femme fatale rather than as a matronly lady.

A key to La Güera's enormous appeal is thus sexism: in a sexist society, strong, intelligent, and irreverent women are admired mainly if they are also feminine, sexy, and beautiful. It helps to have a sense of humor, too, that makes them less threatening. If in some narratives La Güera challenged constricting gender roles by violating the norms of proper sexual conduct and standing up to masculine authority, her hyper-femininity and three marriages safely reinforced traditional gender differences. So did the view that her success could be imputed to her dazzling beauty and liaisons with powerful men. Thus, despite occasionally being portrayed as a transgressive figure, she could also bolster prevailing norms and morality.

La Güera's increasing popularity reflects the contemporary fixation with celebrity, beauty, and the erotic. The contrast with Mexico's two main independence heroines, Leona Vicario and María Josefa Ortiz de Domínguez, is instructive. In these respects, neither the allegedly dour Corregidora nor the proper Vicario can compete with our sensual and photogenic heroine, even though they were equally brave and could potentially have become feminist icons. Indeed, in 1831 Vicario penned a remarkable defense of women's intellectual abilities that challenged the view that women are ruled by emotion rather than reason. In response to Lucas Alamán's charge that her political activities had been motivated not by true patriotism but by love for her future husband, Vicario published an open letter in *El Federalista:* "Love is not the only motive of women's actions," she insisted, for women are fully capable of developing their own opinions "with total independence . . . excepting the very stupid, or those who owing to their education have acquired servile habits. Of both classes there are also many men."[6] Although Leona Vicario—unlike María Ignacia Rodríguez—has become an important player in the official narrative of Mexican history taught to every schoolchild, she has yet to be celebrated in an amusing film, play, or opera, and rarely elicits the same enthusiasm as La Güera Rodríguez. Their divergent trajectories are proof that the public generally prefers entertainment to history lessons.

La Güera's special attraction may also respond to a deep psychological need for superheroes who combat evil. As William Marston, the creator of Wonder Woman, wrote in explaining the popularity of comic book heroes, they appeal to "a universal desire to see good overcome evil, to see wrongs righted, underdogs nip the pants of their oppressors, and . . . right triumphing over not-so-mighty might."[7] La Güera Rodríguez embodied these characteristics because—at least as the legend developed, though not in real life—this petite woman rose above the pettiness of her social class, triumphed over her abusive first husband, vanquished the powerful inquisitors, and helped bring down the colonial regime. Many authors, especially of popular blogs, not only turned her into a defiant rebel but, by claiming to reveal her unjustly ignored role in Mexican history, positioned themselves too as rebels who were defying the historical establishment.

By the twenty-first century La Güera Rodríguez was firmly ensconced as an icon of Mexican history. Yet her portraits contained major inaccuracies. Over time, the stories that began as rumor or fictional anecdotes evolved to achieve the status of historical fact. And, then as now, the more sensational the story, the faster and farther it spread—especially if it confirmed the public's gendered stereotypes or fueled their fantasies. After all, who wouldn't want to believe that there was such a splendid heroine in Mexican history? Or that the history of independence was also a dramatic love story? La Güera's afterlife in popular culture is thus, as Charles Weeks put it in his analysis of the Juárez myth, "only in part history and the other part wish fulfillment."[8] Moreover, the complexity of her life has been erased by depicting her as the archetypal Sexy Dame or Intrepid Heroine.

By separating fact from fiction, this study reclaims the real María Ignacia Rodríguez for the history of Latin American women. Many details in the primary sources support her portrayal as a conventional socialite, battered wife, struggling widow, resilient survivor, social climber, loving family matriarch, patriot, and devout Catholic, to name but a few of her possible identities. Her biography shows how one woman navigated the restrictions placed on her sex during the late colonial and early republican periods. It challenges the idea of a rigid separation of public and private spheres that supposedly prevented women from engaging in civic life. It helps us understand the daily life of the time, for example, by showing the regular presence of illness and death and the litigiousness of her social circle. It illuminates economic history by revealing the numerous times she was in financial straits, for she was not as wealthy as some have supposed, and she shared the reversal of fortune that affected so many elite Mexicans after 1810. It provides new insight into political history by suggesting, at the level of an individual, how difficult it must have been to live through the crisis years of the independence struggle, when the wisest course of action was far from clear and when many individuals only gradually came to support a full separation from the mother country. Indeed, apart from her unusual beauty and charm, La Güera Rodríguez was in many ways typical of women of her time, place, and social class.

It was only long after her death that she became a promiscuous rebel, wise woman, feminist, and major national heroine. Her journey from woman to myth shows how the past is constantly reworked to fit the present, for the stories we tell about our history reveal a great deal about who we are. Generations of Mexicans have interpreted her according to their changing views of gender, class, race, politics, and nation. They have used her to construct the past as they wished it could have been. Thus, doña María Ignacia Rodríguez has an enduring place—although not precisely the one she deserves—in the collective imaginary.

APPENDIX A   Chronology of a Life

1778   November 20 Birth of María Ignacia Rodríguez de Velasco, "La Güera Rodríguez"

1794   September 7 First marriage, to Gerónimo Villar Villamil y Primo

1795   July 7 Daughter Josefa is born

1797   May 14 Daughter Antonia is born

1798   September 9 Son Gerónimo is born

1799   March Simón Bolívar visits Mexico City for eight days

1800   March 2 Son Agustín is born

        November Son Agustín dies

1801   May 28 Daughter Guadalupe is born

        October 21 Villamil accuses La Güera of adultery but withdraws the suit ten days later

1802   July 4 Villamil fires at her with his pistol; she accuses him of attempted murder

        July 5 Viceroy arrests Villamil and deposits La Güera with her uncle, Luis Osorio

        August 29 Villamil is freed from house arrest and sues her for ecclesiastical divorce

December 9 Last filing in the divorce case

1803   June? La Güera leaves her *depósito*

April–January 1804 Humboldt visits Mexico City

1804   ? La Güera reunites with Villamil

1805   January 26 Villamil dies

June 12 Daughter Paz is born

1807   February 10 Second marriage, to Juan Ignacio Briones

August 16 Briones dies

1808   April 8? Briones's siblings file a lawsuit disputing the inheritance

April 22 Daughter Victoria is born

July 19 Mexico City *ayuntamiento* proposes a provisional government of New Spain

September 15 Yermo's coup against Viceroy Iturrigaray

1809   March–April Agustín de Iturbide visits La Güera at her parents' house

Fall? Daughter Victoria dies; La Güera inherits Briones's entire estate

October 28 La Güera denounces Aguirre for plotting to kill the viceroy

December 29 La Güera buys the Hacienda de la Patera

1810   March 9 Banished from Mexico City for her role in the intrigue against Aguirre

May 5 La Güera is permitted to return to the outskirts of Mexico City

September 13 Denounced for contributing funds to Hidalgo's revolution

September 16 Grito de Dolores

December 5 La Güera's father dies

1811   January La Güera is again residing in Mexico City

February? Rebel troops occupy her haciendas in the state of Guanajuato

March 1 Rents the Uluapa mansion from her sister Josefa

March 5 Buys twenty-two dozen stockings on credit to sell at retail

October 4 Agreement with Briones's siblings to resolve the lawsuit over his estate

1812	January 15 Daughter Josefa marries the Conde de Regla
	May? La Güera moves to San Francisco street and sublets her sister's house
	June 6 Daughter Antonia marries the Marqués de Aguayo
1814	June 22 La Güera is denounced for helping the insurgents
1815	May 16 First grandchild is born
1816	May? Sued by sister Josefa over a rental contract and by merchant Lama over a debt
	July 24 Daughter Guadalupe dies
1817	June? Buys twenty-four cases of cigarettes on credit to sell at retail
	September 22 Domingo Malo rents the Molino Prieto, with Iturbide as guarantor
	September 17 La Güera is accused of contact with the rebel priest Ramón Cardeña
1818	January 16 Signs contract with her uncle José Rodríguez to recover what he owes her
	April 13 Lawsuit with her sister Josefa is resolved
	April 30 Her mother dies
	December 4 Lawsuit with the merchant Lama is resolved
1819	April 1 Dictates her first will during a grave illness
1820	September 16 Daughter Paz marries the Marqués de Guadalupe Gallardo
1821	February 24 Iturbide proclaims Mexican independence in the Plan de Iguala
	September 13 Iturbide meets Novella and O'Donojú at La Güera's Hacienda de la Patera
	September 27 Iturbide's triumphal entrance to Mexico City; independent Mexico is governed by a provisional junta and then a congress
1822	May 19 Iturbide is proclaimed emperor of the Mexican Empire; rumors of La Güera's influence on him are spread by his enemies
	December 22 La Güera buys the Hacienda de la Escalera
1823	March 19 Iturbide resigns and leaves for exile; birth of the Mexican republic
1825	September 5 La Güera's third marriage, to Juan Manuel de Elizalde

1826	March 19 Son Gerónimo marries María Guadalupe Díaz de Godoy
1828	June 7 Daughter Josefa dies
	September 15 Daughter Paz dies
1836	February 27 First great-grandchild is born
1839	December 6 Sister Josefa dies
1840	February 1 Meets Fanny Calderón de la Barca
1842	January 2 Last visit to bid adieu to the Calderón de la Barcas
1845	December 26 Sister Vicenta dies
1846	December Helps raise funds for Mexican troops during the war with the United States
1850	August 16 Dictates her last will and testament
	November 1 Death of María Ignacia Rodríguez de Velasco

APPENDIX B Genealogy

Note: *The genealogical information available about La Güera's family is incomplete, especially regarding the children who died in infancy and the families of her parents and husbands. When the sources contradict each other, I have followed the information in wills and parish registers.*

María Ignacia Rodríguez de Velasco y Osorio Barba (b. 20 Nov 1778, d. 1 Nov 1850)

PARENTS (MARRIED 30 JUL 1776)

Antonio Rodríguez de Velasco Jiménez (b. 9 Mar 1747, d. 5 Dec 1810)
    Sister: Bárbara, m. Silvestre Díaz de la Vega (b. 1747, d. 7 Dec 1812)
    Brother: José Miguel, single
María Ignacia Osorio y Barba Bello Pereira (b. 1751, d. 30 Apr 1818)
    Brother: Luis Osorio y Barba (b. 1753), m. Bárbara García de Arroyo 15 Oct 1786

SISTERS

María Josefa Rodríguez de Velasco (b. 27 Nov 1779, d. 6 Dec 1839), m. Antonio
Manuel Alejandro Cosío Acevedo (b. 9 Oct 1780, d. 3 Apr 1810), marqués de
Uluapa V, 10 Jul 1796
María de la Luz, d. infancy
María Loreto, d. infancy
María Guadalupe, d. infancy
Alejandro Mariano (b. 15 Sep 1805, d. 17 Dec 1836), marqués de Uluapa VI,
single
María Vicenta Rodríguez de Velasco (b. 27 Aug 1783, d. 26 Dec 1845), m. José
Marín y Muros 29 Oct 1808
Manuela (b. 30 Nov 1817), m. José Juan Landero 10 Jun 1832
Josefa (b. 1835), m. Ponciano Casas 26 Oct 1864
Paulino (b. ca. 1836), m. Luisa Berra Estrella 21 Mar 1872
María de la Luz (b. 1837)
Pedro Telmo (b. 1838)
Joaquina (b. 1840), m. Juan Francisco Pasquel Andrade 19 Jul 1862
Ana María (b. 1841)
Antonia (1843–1908), m. Francisco Múñoz Cartabuena 23 Nov 1866
María Dolores (b. 1846), m. Manuel Caraza Domínguez 23 Dec 1864
María de la Luz (b. 1849), m. Lorenzo Caraza Domínguez 14 Aug 1868
Ana Josefa (b. 1854)
María de los Dolores (b. 4 May 1829, d. 19 Jan 1898), m. José Rafael Castro
Amalia (b. 1851), m. Everardo Hegewisch Martínez 26 Nov 1873
José Rafael (b. 1855), m. Josefa León Martínez 26 Nov 1881
María Isabel (b. 1860)

FIRST HUSBAND (MARRIED 7 SEP 1794)

José Gerónimo López de Peralta Villar Villamil y Primo (b. 8 Nov 1766, d. 26
Jan 1805)
Father: José Gerónimo López de Peralta de Villar Villamil Alvarado
(1742–1803)
Mother: Maria Josefa Primo Villanueva (b. 1748), m. 1762
Mother's siblings:
María Gertrudis Primo Villanueva, m. Antonio Septién Castillo
José Luis Primo Villanueva (b. 1744), m. María Ignacia Canal Hervás 11
Jul 1764
María Dolores Primo Villanueva, m. Pedro Antonio Septién-Montero
Siblings:

María Guadalupe Villar Villamil y Primo, m. Juan Manuel Velázquez de la
Cadena Cervantes 28 Sep 1787
Dolores (b. 1790)
Loreto (b. 1791)
Rosario (b. 1793)
José Manuel (b. 1795), marqués de la Cadena, m. Rafaela Valdivielso
Vidal de Lorca 27 Oct 1816
Ignacio (b. 1797), priest
María de la Luz Villar Villamil y Primo, m. Rafael Lardizábal Fernández
Silva 8 Jan 1797
Juan Manuel (b. 1775)

CHILDREN

1. María Josefa Villar Villamil Rodríguez (b. 7 Jul 1795, d. 7 Jun 1828), m.
Pedro José Romero de Terreros y Rodríguez de Pedroso (b. 1 Nov 1788, d. 12
Apr 1846), conde de Regla III, marqués de Villahermosa de Alfaro VI, conde
de Xala IV, 15 Jan 1812; divorced by ecclesiastical decree 1826
Pedro José Maria (b. 16 May 1815, d. 8 Jan 1856), conde de Regla IV, m.
Mariana García Conde Vidal de Lorca
Matilde (b. 27 Feb 1836, d. 29 Mar.1876), m. Miguel Cervantes Estanillo
29 Sep 1857
Manuel Pedro Ramón (b. 21 Jul 1816, d. 21 Apr 1878), m. María Guadalupe
Gómez de Parada 24 Dec 1835
Paz (b. 20 Sep 1841, d. 24 Sep 1889), m. Pedro Rincón Gallardo Rosso
20 Sep 1869
Alberto (b. 25 Apr 1844, d. 1 Sep 1898), m. Ana María Vinent y Kindelán
Manuel Romero de Terreros y Vinent (b. 24 Mar 1880, d. 1968),
marqués San Francisco VI
Josefa (b. 1847), m. Francisco de Paula Algara y Cervantes 20 Feb 1872
Pedro
Juan Nepomuceno (b. 3 Feb 1818, d. 28 Feb 1862), duque de Regla I, single
Ramón María (b. 5 Feb 1819, d. 22 Mar 1882), m. María del Refugio
Goríbar y Múzquiz
María del Refugio (1851–1938), m. Eduardo Rincón Gallardo Rosso 19
Dec 1871
Guadalupe (b. 1856), m. Antonio Algara Cervantes 21 Jun 1879
María Antonia Carlota (b. 4 Nov 1820, d. 1840), m. Ramón Samaniego y de
la Canal 21 Nov 1838
María Josefa de Jesus (b. 15 Apr 1822, d. 27 Mar 1824)
Ignacio Antonio (b. 24 May 1824), m. Dolores Ruiz Negrete 4 Aug 1856

Pedro (b. 1860), m. Virginia Almeida Reguera 13 Feb 1884, Concepción
Mendoza Carranza 6 Jun 1885

Ignacio (ca. 1862–1895), m. Virginia Moreno Castañares 8 Dec 1885

2. María Antonia Villar Villamil Rodríguez (b. 14 May 1797, d. 20 Nov 1864),
m. José María Valdivielso Vidal de Lorca (b. 9 Feb 1787, d. 28 Mar 1836),
marqués de San Miguel de Aguayo V, 6 Jun 1812

María Guadalupe (b. 17 Oct. 1815, d. 1882), nun

María Dolores (b. 1822), m. Agustin Gómez Parada 11 Jan 1850

María Concepción (b. 6 Feb 1828, d. 28 Oct 1872), m. cousin Pedro Malo
Valdivielso 29 Jun 1846

Dolores (1847–1911), m. Romualdo Zamora, duque de Heredia, 12 Nov
1870

María (1849–1918), m. Mariano Fortuño Pino 24 Apr 1867

Salvador (1851–1901), m. Ana Rivas Iñigo 31 Oct 1877, Rosa Zayas-
Bazán Hidalgo 26 Jan 1887

Pedro (1853–1878)

María de la Paz (1858–1909), m. José Luis Vidal Araoz 23 Jan 1882

María de la Concepión (b. 1868), m. Francisco Contró Amieva 3 Feb 1897

María del Carmen (b. 20 Nov 1832, d. 15 Mar 1838)

3. Gerónimo Mariano Villar Villamil Rodríguez (b. 9 Sep 1798, d. 1861), m.
María Guadalupe Díaz de Godoy Sandoval Gorráez 19 Mar 1826

Guadalupe (b. 1828, d. infancy)

Manuel Villar Villamil Díaz (1829–1905), m. Carmen Goríbar Ecay-
Múzquiz 15 Jun 1853

Ignacio (1856–1946), m. Isabel Guzmán Zayas 1894, Joaquina Ezpeleta
Alvarez de Toledo 1898

María de la Luz (1859–1945), m. Henri Grandin de Mansigny, conde de
Mansigny, 1882

María de la Paz (b. 1861), m. Jean Roslin, barón d'Ivry

Victoria (b. 1866)

4. Agustín Gerónimo Villar Villamil Rodríguez (b. 2 Mar 1800, d. November
1800)

5. María Guadalupe Villar Villamil Rodríguez (b. 28 May 1801, d. 24 Jul 1816)

6. María de la Paz Villar Villamil Rodríguez (b. 12 Jun 1805, d. 15 Sep 1828),
m. José María Rincón Gallardo, marqués de Guadalupe Gallardo II (b. 25
Jun 1793, d. Sep. 1877) 16 Sep 1820

Francisco Manuel (b. 1821, d. 7 Nov 1822)

María Guadalupe (b. 8 Jan 1823), m. José Tornel Diez de Bonilla

Carolina (1849–1913), m. Ignacio Barajas Parlajás 1880

Agustín, m. Josefina Gallardo 29 Nov 1873

Joaquín María (1824–1844)

Rosa Ramona (b. 31 Aug 1825), m. José Ignacio Palomo y Montúfar 1853

Angelina (1857–1884), m. Francisco Cayo Moncada
Joaquín (b. 1861)
José Ignacio (b. 1863)

SECOND HUSBAND (MARRIED 10 FEB 1807)

Juan Ignacio Briones Fernández de Ricaño Busto (b. 10 Apr 1753, d. 16 Aug
1807)
Siblings:
José Briones (d. 1828)
María Justina Manuela (b. 28 Sep 1760)
María Vicenta (b. 31 Oct 1761), m. Eligio Gil
   María Dolores Gil Briones (b. 26 Aug 1787), m. José María Gadea
Daughter of Briones and La Güera:
7. Victoria Briones Rodríguez (b. 22 Apr 1808, d. 1809)

THIRD HUSBAND (MARRIED 5 SEP 1825)

Juan Manuel de Elizalde y Martinicorena (b. 23 Dec 1791, d. 13 Dec 1870)

SOURCES

Most of these facts come from the Familias Novohispanas (FN) database, which
incorporates information from FamilySearch: FS, "México Bautismos, 1560–
1950," "México, Distrito Federal, registros parroquiales y diocesanos, 1714–1970,"
"Mexico, Distrito Federal, Catholic Church Records, 1514–1970," "Mexico, Veracruz, Catholic Church Records, 1590–1978," and "Chile, bautismos, 1585–1932."
The birth registers of La Güera's children Josefa, Antonia, Agustín, Paz, and
Victoria contain the images of the original records. Gerónimo's baptismal register is in AGN, Oficios Vendibles, contenedor 11, vol. 24, exp. 7 (1810–1817), f.
504. The register of La Güera's marriage to Villamil is in AP, Matrimonios Españoles, libro 35, no. 154, f. 176v; to Briones in AP, Matrimonios, libro 40, no. 34,
f. 10v. Her daughter Josefa's marriage register is in AP, Matrimonios, libro 42,
no. 10, f. 66v.
The death certificate for La Güera's father can be found in AGN, Oficios Vendibles, contenedor 11, vol. 24, exp. 7 (1810–1817), f. 503; the one for Juan Ignacio
Briones in AP, Entierros de Españoles, libro 36, f. 107v; and for María Ignacia
Rodríguez in AP, Entierros, libro 29, no. 2220, f. 30. The dates of La Güera's
father's birth, the death of her first husband, and the birth of her second husband
are in Muñoz Altea, "La Güera Rodríguez," 200, 204–205, 208.

Additional information comes from the wills of *Antonio Rodríguez de Velasco* (October 31, 1810), AHN, Francisco de la Torre #675, vol. 4557 (1803–1816), ff. 448v–450v; *José Miguel Rodríguez de Velasco* (December 24, 1822), AHN, Francisco de la Torre #675, vol. 4558 (1822), ff. 767–768v; *María Ignacia Rodríguez de Velasco* (April 1, 1819, and August 16, 1850), AHN, Francisco de Madariaga #426, vol. 2830, ff. 113–116v (1819) and vol. 2873, ff. 596v–601v (1850); *Pedro Romero de Terreros y Rodríguez de Pedroso* (March 25, 1826, and January 2, 1831), AHN, Manuel García Romero #286, vol. 1774, ff. 221v–222 (1826) and vol. 1775, ff. 13–26v (1831); *Gerónimo Villar Villamil* (May 17, 1838), AHN, Francisco de Madariaga #426, vol. 2854 (1838 tomo I), ff. 519v–524; *María Vicenta Rodríguez de Velasco* (August 28, 1838), AHN, Ignacio Peña #529, vol. 3535 (1838), ff. 160–162; (February 29, 1840), AHN, José López Guazo #361, vol. 2346 (1840), ff. 50–51v; (October 30, 1844), Ramón de la Cueva #169, vol. 1001, ff. 685–688; and *María Josefa Rodríguez de Velasco* (August 9, 1839), AHN, Francisco de Madariaga #426, vol. 2857 (1839 tomo II), ff. 678–680v.

Glossary

abogado   Lawyer

audiencia   Royal court; high court

ayuntamiento   City council; municipal government

bienes libres   Property outside of entail

caballero   Knight in a chivalric order

castizo   Person of mestizo and white parents, in theory of three-quarters European descent

colegio   School; also professional association

compadre   Godfather of a child, therefore spiritual kin of the family

corregidor   Chief magistrate or provincial governor

criollo   Creole; a Mexico-born person of Spanish ancestry

depósito   Safehouse where women were placed during court proceedings

doncella   Single maiden, virgin

esponsales   Promise to marry; betrothal

gananciales   Property and earnings accrued during marriage; community property

güera   Mexicanism for someone who is fair-skinned and European looking, sometimes blonde

hacendado   Owner of a hacienda or rural estate

legítima   Portion guaranteed to each child from a parent's estate

licenciado   Honorific for a university graduate

mayorazgo   Entail; also the person possessing an entail

oidor   A judge in the audiencia
patria   Homeland, both as nation and native city
peninsular   Refers to Spain or a person born in Spain
provisor vicario, also *provisor*   Ecclesiastical judge
rayas   Wages paid to laborers on haciendas
regidor   Councillor of the ayuntamiento; alderman, councilman
tertulia   Social gathering
tierra adentro   Area north of Mexico City, roughly "the outback"
zócalo   Main square of Mexico City, in the city center

Notes

INTRODUCTION

1. Calderón de la Barca, *Life in Mexico*, 141.

2. Quote from the prologue, "Isagoge," in Valle-Arizpe, *Güera Rodríguez*.

3. "Don José Villamil y Primo contra doña María Ignacia Rodríguez, 1802," in Arrom, *Mujer mexicana*, 63–107.

4. See, for example, the exhibit at the Galería de Historia, Museo del Caracol (part of the Museo Nacional de Historia in Mexico City), visited on February 25, 2018; and history textbooks online in Secretaría de Educación Pública, Catálogo digital de libros de texto gratuitos, ciclo escolar 2018–2019. https://libros .conaliteg.gob.mx/content/common/consulta-libros-gb/, accessed January 15, 2019.

5. Molly, "Alebrijes."

6. Museum exhibit visited by the author in March 2015. See Galeana, *Museo de la Mujer*, 65–75.

7. Garci, *Más pendejadas célebres*, 14–18; Rivera, "La Güera Rodríguez"; and Díaz, "La Güera Rodríguez."

8. Yorch, "La Güera Rodríguez"; Reznik, "¿Quien fue la Güera Rodríguez?"; and Dávila, "Conozca a las 10 prostitutas."

9. For an introduction to the English-language literature on Mexican women in the late colonial and early republican periods, see, for example, Arrom, *Women of Mexico City;* Francois, *Culture of Everyday Credit;* Lavrin, *Latin American*

Women; Stern, *Secret History;* Tuñón Pablos, *Women in Mexico;* and Twinam, *Public Lives, Private Secrets.*

10. Excellent examples of recent biographies of Mexican women include Bazant, *Laura Méndez de Cuenca;* Cano, *Se llamaba Elena Arizmendi;* Chassen-López, "Patron of Progress"; and Townsend, *Malintzin's Choices.* For discussions of the "new" biography, see the AHR Roundtable "Why Biography," *American Historical Review* 114: 3 (2009): 573–652; and the issue on biography in the Mexican journal *Secuencia* 100 (2018): 8–162.

11. On changing representations of historical figures, see esp. Brunk, *Posthumous Career of Emiliano Zapata;* Cypess, *Malinche in Mexican Literature;* Núñez Becerra, *La Malinche;* Velasco, *Lieutenant Nun;* and Weeks, *Juárez Myth.*

CHAPTER 1. LA GÜERA AS A YOUNG WOMAN, 1778–1808

1. See Bustamante's *Diario* entries of June 12, 1826; August 2, 1828; May 16, 1830; April 2, 1832; January 8, 1835; October 26, 1838; December 5, 1839; February 1, 1846; and September 4, 1846.

2. Calderón de la Barca, *Life in Mexico,* 142.

3. "Extracto de algunos pasages de la confesión de Ignacio José Allende, uno de los principales cabecillas de la insurrección," May 1811, AGI, Archivos Estatales, ES.41091.AGI/21/ESTADO.39.N.9, http://pares.mecd.gob.es.

4. See, for example, the July 1812 letter written by the Marquesa de Villahermosa to the ex-vicereine Inés de Jáuregui in Spain, in which she identifies her daughter-in-law Josefa Villamil as "hija de la Güera." Cited in Romero de Terreros, *Ex-antiquis,* 234.

5. For detailed information on both families, see Muñoz Altea, "La Güera Rodríguez," 200–201. María Ignacia Rodríguez's birth certificate is in FS, "México bautismos, 1560–1950," Ref. 2: CH01KG, FHL microfilm 35,190.

6. Although Ladd was describing the titled nobility, her comment applies just as well to the elite circles in which La Güera's family traveled; *Mexican Nobility,* 163.

7. The secondary sources provide contradictory information about her sisters' ages. I have followed the information in the FS and FN databases (see appendix B). One author also mentions a brother, José, who must have been among the "others that died" in infancy referred to by her father in his will, where he declares that he only has three daughters and identifies Vicenta's husband as José Marín, an *empleado de vista* of the Real Aduana de Guadalajara. Testament of Antonio Rodríguez de Velasco (October 31, 1810), AHN, Francisco de la Torre #675, vol. 4557, ff. 448v–450v. In 1833 Vicenta refers to her deceased husband as an

administrador cesante of the Aduana de Valladolid; AHN, Ignacio Peña #529, vol. 3530 (August 6, 1833), ff. 55–155v.

8. All citations from the divorce case are in the selection published in Arrom, *Mujer mexicana,* 63–107.

9. AGN, Inquisición, vol. 1468, exp. 26 (1800), ff. 297–298.

10. García, *Leona Vicario,* 35–44; Calderón de la Barca, *Life in Mexico,* 286–288.

11. The entail also included jewelry, the wheat- and flour-producing Hacienda del Molino Prieto, two cattle ranches (the Hacienda de la Soledad in the pueblo of Dolores and the *agostadero* of San Cristobal de Cabezones in Monterrey), the Rancho de Santiago in Tenosotlán, and the Hacienda de San Nicolás Zasni adjacent to Bojay. These properties were supposed to produce annual revenues of at least 9,025 pesos in 1794, although the elder Villamil claimed that their revenues were less because some of these were not under contract or were involved in lawsuits. (He was, in fact, involved in ten lawsuits, including one with the tenant of the Bojay hacienda, who charged that he had deceived her.) Villamil Senior also possessed *bienes libres* (property outside the *mayorazgo*) valued at 52,060 pesos. See "Autos sobre alimentos," esp. ff. 8–8v and 11–12v; AGN, Vínculos y Mayorazgos, vol. 214, exp. 7, and vol. 215, exp. 8, esp. ff. 8–8v and 11–12v; and Romero de Terreros, *Condes de Regla,* 86.

12. On the Villar Villamil family, see Muñoz Altea, "La Güera Rodríguez," 201–203.

13. "Autos que sigue Don José Gerónimo López de Peralta Villar y Villamil, apelando al matrimonio que pretende contraer su hijo" (July 1794), AGN, Matrimonios, caja 1185, exp. 1, esp. ff. 2v and 3v.

14. AP, Matrimonios Españoles, libro 35, no. 154, f. 176v. On Rivero, see Aguirre Salvador, *El mérito,* 431.

15. "Autos sobre alimentos" (1794–1798), AGN, Vínculos y Mayorazgos, vol. 215, exp. 8, f. 104v.

16. Villamil was appointed to the position of *subdelegado* in October 1796; AGN, Correspondencia de Virreyes, 1ª Serie, Marqués de Branciforte (1796), vol. 185, ff. 80–80v. According to Josefa's baptismal record, he was already a Maestrante de Ronda in July 1795 but still not a Caballero de Calatrava in March 1800 when Agustín was born. Villamil's military title is sometimes listed as Teniente de Granaderos y Ayudante del Regimento de Infantería de Milicias Provinciales.

17. In 1794 the properties of the *mayorazgo* were mortgaged for at least 46,251 pesos (Ladd, *Mexican Nobility,* 85). The lawsuit against the villagers from Cerro, Denqui, and Múñi over the boundaries of Bojay had already begun by the end of 1800 and continued through at least January 1803. AGN, Tierras, vol. 2583, exp. 2 and vol. 3584, exp. 2 (1800–1803).

18. Testament of María Ignacia Rodríguez (August 16, 1850), AHN, Francisco de Madariaga #426, vol. 2873, art. 6.

19. See AGN, Bienes Nacionales, leg. 1644, exp. 2 (1808), ff. 2-2v.

20. A copy of the criminal case appears in the files of the divorce case: "Cuaderno reservado contra D. Josef Villamil y Primo, 1801," inserted in "Causa de divorcio del Capitán don José Villamil y su muger da. María Ignacia Rodríguez," AGN, Criminal, vol. 582, exp. 1 (1802). For a selection of these documents, see Arrom, *Mujer mexicana*, 63-107. For my analysis of ecclesiastical divorce, see Arrom, *Women of Mexico City*, chap. 5.

21. "Súplica del Conde de Regla," AGN, Matrimonios, caja 159, exp. 47 (1811-1812), f. 6v.

22. The king's ruling dated May 2, 1803, took several months to arrive in Mexico. AGN, Reales Cédulas Originales y Duplicadas, vol. 188, exp. 94, ff. 101-101v.

23. The witnesses were chosen by the *audiencia*'s *alcalde del crimen*, José Arias Villafañe, "who knows the couple intimately." The Conde de Contramina also testified, but his declaration is not included in the file because it was oral rather than written. For a complete list of the witnesses, see Arrom, *Mujer mexicana*, 92-93.

24. There may have been later filings in the divorce case that are not included in the documents I located, which were the *audiencia*'s copy. The ecclesiastical court's copy appears to have been lost. Some related records in the military court appear in "Causa formada al Capitán Don José Villamil a pedimento de su mujer Da. María Ignacia Rodríguez de Velasco, por haberla tirado un pistoletazo" (1802-1804), AGN, Criminal, contenedor 214, vol. 454, exp. 6, ff. 201-232.

25. "Cuaderno reservado contra D. Josef Villamil y Primo."

26. On Villamil's death and will, see Muñoz Altea, "La Güera Rodríguez," 204-205.

27. AGN, Vínculos y Mayorazgos, vol. 225, exp. 1 (1816), ff. 17-17v.

28. The 2,000-peso loan dated from 1796. AGN, Bienes Nacionales, leg. 1644, exp. 2 (1808), ff. 4-4v. See also La Güera's wills of 1819 (arts. 4 and 6) and 1850 (art. 6). The 1819 will is in AHN, Francisco de Madariaga #426, vol. 2830, ff. 113-116v.

29. Testament of María Ignacia Rodríguez (1819), art. 10.

30. AGN, Vínculos y Mayorazgos, vol. 215, exp. 10 (1818), f. 5v.

31. According to her 1819 will, La Güera only received this pension during the two years that she was a widow (art. 10). The annual income from the *mayorazgo* is from 1794; "Autos sobre alimentos," f. 11.

32. See Arnold, *Bureaucracy*, 131-137.

33. See Testament of María Ignacia Rodríguez (1850), arts. 12 and 16; and AHN, Francisco de Madariaga #426, vol. 2855 (November 2, 1838), ff. 1205-1208v.

34. On Briones's career, see the certificates of marriage, baptism, and death in the following notes, and AGN, Colegios, caja 5078, exp. 5 (1779) and caja 141,

exp.18 (1781); AGN, Real Audiencia, caja 5436, exp. 22 (1790), f. 4 and caja 2485, exp. 33, ff. 1–5v; Jiménez Gómez, "Creencias y prácticas," 136; and Múñoz Altea, "La Güera Rodríguez," 205–206. He was named *censor regi* in 1802; AGN, Real Audiencia, caja 2485, exp. 33, ff. 1–5v.

35. AP, Matrimonios, vol. 40, no. 34, f. 10v (February 10, 1807).

36. Briones's death certificate in AP, Entierros de Españoles, libro 36, f. 107v (August 16, 1807); and Victoria's baptism record in FS, "México, D.F., registros parroquiales y diocesanos, 1514–1970," 61903/:1:QJ8Y-TJGN.

37. Muñoz Altea writes that Briones dictated his will in Querétaro on July 11, 1811, to notary José Domingo Vallejo ("La Güera Rodríguez," 205–206), but this date must be a typographical error, since Briones died in 1807. Perhaps the will dates from 1801.

38. I have not been able to locate Briones's will or the records of the lawsuit. Details emerge in AHN, José Ignacio Moctezuma #158, vol. 959 (August 29, 1807), ff. 130–131; and AGN, Criminal, caja 5122, exp. 018 (May 31, 1808), ff. 1–2v.

39. When they settled the case on October 4, 1811, a fifth of the estate was valued at 64,000 pesos and La Güera agreed to pay interest on this sum from April 8, 1808, which was probably the date when she started to manage the legacy. See summaries of the case in her 1819 will, arts. 5 and 12; and AHN, Francisco de Madariaga #426, vol. 2838 (January 12, 1827), ff. 26–31, and vol. 2860 (January 11, 1841), ff. 587–592v.

40. Bustamante, *Suplemento*, vol. 3, 268–269.

CHAPTER 2. LA GÜERA ON HER OWN, 1808–1820

1. Mortgages normally charged 5 percent interest. See testaments of María Ignacia Rodríguez, (1819) AHN, Francisco de Madariaga #426, vol. 2830, art. 7 and (1850) AHN, Francisco de Madariaga #426, vol. 2873, art. 14; see also AHN, Francisco de Madariaga #426, vol. 2838 (January 12, 1827), f. 27, vol. 2848 (June 12, 1835), ff. 481–481v, and vol. 2860 (June 11, 1841), ff. 587–587v.

2. AGN, Inquisición, vol. 1446, exp. 4, ff. 32–35; and Carbajal López, "Tras los pasos."

3. See La Güera's petition to the viceroy on April 14, 1810, in "Averiguación que hace Bernardo de Prado, Inquisidor decano, contra María Ignacia Rodríguez de Velasco, sobre un atentado al virrey de la Nueva España" (1809–1810), AGN, Indiferente Virreinal, caja 4452, exp. 1, f. 108v.

4. I thank Rodrigo Amerlinck for sharing Iturbide's letters from his private collection.

5. Ladd, *Mexican Nobility*, 264, note 119.

6. AHN, Francisco de Madariaga #426, vol. 2834 (1823), ff. 208v–213.

7. Testament of Pablo Cortés, AHN, José Ignacio Montes de Oca #417, vol. 2780 (1930), art. 8, f. 29. Both Cortés and Malo signed a contract to buy the neighboring Hacienda del Santo Cristo on December 17, 1818; AGN, Vínculos y Mayorazgos, vol. 215, exp. 10, f. 18v.

8. Testament of María Ignacia Rodríguez (1819), arts. 7, 12, and 15.

9. "Extracto de algunos pasages de la confesión de Ignacio José Allende, uno de los principales cabecillas de la insurrección," May 1811, AGI, Archivos Estatales, ES.41091.AGI/21/ESTADO.39.N.9, http://pares.mecd.gob.es.

10. Alamán, *Historia*, vol. 1, 283; Bustamante, *Suplemento*, vol. 3, 268–269.

11. "Averiguación," exp. 1 and exp. 7. La Güera's testimony appears in exp. 1, ff. 117–119.

12. Declaration by Lic. José María Espinosa (October 31, 1809), in "Averiguación," exp. 1, f. 46v.

13. Reports of January 18 and February 6, 1810, in "Averiguación," exp. 1, ff. 23–24v and exp. 7, ff. 160–64.

14. "Averiguación," exp. 1, ff. 97–99.

15. Carlos Mejía Chávez speculates that La Güera was collaborating with the conspirators of Valladolid, but I have not found any evidence for this theory. ("'¡Qué le quieren dar veneno al señor Arzobispo-Virrey!'" 100–101.) His only proof is Ignacio Allende's 1811 declaration that he had heard that she gave the viceroy bad advice.

16. Letter from María Ignacia Rodríguez to Viceroy Lizana (March 17, 1810), in "Averiguación," exp. 1, ff. 100–100v.

17. Letters from Maria Ignacia Rodríguez to Viceroy Lizana (March 17 and April 28, 1810), in "Averiguación," exp. 1, ff. 101 and 106v. On her ties to Villamil's relatives in Querétaro, see AHN, Francisco de Madariaga #426, vol. 2829 (July 7, 1818), ff. 231–32, and vol. 2862 (April 5, 1842), ff. 263–65; and Testament of Gerónimo Villamil (May 17, 1838), AHN, Francisco de Madariaga #426, vol. 2854 (1838 vol. I), ff. 519v–524.

18. "Averiguación," esp. exp. 1, ff. 95, 100–109v.

19. I am grateful to Dr. Ann Carmichael, a historian of medicine, for helping me understand the medical certificate.

20. The description of her father comes from her petition of April 14, 1810, in "Averiguación," exp. 1, f. 109v; his death certificate is inserted in AGN, Oficios Vendibles, contenedor 11, vol. 24, exp. 7, f. 503. On the death of her brother-in-law, see Zárate Toscano, *Los nobles*, 463.

21. AGN, Civil Legajos, vol. 208, exp. 4 (1826), ff. 1–11v.

22. "La Marquesa viuda de Uluapa contra doña María Ignacia Rodríguez su hermana sobre que haga la obra y le satisfaga la renta de la casa" (1816–1818), AGN, Vínculos y Mayorazgos, vol. 225, exp. 1, n.p. The summary of the case appears following f. 52.

23. AGN, Oficios Vendibles, contenedor 11, vol. 24, exp. 7, esp. ff. 502v, 509.

24. It was casa no. 1 of the 2nd Calle de las Damas, on the corner with Ortega. Aguirre had rented it since at least 1800 and the interim director of the Ramo de Tabaco, don Francisco de Paula Bernal, had also lived there "in the company of the Sr. Regente" since 1803; he left it on the last day of February 1811 so that La Güera could move in. AGN, Vínculos y Mayorazgos, vol. 225, exp. 1, and vol. 223, exp. 6, esp. ff. 34, 40v, 45.

25. Until she married Elizalde, La Güera rented a house on the 1st Calle de San Francisco from the Padres Carmelitas del Desierto. Testament of María Ignacia Rodríguez (1850), art. 12.

26. The three siblings were still alive in 1819. By 1827 only two heirs remained: don José Briones and Vicenta's daughter, doña Dolores Gil Briones viuda de Gadea. After José died in 1828, the sole heir was Dolores. Testament of María Ignacia Rodríguez (1819), art. 12; AHN, Francisco de Madariaga #426, vol. 2838 (January 12, 1827), ff. 27–28 and vol. 2852 (February 21, 1837), ff. 191–193.

27. AGN, Ramo Inquisición, vol. 1453, ff. 197–98v.

28. Lizana y Beaumont, *Instrucción pastoral*.

29. Guedea, *Prontuario*, 364.

30. "La Marquesa viuda . . . contra . . . su hermana," esp. entries of July 12, 1816 (f. 15) and the case summary of September 26, 1817 (n.p.).

31. For example, Joel Poinsett, who met Josefa in 1822 (*Notes on Mexico*, 56–57); and H. G. Ward, who met Paz between 1825 and 1827 (*Mexico in 1827*, vol. 2, 313, 400).

32. "Súplica del Conde de Regla," AGN, Matrimonios, caja 159, exp. 47 (1811–1812), f. 6v.

33. La Güera gave her fifteen-year-old daughter permission to marry on August 25, 1820. AHN, Francisco de Madariaga #426, vol. 2831, ff. 304v–305.

34. There were at least eighteen millionaires in New Spain at the time; Ladd, *Mexican Nobility*, 25, 122, 184–185.

35. Letter from Fanny Calderón de la Barca to William H. Prescott, June 5, 1840, in Wolcott, *Correspondence*, 128.

36. Testament of María Ignacia Rodríguez (1850), arts. 19 and 20; "Autos sobre alimentos" (1794–1798), AGN, Vínculos y Mayorazgos, vol. 215, exp. 8, f. 12; and "Súplica," f. 23v.

37. Zárate Toscano, "Los privilegios del nombre," 349–350.

38. See "Súplica," esp. ff. 6v–7, 11.

39. The wedding took place in the Uluapa house that La Güera was renting at the time. "Partida de Matrimonio," AP, libro 42 (1812), no. 10, f. 66v.

40. He also explained that he had not been able to give his wife *arras* because he had not yet inherited his *mayorazgo* and his father's *bienes libres* "were diminished by the independence war." Testaments of Conde de Regla (March 25, 1826), AHN, Manuel García Romero #286, vol. 1774, arts. 4 and 5, f. 222, and

(February 1, 1831), vol. 1775, arts. 4 and 5. Josefa later inherited a *mayorazgo* from a line of the Villamil family that died out without succession; Fernández de Recas, *Mayorazgos,* 80.

41. "Súplica," ff. 10v–11.

42. Letter from María Ignacia Rodríguez to don Pedro Gutiérrez de Salcedo, February 10, 1812, in "Tente don Juan Manuel Lama con Maria Ignacia Rodriguez sobre pesos," AGN, Civil, exp. 2 (1816), f. 92v; and "Quien Llama al Toro, Sufre la Cornada" (Mexico City: Oficina de la Testamentaria de Ontiveros, 1826), inserted in Bustamante, *Diario,* following the entry of June 12, 1826.

43. Cited in Romero de Terreros, *Ex-antiquis,* 232–234.

44. Testament of María Ignacia Rodríguez (1819), art. 11.

45. The payment was due on January 11, 1817. AGN, Oficios Vendibles, contenedor 11, vol. 24, exp. 6, ff. 511–511v.

46. See AHCM, Ayuntamiento: Comisiones, 1728–1856, vol. 406, exp. 11 (1818), ff. 28 and 4; AHCM, Ayuntamiento: Regidores Honorarios, vol. 1, exp. 38; and AGN, Vínculos y Mayorazgos, vol. 215, exp. 10 (November 1818), f. 3.

47. See AHN, Francisco de Madariaga # 426, vol. 2834 (1823), f. 210; and Ladd, *Mexican Nobility,* 155–157, 167–168.

48. FS, "México Matrimonios, 1570–1950," FHL #657, 686.

49. Although Gerónimo received a legal notification in "the pueblo of Atitalaquia" on June 12, 1823, he identified himself as a *vecino* of the capital in several documents. The census of 1842 listed his residence as no. 23, 2nd Calle de Mesones Norte, and identified him as a *labrador,* a synonym of *hacendado* at that time. See Padrón Municipal de 1842, banco de datos digital, courtesy of Linda Arnold. See also Bustamante, *Diario,* June 12, 1832, and January 8, 1835; AHN, Francisco de Madariaga #426, vol. 2854 (1838, tomo I), f. 630; and AHN, José López Guazo #361 (1835), vol. 2344, f. 191.

50. See, for example, the baptismal certificates of two of Paz's children from January 8, 1823, and August 31, 1825 (FS, "México, Distrito Federal, registros parroquiales y diocesanos, 1514–1970," database with images, #35199 and #35826); and Romero de Terreros, *Condes de Regla,* who identifies La Güera as Manuel's godmother in 1816 (99).

51. Romero de Terreros cites a letter of August 1, 1815, in which Fagoaga sent the news. *Condes de Regla,* 80.

52. José had pawned jewels and silver worth over 13,000 pesos, among them some belonging to his sister Bárbara, without her permission. Testament of José Miguel Rodríguez de Velasco (December 24, 1822), AHN, Francisco de la Torre #675, vol. 4558, art. 4.

53. "Convenio" (January 16, 1818), AHN, Francisco de Madariaga #426, vol. 2829, ff. 33v–35v. See also the wills of Antonio Rodríguez de Velasco (October 31, 1810) and of José Miguel Rodríguez de Velasco (October 30, 1810), in AHN, Francisco de la Torre #675, vol. 4557 (1803–1816), ff. 448v–450, 447–448v.

54. Testament of María Ignacia Rodríguez (1819), art. 8; and Carbajal López, "Tras los pasos."

55. Letters of María Ignacia Rodríguez to don Pedro Gutiérrez de Salcedo, December 8, 1811, February 10, 1812, and March 1812, in "Lama con Rodríguez sobre pesos" (1816–1818), AGN, Civil, vol. 473, exp. 2, ff. 91–92, 108–109.

56. In 1827 Elizalde noted that the insurgents had occupied the properties from 1810 to 1820; another document suggests that the rebels Liceaga and Verduzco took them in 1813. It is possible that other rebels held them before that date. See AHN, Francisco de Madariaga #426, vol. 2838 (January 12, 1827), f. 27v; and Guedea, *Prontuario,* 364.

57. AGN, Vínculos y Mayorazgos, vol. 215, exp. 10 (November 5, 1818), esp. f. 5.

58. AHN, Francisco de Madariaga #426, vol. 2848 (June 12, 1835), f. 481v.

59. AGN, Operaciones de Guerra, vol. 367, exp. 18 (1818), ff. 234v–235v. It is unclear whether she obtained the exemption, but at least she did not have to pay until 1819 at the earliest, while her petition was being considered (exp. 19).

60. Testament of María Ignacia Rodríguez (1819), art. 12.

61. In 1827 she still owed 42,000 pesos on the principal plus 13,000 in accumulated interest. AHN, Ignacio de la Barrera #90, vol. 582 (December 29, 1819), ff. 71–73; Francisco de Madariaga #426, vol. 2831 (March 3, 1820), ff. 108v–110, vol. 2838 (January 12, 1827), ff. 27v–28; and Testament of María Ignacia Rodríguez (1850), arts. 5, 7, and 8.

62. AHN, Francisco de Madariaga #426 (January 10, 1818), vol. 2829, ff. 9v–11v.

63. "Lama con Rodríguez sobre pesos," AGN, Civil, vol. 473, exps. 2–4 (1816–1818). The quotes are from exp. 2, f. 133v.

64. "La Marquesa . . . contra . . . su hermana," vol. 225, exp. 1; and "Da. María Ygnacia Rodríguez sobre la entrega de una casa que tuvo arrendada" (1817–1818), AGN, Vínculos y Mayorazgos, vol. 223, exp. 6.

65. See esp. the summary of the case on September 26, 1817, "La Marquesa . . . contra . . . su hermana," n.p. and ff. 15–15v, 17, 30–31, 117; and Josefa's petition of April 8, 1818, "Da. María Ygnacia Rodríguez sobre la entrega de una casa," ff. 55v–57v.

66. She was referring to the purchase of the Rancho del Cristo adjacent to the Molino Prieto, part of the Villamil mayorazgo. "La Marquesa . . . contra . . . su hermana," esp. ff. 15v, 41; and "Da. María Ygnacia Rodríguez sobre la entrega de una casa," esp. ff. 54–55, 66v–67.

67. See esp. "Da. María Ygnacia Rodríguez sobre la entrega de una casa," ff. 21, 79–80v.

68. See the case summary of January 23, 1818, in "La Marquesa . . . contra . . . su hermana," n.p.

69. Josefa's accusations are in the filing of April 8, 1818 ("Da. María Ygnacia Rodríguez sobre la entrega de una casa," f. 56v). Her version of how La Güera

bought La Patera is contradicted by later documents, for example, AHN, Francisco de Madariaga #426, vol. 2848 (June 12, 1835), f. 481; and Testament of María Ignacia Rodríguez (1819), arts. 6 and 7.

70. On April 9, 1818, her mother had received permission to install an *oratorio* with a portable altar in her residence because she was too sick to leave the house to attend mass and "wanted to enjoy this spiritual benefit." AGN, Bienes Nacionales, vol. 1070, exp. 20 (1818), f. 3.

71. Testament of María Ignacia Rodríguez (1819), art. 7.

72. Testament of María Ignacia Rodríguez (1850), arts. 19 and 20.

73. Testament of María Josefa Rodríguez y Osorio (August 9, 1839), AHN, Francisco de Madariaga #426, vol. 2857 (1839, tomo II), art. 6.

74. AHN, Francisco de Madariaga #426, vol. 2840 (April 28, 1829), f. 482v.

75. She still owed 8,000 pesos to the Archicofradía del Rosario in 1836, when she transfered that obligation to the Hacienda de San Isidro, by then belonging to Dolores Gil, who promised to pay the debt. AHN, Luis Calderón #160, vol. 164 bis (February 11, 1820), ff. 7v–11v; Francisco Calapiz #170, vol. 1051 (November 15, 1833), ff. 11v–14; and Francisco de Madariaga #426, vol. 2852 (February 23, 1837, tomo I), f. 193v.

76. Martínez Núñez speculated that the mystery person might have been Villamil's illegitimate daughter ("Biografía crítica," 50, 53), but I have not been able to corroborate this theory. He based it on the fact that a Guadalupe Villamil who married in 1797 listed her father as José Gerónimo Villamil. This was actually his sister Guadalupe. The confusion arises because both father and son often used the same name in legal documents.

CHAPTER 3. INDEPENDENCE HEROINE?

1. Calderón de la Barca, *Life in Mexico*, 329.

2. "Compendio de la denuncia del tambor mayor" (September 13, 1810), cited in Castillo Ledón, *Hidalgo*, vol. 1, 176.

3. Rodríguez, "Royal Subject," 30.

4. In 1794 don Bernardo Abasolo leased the Hacienda de la Soledad from the Villamil *mayorazgo* for 1,100 pesos a year. "Autos seguidos por Don José Villar Villamil con Don José Villamil y Primo sobre alimentos," AGN, Vínculos y Mayorazgos, vol. 215, exp. 8 (1794–1798), f. 11.

5. Letter to Pedro Gutiérrez de Salcedo, the merchant Lama's agent, on December 8, 1811, in "Lama con Rodríguez, sobre pesos," AGN, Civil, vol. 473, exp. 2, ff. 91–91v.

6. The testimony is missing from the file; only the descriptive cover sheet has been preserved. AGN, Operaciones de Guerra, vol. 944, exp. 12 (June 22, 1814), ff. 30–30v.

7. Reproduced in García, *Documentos históricos,* vol. 5, 461–462.

8. Guedea, *Prontuario,* 361–365. On the history of the text, see "Introducción," xiii–xxiv.

9. Torre Villar did identify seven women among its members; *Los 'Guadalupes,'* lxxv–lxxix. The quote about Betancourt is in Guedea, *Prontuario,* 362.

10. "Denuncia del alcaide," 334.

11. On Antonia's wedding, see Romero de Terreros, *Ex-antiquis,* 236; on Josefa's, see AP, Matrimonios, libro 42, no. 10, f. 66v (January 15, 1812).

12. Romero de Terreros, *Condes de Regla,* 84–88.

13. Ladd, *Mexican Nobility,* 197; "Orden de Isabel la Católica," Wikipedia en español, https://es.wikipedia.org/wiki/Orden_de_Isabel_la_Cat%C3%B3lica, accessed August 8, 2018.

14. Ladd, *Mexican Nobility,* 264 note 119; Martínez Núñez, "Biografía crítica," 128, 140.

15. Alamán, *Historia,* vol. 5, 154; Robertson, *Iturbide,* 125–126.

16. Capitán Joaquín Sánchez Badajoz's testimony of March 21, 1821, reproduced in Valle, "Redescubriendo a Iturbide," 7.

17. José Manuel Velázquez de la Cadena y Villar Villamil received the title of Marqués de la Cadena in February 1822. As the son of her first husband's sister Guadalupe, he was La Güera's *sobrino político.* Ladd, *Mexican Nobility,* 122–123, 192–193, 268 note 163. On her children's persistent ties with their cousins, see, for example, AHN, Francisco de Madariaga #426, vol. 2854 (1838, tomo I), ff. 520–520v.

18. Romero de Terreros, *Corte de Agustín,* 20–21; Zárate Toscano, *Los nobles,* 385–386, 401; Ladd, *Mexican Nobility,* 122–124, 192.

19. Bustamante, *Cuadro histórico,* vol. 5, 323.

20. Guedea, "Rodríguez de Velasco," in *Encyclopedia of Mexico.*

21. Torre accompanied Capitán General O'Donojú on his trip to New Spain in 1820. His unpublished diary was brought to light in 1960, when Carlos Olmedilla cited parts of it in "México, 1808–1821," 599–600.

22. "Dudas, para el que quisiere responderlas, que le han ocurrido á un triste Evangelista" (Mexico City: Imprenta Imperial [contra el despotismo] de D.N.F., 1822). I have been unable to locate the original, and it is possible that the document is fraudulent because this publishing house never published anything else—although there was an Imprenta (contraria al despotismo) de D. J. M. Benavente. A handwritten copy is included in the Juan E. Hernández y Dávalos Collection, UT, HD 15–1.1697. It must have been copied before 1943, when the University of Texas acquired the collection, and probably dates to at least 1893, when Hernández y Dávalos died. Valle-Arizpe reproduces it with another signature (D.B.T.) and says he saw it among General Almazán's papers; *Güera Rodríguez* (1960), 205–207.

23. Rocafuerte, *Bosquejo ligerísimo,* 21, 41–42, 81.

24. Torrente, *Historia de la Revolución*, vol. 3, 135–136.

25. Beruete, *Elevación y caída*, 51, 70.

26. Bustamante, *Suplemento*, vol. 4, 207–208, and *Diario*, October 26, 1838.

27. Pi y Margall and Pi y Arsuaga, *Historia de España*, 646.

28. Alamán, *Historia*, vol. 5, 53 note 51.

29. Prologue by the publisher in Torrente, *Historia de la Independencia*.

30. Bustamante, *Suplemento*, vol. 3, vi.

31. Beruete's diary was discovered in 1932 and Torre's is still unpublished. Bustamante's complete diary was only published in 2001. On the history of these texts, see the prologues to the published editions and Olmedilla, "México 1808–1821," 595–600.

32. Fossey, *Le Mexique*, 282.

33. In her 1850 will La Güera declared that she only put down 10,000 pesos to buy the hacienda, valued at 147,000, and mortgaged the rest at 5 percent interest; AHN, Francisco de Madariaga #426, vol. 2873, arts. 9 and 11, f. 598. Her uncle was still alive when he sold her the hacienda, since he made a will on December 24, 1822; AHN, Francisco de la Torre #675, vol. 4558 (1817–1824), ff. 767–768v. On Elizalde's contribution, see AHN, Francisco de Madariaga #426, vol. 2846 (1834, tomo I), ff. 229–232.

34. Poinsett, *Notes on Mexico*, 56–57.

35. Bustamante, *Diario*, July 27, 1826.

36. Romero de Terreros, *Condes de Regla*, 105–108.

37. Bustamante, *Diario*, September 16, 1825.

38. See Couturier, who references a memo from Joel Poinsett in the U.S. National Archives, "Women in a Noble Family," 143–144; and Bustamante, *Diario*, August 16, 1824.

39. Rippy, *Joel R. Poinsett*, 110.

40. See Testament of Gerónimo Villamil (May 17, 1838), AHN, Francisco de Madariaga #426, vol. 2854 (1838, tomo I), ff. 519–524v; Bustamante, *Diario*, January 8, 1835, and annex of July 12, 1836.

41. Testament of Pedro Romero de Terreros (February 1, 1831), AHN, Manuel García Romero #286, vol. 1775 (1831), f. 13; Romero de Terreros, *Condes de Regla*, 90, 96–97.

42. Manuel Romero de Terreros was governor of the Federal District in 1862 and served in congress several times. See Ladd, *Mexican Nobility*, 209; Zárate Toscano, *Los nobles*, 426; Romero de Terreros, *Condes de Regla*, 100–103; and Pani, "El proyecto de estado," 450.

43. Ortega y Pérez Gallardo, *Historia genealógica*, vol. 2, 41. It is possible that Ortega confused the father and son in listing Manuel's positions.

44. In 1822 congress authorized Gerónimo to manage his *mayorazgo*. AHN, Francisco de Madariaga #426, vol. 2834 (June 12, 1823), ff. 208v–213, and vol. 2855 (November 2, 1838), ff. 1205–1208v.

45. Guridi y Alcocer represented her until 1826, when she revoked his power of attorney to give it to her husband. AHN, Francisco de Madariaga #426, vol. 2833 (April 29, 1822), ff. 298–300v and vol. 2837 (July 13, 1826), ff. 336v–338.

46. Letter from Fray Francisco Calzada (December 20, 1822) reproduced in Valle, "Redescubriendo a Iturbide," section entitled "Deudas de la Güera Rodríguez."

47. See Kentner, "Role of Women," and Senado de la República, *Mujeres insurgentes.*

48. Bustamante, *Cuadro histórico,* vol. 1, 16 and vol. 2, 200.

49. Yorch, "La Güera Rodríguez."

CHAPTER 4. AN ARISTOCRATIC LADY, 1825–1850

1. Calderón de la Barca, *Life in Mexico,* 776, note 17.

2. Box no. 18 in the first row of the Coliseo had been in her family's possession since 1800; the monthly rent in 1825 was 34 pesos. AGN, Civil Legajos, vol. 208, exp. 4 (April 1826), ff. 1–11v.

3. Padrón municipal in AHCM, Fondo Ayuntamiento y Gobierno del Distrito Federal, Padrones (1842), vol. 3407, exp. 1, f. 862; and (1848), vol. 3408, tomo II, exp. 1, f. 1v of the manzana no. 47, cuartel mayor 2, menor 5.

4. Burkholder and Chandler, *Biographical Dictionary,* 108; Muñoz Altea, "La Güera Rodríguez," 206–207.

5. Arnold, *Bureaucracy,* 68, 125, 165.

6. Bustamante noted that in 1830 some deputies wanted to disqualify Elizalde because he did not fulfill the property-owning requirement, since the estates he managed were his wife's. Congress decided in his favor. *Diario,* December 20, 1830.

7. See Mateos, *Historia parlamentaria,* vol. 1, 103, 179; *Diccionario Porrúa* (1995), 1175–1176; AHN, Francisco de Madariaga #426, vol. 2837 (1826), f. 336v; vol. 2838 (1827), f. 26v; vol. 2852 (1837), f. 177v; vol. 2846 (1834), ff. 229–232; AHCM, Ayuntamiento: Comisiones, 1728–1856, vol. 406, exp. 13 (1826) and AHCM, Municipalidades, Sección San Ángel, Serie Comunicados, Bandos (1830), caja 25, exp. 780, f. 1; BNM, Colección Lafragua #2850 (1832), #3296 (1835), #3469 (1836), #3570 (1836) and #3573 (1837); and Malo, *Diario,* vol. 1, 128, 134.

8. Arrom, *Containing the Poor,* 296.

9. AHN, Francisco Miguel Calapiz #170, vol. 1050 (1836), ff. 244–246v (August 23, 1836), ff. 333v–335v and (October 6, 1836), ff. 432–437; and Manuel García Romero #286, vol. 1779 (December 13, 1839), ff. 474v–478.

10. Testament of María Ignacia Rodríguez (1850), AHN, Francisco de Madariaga #426, vol. 2873, art. 12; and Padrón municipal (1848).

11. Testament of María Ignacia Rodríguez (1850), art. 23.

12. Septién (a relative of Villamil's mother) also owed her several years' worth of interest. Testament of María Ignacia Rodríguez (1850), art. 10.

13. See esp. Testament of María Ignacia Rodríguez (1850), arts. 9–12 and 19–20.

14. San Isidro's value is approximate because we only know that the two haciendas in Guanajuato together were worth 280,000 pesos in 1811. Santa María apparently sold for 36,201 pesos around 1820. AHN, Francisco de Madariaga #426, vol. 2838 (1827), f. 27v.

15. Bustamante, *Diario*, February 1, 1846.

16. AHN, José Ignacio Montes de Oca #417, vol. 2782 (July 5,1832), f. 226.

17. Testament of María Ignacia Rodríguez (1850), art. 19.

18. They reached a new agreement on September 21, 1826, which included not only the hacienda but its *casa anexa*. The transfer of property was completed in 1828. See AHN, Francisco de Madariaga #426, vol. 2838 (January 12, 1827), ff. 26v–31; vol. 2840 (October 16, 1829), ff. 482–486v; vol. 2852 (December 1, 1837), ff. 191–198v; and vol. 2860 (June 11, 1841), ff. 287–292v.

19. AHN, Francisco Miguel Calapiz #170, vol. 1051 (1837), f. 11v.

20. She apparently stopped paying the mortgages on La Patera (due to the Colegio de San Gregorio and the Religiosas de Santa Clara) in 1824. She obtained extensions in 1835 and 1840, with permission from the Fondo de Capellanías y Obras Pías. AHN, Francisco de Madariaga #426, vol. 2846 (February 19, 1834), f. 229v and vol. 2848 (June 12, 1835), ff. 479–484v; AGN, Capellanías, vol. 109, exp. 1508 (1775–1840), ff. 1–14v, and vol. 1834, exp. 5 (1839), ff. 1–8v; and AGN, Bienes Nacionales, leg. 1834, exp. 6 (1848), f. 3.

21. AHN, Francisco de Madariaga #426, vol. 2838 (1827), ff. 26v–31; vol. 2852 (1837), ff. 177v–179v and 191–198v; vol. 2862 (April 5, 1842), ff. 263–265; and AHN, José López Guazo #361, vol. 2347 (1842–43), ff. 56–69v, 125–126v, 236–249, 263–265.

22. AGN, Bienes Nacionales, leg. 1834, exp. 6 (June 17, 1848), f. 2.

23. AHN, José María Ramírez #612, vol. 4129 (1842), ff. 74–76 and ff. 78v–80.

24. A brief statement in La Güera's 1850 will suggests that her sisters may have taken her to court. AHN, Francisco de Madariaga #426, vol. 2859 (October 14, 1840), ff. 894–898, and vol. 2851 (November 25, 1836), ff. 1193–1205; and Testament of María Ignacia Rodríguez (1850), arts. 19, 20.

25. AHN, Francisco de Madariaga #426, vol. 2855 (November 2, 1838), ff. 1205–1208v; and Testament of María Ignacia Rodríguez (1850), arts. 12 and 16.

26. The language sometimes varied. This example is from AHN, Francisco de Madariaga #426, vol. 2846 (February 19, 1834), ff. 229 and 231v. It cited the Fuero Real and Leyes del Toro.

27. AHN, Francisco de Madariaga #426, vol. 2852 (February 23, 1837, tomo I), esp. f. 193, and vol. 2840 (October 16, 1829), ff. 483–483v.

28. AHN, Francisco de Madariaga #426, vol. 2852 (February 23, 1837, tomo I), f. 192v.

29. Gerónimo as explaining why there had been no *gananciales* in his marriage. Testament of Gerónimo Villar Villamil, AHN, Francisco de Madariaga #426, vol. 2854 (May 17, 1838), art. 3.

30. AGN, Bienes Nacionales, leg. 1834, exp. 6 (1848), f. 1v.

31. Padrón municipal (1842). Another *entresuelo* and *accesoria* were occupied by doña Secundina Villarria, a single woman of thirty-two years of age who did not list an occupation.

32. Testament of Pablo Cortés (January 27, 1830), AHN, José Ignacio Montes de Oca #417, vol. 2780, ff. 27v–30; and a later will that lists the products of the haciendas, vol. 2782 (July 5, 1832), ff. 225–228.

33. *Padrón general ... 1813*, 37. The 1848 municipal census notes that Elizalde's rent had risen to 528 pesos in 1841, so the decline after 1813 must have been even steeper.

34. The 1848 census shows that the three servants were all different from those registered in 1842. Unlike the 1842 census, it does not specify their duties. Padrón municipal (1842) and (1848).

35. Ward, *Mexico in 1827*, vol. 2, 593. Waddy Thompson, plenipotenciary minister of the U.S. to Mexico in 1842–1844, also mentions her ("I am disposed to think that La Guera Rodriguez, the beautiful lady who enchanted him [Humboldt] so much, was not the only thing in Mexico which he saw couleur du rose") but apparently never met her and only based his statement on what he read in *Life in Mexico*. Thompson, *Recollections of Mexico*, 147.

36. The Calderón de la Barcas arrived in Mexico on Christmas Day 1839 and left shortly after New Year's in 1842. La Güera appears in *Life in Mexico* on 141–143, 276–277, 456–457, 472–475, and 607.

37. Letter to William H. Prescott, June 5, 1840, in Wolcott, *Correspondence*, 128–133.

38. Zeuske, *Simón Bolívar*, 75.

39. Fossey went to Mexico in 1831 as a colonist, had a distinguished career as a teacher, and left Mexico in 1866. See Burton, "Did You Know?" and Fossey, *Le Mexique*, 282.

40. Bustamante, *Diario*, January 8, 1835, July 12, 1836.

41. Despite being an eyewitness to events, Bustamante occasionally confused facts, as when he wrote that the "guera Velasco" was named Josefa or that her daughter Josefa died in Baltimore instead of Brooklyn. *Diario*, October 26, 1838, September 13, 1833.

42. See Bustamante, *Diario*, July 27, 1826, September 16, 1828, and October 26, 1838.

43. On Josefa's divorce, see Bustamante, *Diario,* February 20 and 22, April 24, June 12 and 27, and July 27, 1826; August 7, 1828; and the pamphlet inserted after the entry of June 19, 1826, titled "Quien llama al toro, sufra la cornada."

44. Couturier, *Silver King,* 180.

45. In addition to Bustamante's *Diario,* see AHN, Francisco de Madariaga #426, vol. 2837 (February 22, 1826), ff. 110–111; and Testament of Pedro Romero de Terreros (March 25, 1826), AHN, Manuel García Romero #286, vol. 1774, art. 3.

46. On Josefa's death, see Bustamante, *Diario,* August 2, 7, and 8, 1828; and Romero de Terreros, *Condes de Regla,* 93–96. The dates of her journey are unclear. She was in Mexico City on January 2, 1828, when she appeared before notary José Vicente Maciel to give her power of attorney to don José María Icaza. AHN, José Vicente Maciel #427, vol. 2901 (1828), ff. 1–1v.

47. Bustamante, *Diario,* February 20, 1826, and August 11, 1828.

48. Bustamante, *Diario,* September 16, 1828.

49. Calderón de la Barca, *Life in Mexico,* 142.

50. Couturier, *Silver King,* 180–181.

51. The 1842 census recorded the household as consisting of Gerónimo, identified as a thirty-eight-year-old, his twenty-eight-year-old wife Guadalupe Díaz, his twelve-year-old son Manuel, and twelve *dependientes,* many of them likely his servants, nine of them born on his Hacienda de Bojay. Padrón Municipal de 1842, banco de datos digital, courtesy of Linda Arnold.

52. Romero de Terreros, *Condes de Regla,* 95.

53. Antonia rented casa no. 8 on the 1st Calle de San Francisco from the Tercer Orden de San Francisco for 60 pesos a month. AHN, Manuel García Romero #286, vol. 1778 (May 9, 1838), ff. 205–206.

54. The description is from Fanny's letter of February 1, 1840; *Life in Mexico,* 141.

55. "Avisos: Gran Concierto."

56. AHN, Francisco de Madariaga #426, vol. 2851 (July 20, 1836), ff. 702v–704v; AHN, Manuel García Romero #286, vol. 1778 (May 9, 1838), ff. 205–206, and vol. 1781 (January 29, 1841), ff. 38–40; AHN, José López Guazo #361, vol. 2344 (July 21, 1835), ff. 190v–193v.

57. AP, Entierros, libro 29, no. 2220, f. 30. Her 1850 will is transcribed in Muñoz Altea, "La Güera Rodríguez," 212–217.

58. Despite the 1842 law prohibiting burials in the city center, the nobility continued this old tradition. See the death certificates cited in appendix B and Zárate Toscano, *Los nobles,* 265–267, 402.

59. Romero de Terreros, *Ex-antiquis,* 230; FS, "México, Distrito Federal, registros parroquiales y diocesanos, 1514–1970," database with images (https://familysearch.org/ark:/61903/1:1:ND3V–NYL : 9 March 2018).

60. Valle-Arizpe, "Supervivencias inánimes," *Güera Rodríguez,* chap. 14.

61. Interview with church spokesman, Iglesia de San Francisco, March 1, 2018.

CHAPTER 5. THE FIRST HUNDRED
YEARS AFTER HER DEATH

1. See esp. Fernández de Lizardi, *Calendario;* Bustamante, *Cuadro histórico,* vol. 1, 16, and vol. 2, 200; Tecuanhuey, "Imagen de las heroínas"; and Guzmán Pérez, "Gertrudis Bocanegra."

2. Alvarado, *Educación,* esp. 30–31; Pouwels, *Political Journalism,* 29–44.

3. Chapter XXIII, titled "Heroínas de la Independencia," was entirely based on Fernández de Lizardi's *Calendario* of 1825. González Obregón, *México viejo,* 281–294.

4. Moreno Juárez, "Presencia."

5. Agüeros, *Episodios,* vol. 1, 259–269, and vol. 2, 213–230, 253–260.

6. Prieto, *Memorias de mis tiempos,* vol. 1, 237, and vol. 2, 318.

7. Alamán, *Historia,* vol. 5, 167.

8. Curiel, "Prólogo," 46.

9. Romero de Terreros, *Condes de Regla,* 85, and the image of María Ignacia Rodriguez de Velasco between 86 and 87.

10. Romero de Terreros, *Ex-antiquis,* 224–236. The second edition, titled *Bocetos de la vida social en la Nueva España,* was published by Porrúa (1944) and thus gained a wider distribution than the first edition, published in Guadalajara by Jaime.

11. Compare chap. 15 of the 1950 edition of *Güera Rodríguez,* 409, with the 1960 edition, 286.

12. Valle-Arizpe claimed to have read in a letter included in the papers of the investigation (*visita*) of Viceroy Revillagigedo that he wrote the Consejo de Indias "que don Antonio Rodríguez de Velasco lo acusaba porque se había visto obligado a casar a sus hijas con unos militares de la guarnición de México," but I have been unable to verify the reference. Valle-Arizpe cites the Sección de Consejos, Archivo Histórico Nacional, Madrid. *Güera Rodríguez* (1960), chap. 1, 18–19.

13. Testimony of Lieutenant Colonel Mariano Soto Carrillo on December 6, 1802, and filing of September 4, 1802, cited in Arrom, *Mujer mexicana,* 96, 70.

14. Zárate Toscano, *Los nobles,* 105.

15. Jesús Galindo y Villa in 1923 recalled having heard another version of the story from General Vicente Riva Palacio: that it was she who had given him the feathers of three colors with which he decorated his hat. *Polvo de historia,* vol. 1, 45.

16. Although the book began to be translated soon after it was published in Boston in 1843, the project was aborted because of its negative comments about Mexico. The first complete Spanish edition appeared in 1920. See the essay by the Fishers, editors of the expanded edition of *Life in Mexico,* 629–636.

17. Conversation with González Obregón recounted by Peza in "La bella 'Güera' Rodríguez."

18. On mortuary customs, see Zárate Toscano, *Los nobles,* 231–235, 270.

19. Romero de Terreros, *Ex-antiquis*, 230.

20. Romero de Terreros claims that the portrait of La Güera and her daughters was painted by a famous artist and sent to Madrid (*Ex-antiquis*, 226–227). The curator of the royal collection could not locate any record of the painting and doubts it was ever in the royal collection. Communication with Carmen Díaz Gallegos, April 3, 2017.

21. Romero de Terreros, *Corte de Agustín*, 5–10.

22. Valle, *Cómo era Iturbide*, 17. Valle refers to La Güera's influence over Iturbide in only three sentences and cites as his sources Prieto's *Memorias de mis tiempos*, Romero de Terreros's *Condes de Regla*, and Torrente's *Historia*. Valle notes that these stories were not documented with evidence.

23. Peza, "La bella 'Güera' Rodríguez."

24. See, for example, Orozco y Berra, *Diccionario universal*, vol. 5, 167; and Thompson, *Recollections of Mexico*, 122. The story is likewise absent from González Obregón's description of the inauguration of the monument in *México viejo y anecdótico*, 42.

25. Krumm-Heller, "Esbozo biográfico," 20, 23–25.

26. See the Fishers' endnote in Calderón de la Barca, *Life in Mexico*, 696 note 43.

27. Alessio Robles, "Introducción," 80–82.

28. González Obregón, *Calles de México*, 173.

29. This volume contains documents pertaining to hundreds of insurgent women. On La Güera, see "Oficio de D. José Antonio de Noriega" (July 19, 1814), in García, *Documentos históricos*, vol. 5, 461–462.

30. "Denuncia del alcaide," 334–345.

31. Amador, *Noticias biográficas*, 51.

32. Castillo Ledón, *Hidalgo*, vol. 1, 176.

33. La Güera Rodríguez does not appear in Hernández, *Mujeres célebres de México* (1918), Vázquez Santa Ana, *Bosquejos biográficos* (1920), Rubio Siliceo, *Mujeres célebres en la independencia* (1929), Peral, *Diccionario biográfico mexicano* (1944), or Gómez, *Epopeya de la independencia* (1947).

34. Guzmán Pérez, "Mujeres de amor," 91. Only one woman has been added to the wall of honor since then: Carmen Serdán, heroine of the 1910 Revolution.

35. García, "La Güera Rodríguez y el coronel Iturbide" and "La influencia de la Guerra [sic] Rodríguez sobre Iturbide y la Independencia." A third article in the series refers to "his loves with doña Ignacia Rodríguez de Velasco" but does not give any details: "¿Por qué hizo la Independencia Iturbide?"

36. García also cites Romero de Terreros and a certain "Ingeniero Torres," whom I have been unable to identify.

37. Alamán, *Historia*, vol. 5, 53 note 51.

38. Zamora Plowes, *Comedia mexicana Quince Uñas*, vol. 1, 5–6, 9–10, 22, 439, 444.

39. The complete work was reproduced in 1984 with the shorter title *Quince Uñas y Casanova aventureros* (2 vols., Mexico City: Patria, 1984), and a condensed version edited by Pilar Tapia appeared in 2007.

40. In his bibliography Zamora cited only Calderón de la Barca and Torrente as his sources on La Güera, but the source of the nickname "La Venus Mexicana" must have been Prieto or Romero de Terreros.

CHAPTER 6. THE LEGEND CRYSTALLIZED IN
VALLE-ARIZPE'S *LA GÜERA RODRÍGUEZ,* 1949

1. The last edition with revisions is 1956. The 2011 edition is an exact copy of the 9th edition of 1960, although with different pagination. All the references below are based on the 1960 edition.

2. In recognition of his historical as well as literary works, Valle-Arizpe was named Cronista de la Ciudad de México and member of the Academia Mexicana de la Lengua. *Diccionario Porrúa* (1964), 1530; and Oropeza Martínez, *Apuntes autodidácticos,* 7–15.

3. Valle-Arizpe, *Güera Rodríguez,* chap. 1, 11–12, 16, 18–19.

4. Valle-Arizpe, *Güera Rodríguez,* chap. 7, esp. 97, 99.

5. Valle-Arizpe, *Güera Rodríguez,* chap. 2, 23–24, 26–28.

6. Valle-Arizpe also offered an alternative—and equally speculative—theory: that Briones became ill when "La Güera, inadvertently, rolled over in bed and left him uncovered . . . on a freezing night." *Güera Rodríguez,* chap. 4, 52.

7. Valle-Arizpe, *Güera Rodríguez,* chap. 3, 33.

8. Valle-Arizpe, *Güera Rodríguez,* chap. 6, 79.

9. The first time Valle-Arizpe raised Villamil's charges he rejected them as "surely lies" amplified by his imagination (*Güera Rodríguez,* chap. 3, 36). In chaps. 7 and 8, however, the author abandoned such caution and presented them as true.

10. Valle-Arizpe, *Güera Rodríguez,* chap. 7, 89–93, 99; chap. 8, 103, 105, 107–108.

11. Valle-Arizpe, *Güera Rodríguez,* chap. 8, 110–112, 125–126, 130–131; chap. 3, 31; chap. 7, 93.

12. Valle-Arizpe, *Güera Rodríguez,* chap. 9, 38–39, 141, 148–149.

13. Valle-Arizpe, *Güera Rodríguez,* chap. 9, 146–147.

14. According to Andrés Henestrosa's prologue to Beruete's diary, it was first published in New Orleans in 1932 and was immediately reviewed by Rafael Heliodoro Valle (*Elevación y caída,* 9–10). William Spence Robertson also cites it in 1952 (*Iturbide,* 187). Valle-Arizpe was evidently unfamiliar with these texts.

15. Valle-Arizpe, *Güera Rodríguez,* chap. 11, 181, 186–187, 197, 207.

16. Valle, *Bolívar en México,* ix.

17. Valle, *Bolívar en México*, ix; González Obregón, *México viejo y anecdótico*, 37–38; Romero de Terreros, *Condes de Regla*, 86.

18. Valle-Arizpe, *Güera Rodríguez*, chap. 6, 80–81, 84–85.

19. Valle-Arizpe, *Güera Rodríguez*, chap. 10, 170–172.

20. This reference is to *El médico de su honra* by Pedro Calderón de la Barca, in which a husband kills his wife because he believes the false rumors of her adultery. Valle-Arizpe, *Güera Rodríguez*, chap. 8, 114.

21. See Mandrell, *Don Juan and the Point of Honor*. In Mexico, Salvador Toscano made a silent movie, *Don Juan Tenorio*, around 1900, and another version was filmed during Mexican cinema's Golden Age, in 1937. See http://www.imdb.com/title/tt2370830/ and http://www.imdb.com/title/tt0228227/, accessed September 8, 2018.

22. Valle-Arizpe, *Güera Rodríguez*, chap. 5, 64–65; chap. 11, 192; chap. 12, 213.

23. Valle-Arizpe, *Güera Rodríguez*, chap. 2, 23.

24. Valle-Arizpe, *Güera Rodríguez*, chap. 10, 161, 171.

25. Valle-Arizpe, *Güera Rodríguez*, chap. 3, 34–35.

26. Valle-Arizpe, *Güera Rodríguez*, chap. 10, 153–55.

27. Valle-Arizpe, *Güera Rodríguez*, chap. 10, 156–157.

28. Valle-Arizpe, *Güera Rodríguez*, chap. 10, 159–163.

29. Valle-Arizpe, *Güera Rodríguez*, chap. 11, esp. 197–199.

30. Valle-Arizpe, *Güera Rodríguez*, chap. 11, 204.

31. Valle-Arizpe, *Güera Rodríguez*, chap. 11, 207–208.

32. María Guadalupe Sánchez Robles notes that the repeated use of superlatives was one of the strategies used by Valle-Arizpe to make her a mythical figure; "La Güera Rodríguez," 365–368.

33. Valle-Arizpe was not the first author to represent the Don Juan figure as a woman. See, for example, Rafael María Liern y Cerach, *Doña Juana Tenorio* (1875) and Jacinto Octavio Picón, *Juanita Tenorio* (1910), both cited by Singer in his enormous bibliography, *The Don Juan Theme*.

34. Valle-Arizpe, *Güera Rodríguez*, chap. 10, 172.

35. Valle-Arizpe, *Güera Rodríguez*, chap. 14, 257–258.

36. Valle-Arizpe, *Güera Rodríguez*, chap. 14, 263.

CHAPTER 7. LA GÜERA AFTER VALLE-ARIZPE:
THE POWER OF FICTION

1. María y Campos, "Estreno de *Hoy invita la Güera*." In 1967 Arturo Sotomayor noted that the book had been received "with unanimous applause"; *Don Artemio*, xvii.

2. The alleged incident could have occurred between 1952 and 1957, when Adolfo López Mateos was the Secretario de Trabajo y Previsión Social. See Blanco, *Álbum de pesadillas*, 18–19.

3. Ortega y Medina, *Humboldt desde México*, 167–73, 217.

4. Blanco, *Álbum de pesadillas*, 21–22.

5. Muñoz Altea, "La Güera Rodríguez," 203. The author nonetheless repeats some of Valle-Arizpe's inventions (such as her great friendship with Bolívar and the erroneous date of her alleged Inquisition trial) and introduces new errors. A few incorrect dates are probably typographical errors that the author was unable to correct because he died before the book's publication. Another error is his confusion of ecclesiastical divorce (a Church-authorized separation) with annulment, which was the only way to dissolve a marriage.

6. Oropeza Martínez, *Apuntes autodidácticos*, 6, 60–61, 66; Valle Arizpe, *Güera Rodríguez* [selection].

7. See, for example, Martínez Serrano, "Manuel Tolsá inmortalizó el rostro de la Güera Rodríguez"; and Garci, *Más pendejadas célebres*, 18. An official website of Mexico City denied the legend: Ruvalcaba, "La Profesa: Un estuche de lujo."

8. According to a program on the Yolo Camotes YouTube channel, she was "La Güera Rodríguez: La seductora de la Independencia."

9. Bautista, "La 'Güera' Rodríguez, la feminista desconocida"; Xakan, "María Ignacia Rodríguez"; and TeleSur, "La Güera Rodríguez."

10. This invention may be partly due to confusion of the third orders of laypeople with the second orders of nuns—although there is in any case no evidence confirming her membership in the Third Order of San Francisco favored by her husband. Martínez Núñez, "La redención de La Güera," 20.

11. Valle, "Redescubriendo a Iturbide" and "Deudas de la Güera Rodríguez."

12. Although *Hoy invita la Güera* was presented in 1955, it was not published until 1956, and it was then reproduced in a joint edition with Salvador Novo's *La culta dama* in 1984 (reprinted in 1997). The author went by the name Federico S. Inclán until at least 1997; when the play was revived in 2010, he used the name Federico Schroeder. Galván, "Federico Schroeder Inclán." For reviews of the 1962 and 2010 productions, see Solórzano, "Hoy invita la Güera," and Velasco, "Enredos amorosos" and "La Güera Rodríguez."

13. The quotes are from Schroeder Inclán, *Hoy invita la Güera*, 84, 65, 68.

14. María y Campos, "Estreno de *Hoy invita la güera*."

15. See the two reviews by Karina Velasco.

16. Barrios Gómez, "Ensalada Popoff," and Flórez, "El México de antaño."

17. The article is signed by Eliot Gibbons, whom I have not been able to identify. It is possible that the true author was Anita Brenner, who often wrote under assumed names. Gibbons, "'La Güera' Rodríguez," 11, 24; and López Arellano, *Anita Brenner*, 146–149.

18. Sotomayor's book was published by UNAM in its series Biblioteca del Estudiante Universitario; *Don Artemio* (1967).

19. Olmedilla, "México, 1808–1821," 599–600.

20. Calvillo, *República Federal*, vol. 1, 300.

21. *Diccionario Porrúa* (1964), 1224–1225.

22. Miquel i Vergés, *Diccionario de insurgentes*, 502.

23. The quote is from Casasola, *Seis siglos de historia gráfica*, vol. 1, 497. The miniature, reproduced in color for the first time, is in the catalogue of an art exhibit sponsored by the Instituto Mexicano Norteamericano de Relaciones Culturales in 1974; see *Veinte mujeres notables en la vida de México*.

24. La Güera did not appear in Villaseñor y Villaseñor, *Biografías de los héroes* (1962), although the revised edition of that 1955 work added three women to the original male pantheon; nor did she appear in López de Escalera, *Diccionario* (1964). Fernández's *Mujeres que honran a la patria* (1958) did include Vicario, Bocanegra, and Ortiz de Domínguez.

25. Kentner, "Role of Women," 258–259. La Güera is also mentioned briefly in two English-language works by professional historians: Doris Ladd in 1976 (*Mexican Nobility*, 82, 210, 264 note 119) and Edith Couturier in 1978 ("Women in a Noble Family," 143).

26. I also included her in *Women of Mexico City*, 215, 233, 238, and 248. Because I was relying on secondary sources, I gave mistaken ages of marriage and death for her on 127.

27. See the film script and "Datos de la Ficha," CONACULTA Cineteca Nacional, FILMOTECA, G.O.-439 and A-00399; interview with Felipe Cazals, "La Güera Rodríguez," in García Tsao, *Testimonios*, 185–195; and Bloch, "La Güera Rodríguez y Gertrudis Bocanegra," 30–33. The film is archived in the FILMOTECA, O.-439, although one reel is missing. A segment can be viewed on YouTube: https://www.youtube.com/watch?v = Q7vEDT2iqag, accessed July 6, 2017.

28. Amador and Ayala Blanco, *Cartelera cinematográfica*, 383. Cazals later disowned the film because he said it gave too much credit to the *criollo* upper classes in the fight for independence and explained that he made it only to earn money. See interview with García Tsao, *Testimonios*, 185–186.

29. Interview with Fanny Cano, "La Güera Rodríguez, el film será todo un éxito, afirma F. Cano," *Cine Mundial* (May 13, 1977), inserted in "Datos de la ficha." It seems that the actress Silvia Pinal had also wanted to play the role of La Güera: García Tsao, *Testimonios*, 185.

30. Tuñón Pablos, "Heroínas en celuloide," 311.

31. See quote from an interview with the soprano Lorena von Pastor in Sevilla, "Las dos Güeras."

32. See Sosa, *Diccionario de la ópera*, pp. 189–196. An aria sung by Guillermina Higareda and Rodolfo Acosta is posted to YouTube: https://youtu.be/raY2xiH-FHA, accessed July 2, 2017.

33. Although it is undated, the issue titled *La Güera Rodríguez* is dated as año 1, núm. 15 of *Cuadernos Mexicanos*, which means it appeared in 1982. It was a joint publication of the Secretaría de Educación Pública and CONASUPO in collaboration with the Museo Nacional de Historia (INAH) and sold for six pesos.

34. "Rodríguez de Velasco y Osorio Barba, María Ignacia," in Álvarez, *Enciclopedia de México*, vol. 11, 341–342; and Musacchio, *Diccionario enciclopédico*, vol. 4, 1760. She also appears in the 1981 *Historical Dictionary of Mexico* edited by Donald Briggs and Marvin Alisky (195).

35. For an example of comic books with brief but accurate references to La Güera, see the series *Episodios Mexicanos* produced by Guadalupe Jiménez Codinach and other historians, esp. nos. 28–35 (1981). No. 34 questions the story of her romance with Iturbide (30).

36. The first Spanish edition of Tuñón's work appeared in 1987. The citation is from the later English-language edition. Tuñón Pablos, *Women in Mexico*, 41.

37. *La antorcha encendida* aired on the Televisa channel from May 6 to November 15, 1996. See Wikipedia, "La antorcha encendida," and the DVD distributed by Xenon Pictures under license to Televisa in 2005 (Alonso and Sotomayor, prods., *La antorcha encendida*).

38. Fuentes Mares, *Mil y una noches mexicanas*, vol. 1, 41–50.

39. Bastien et al., *La Güera Rodríguez: Bella conspiradora mexicana*. On the series, see *Hombres y Héroes*.

40. Guedea, *Prontuario*, 361–365.

41. Some of these statements, though plausible, are speculative. For example, it is unclear whether La Güera was already a firm supporter of independence in 1810, whether the money she gave the insurgents was loaned or donated, and whether her salon was a formal part of the imperial court. Moreover, many elites were autonomists. Guedea, "Rodríguez de Velasco" in *Encyclopedia of Mexico*. Guedea also wrote the entry on La Güera in the *Encyclopedia of Latin American History and Culture* (1996).

42. Villalpando, *Amores mexicanos*, 19. This book was so popular that it was reprinted in 2010.

43. The author also listed other affairs mentioned by Valle-Arizpe. Martín Moreno, *Las grandes traiciones*, 17–32.

44. Blanco also included the scene where she allegedly called in strangers to witness the birth of Briones's posthumous child, and noted that one of her contributions to Mexican culture was to coin the phrase "Fuera de México todo es Cuautitlán." Blanco, *Álbum de pesadillas*, 18–24.

45. Galí Boadella, *Historias del bello sexo*, 37–55. Galí briefly considered—but rejected—the possibility that her illicit affairs were fictitious (52).

46. Another example is the 2007 edition of *Quince Uñas y Casanova aventureros*, condensed and annotated for young readers. A marginal note identifying

La Güera does not mention her contributions to independence, but only affirms that she had three husbands and "it is said that she had love affairs with the baron Alexander von Humboldt, the young Simón Bolívar, and Agustín de Iturbide; the latter marched past her balcony when he led the Ejército Trigarante into the capital in 1821" (Zamora Plowes, *Quince Uñas y Casanova aventureros*, 16).

47. See Arrioja Vizcaíno, *Águila en la alcoba*, 339, 342.

48. Fuentes Aguirre Catón, *La otra historia de México*, vol. 1, 15–34, and vol. 2, 40–67, 220–222. In addition to citing Valle-Arizpe as the source of his information, Aguirre Catón opens the book with a subtitle that copies the first sentence of Valle-Arizpe's book: "Eran dos doncellas muy godibles." On the next page he jokes that the phrase should be "Eran dos doncellas muy jodibles."

49. Alaniz, *Mujeres por la Independencia*, 59–72. Alaniz confused many facts, for example, affirming that she only had two daughters and one son. For a short portrait of La Güera as one of seven heroines deserving a full chapter, see Huerta-Nava, *Mujeres insurgentes*, 40–42.

50. The comedy *La Güera Rodríguez* was directed by Jorge Ortiz de Pinedo and the part of La Güera was played by the telenovela actress Chantal Andere. It was presented in the Teatro Helénico de la Ciudad de México in August and September 2010. See television ad for the play, https://www.youtube.com/watch?v = 5kbKLJl0, accessed June 28, 2017; two reviews by Karina Velasco; and Macías Galland, "Una Güera, que rockea."

51. The opera *La Güera Rodríguez* was presented in a "concert for the bicentennial of Independence" with the Orquesta Sinfónica Instituto Politécnico Nacional in September 2010. See reviews by Vargas, "Después de casi tres décadas," and Sevilla, "Las dos Güeras." Scenes from the opera are available on YouTube, for example, the duet "Tengo que decirte adiós," https://youtu.be/6oG5yF6mqOg, accessed September 7, 2019.

52. The play was presented in September 2010 in the Teatro Ocampo in Morelos and won a prize in the Los Centenarios competition. See *Antorcha y cenizas*, https://www.youtube.com/watch?v = KkunU9kDIg8, accessed September 7, 2019; review by Silvia Vargas, "Cuentan la historia de manera divertida"; and interview with the author in Flores Acevedo, "Sobre *Antorcha y Cenizas*."

53. The monologue "La Güera Rodríguez," directed by Francisco Hernández and with Ericka Ramírez in the title role, was presented on October 1, 2010, in the Pinacoteca de La Profesa by the Fénix Novohispano Compañía Nacional de Teatro Clásico. Hernández, "La Güera Rodríguez."

54. Sunderland Guerrero, "Olor a almizcle."

55. Crononautas Tijerina, "Corrido a la Güera Rodríguez."

56. The first online texts were newspaper articles, such as the often-cited article by Otto Schober, "La reinvindicación de 'La Güera' Rodríguez." By 2010 blogs proliferated, such as Reyes Hernández, "'La Güera Rodríguez,' eterna seductora"; Nina, "La famosa 'Güera Rodríguez'"; and Batista, "La célebre 'Güera Rodríguez.'"

57. Palacio, *Adictas a la insurgencia*. Cited from the Kindle edition, loc. 2593.

58. See, for example, "El Ocaso de la Nueva España," a *Tele Historia* episode; Casa Telmex Cuicuilco, prod., "La Güera Rodríguez"; and Salinas Basave, "Los mitos del bicentenario 22: La Güera."

59. Martín Moreno, *Arrebatos carnales II*, 15–108, quote on 55. The book was reprinted by Editorial Diana in 2011 and the long chapter on La Güera Rodríguez is available as a separate e-book. The 2010 text expands on the author's short section on La Güera in *Las grandes traiciones* (2000), 17–32.

60. Martínez Núñez's thesis shows the difficulty of separating fact from fiction. Although he located many relevant primary documents and challenged several myths that have circulated about La Güera (such as the story of her Inquisition trial and of Iturbide's changing the route of his procession), at some critical junctures he falls back on Valle-Arizpe's narrative as well as on Rocafuerte's rumors ("Biografía crítica"). Martínez Núñez later published a fictitious story full of falsehoods, "La redención de la Güera."

61. Guardia's *Las mujeres*, published in Peru, contained a full chapter on La Güera, and she received brief mentions in two other chapters in that book: Sánchez Robles, "La Güera Rodríguez," 364–369, and Tuñón Pablos, "Heroínas en celuloide," 310–311. On her international visibility, see also two texts published in Spain: García López, *Heroínas silenciadas*, esp. 168, 178–80; and the short reference in Rodríguez, "Los caudillos," 321.

62. Her Spanish-language Wikipedia page was created in 2010 ("María Ignacia Rodríguez de Velasco") and the English-language page in 2006. Some of the early mistakes have since been corrected (for example, the mistaken date of her death). The English version inexplicably includes her under the category of "Mexican people of Portuguese-Jewish descent," a new invention.

63. See Molly, "Alebrijes." This blog also mentions that a "goofy-looking historical docu-drama" about La Güera was advertised all over Mexico City.

64. See, for example, Parbst, "La Güera Rodríguez"; Velázquez Moreno, "'La Güera' Rodríguez"; Escamilla Dimas, "La Güera Rodríguez"; Ríos, "Romance de la Güera"; and Rosas, *99 pasiones*, 29–31. La Güera is also the subject of two long novels: Martínez Villaseñor, *El viento no es para siempre*, and Barba, *La conspiradora*.

65. The exhibit catalogue adds a fifth heroine: Gertrudis Bocanegra (Galeana, *Museo de la Mujer*, 65–75). The brief biographical sketch contains two apocryphal stories (that La Güera was Bolívar's friend, and that Iturbide changed the route of his triumphal procession to give her a feather from his hat) and repeats the falsehood that she was the model for the statue of the Virgen de Dolores in the Profesa church.

66. Yorch, "La Güera Rodríguez."

67. La Güera was the subject of the first chapter in Garci, *Más pendejadas célebres* (a sequel to his 2010 book *Pendejadas célebres en la historia de México*),

billed as "a hysterically funny book to cure the hangover of the bicentennial celebrations," 14–18.

68. Rivera, "La Güera Rodríguez."

69. Díaz, "La Güera Rodríguez."

70. Urena, "La Güera Rodríguez."

71. Ríos, "La Güera estrenó a Simón Bolívar"; Yolo Camotes, "La Güera Rodríguez"; Reznik, "¿Quién fue la Güera Rodríguez?"; Lozano Torres, *Bolívar*, 35–38; Yorch, "La Güera Rodríguez"; and Dávila, "Conozca a las 10 prostitutas," where she is the first "prostitute" on the list, followed by Madame de Pompadour and eight others.

CONCLUSION

1. Blanco, *Álbum de pesadillas*, 19–20.

2. Julio Alejandro and Emilio Carballido, film script of "La Güera Rodríguez," FILMOTECA, G.O.-439, 16.

3. Tuñón Pablos, "Heroínas en celuloide," 311. On the role of films in maintaining cultural symbols, see 306.

4. See esp. Cypess, *Malinche in Mexican Literature*; Núñez Becerra, *La Malinche*; and Townsend, *Malintzin's Choices*.

5. Vigil Talavera, *La puta libertadora*.

6. Quoted in García, *Leona Vicario*, 188.

7. Marston, "Why 100,000,000 Americans Read Comics."

8. Weeks, *Juárez Myth*, 135.

Bibliography

ARCHIVES

AGI	Archivo General de Indias (Seville)
AGN	Archivo General de la Nación (Mexico City)
AHCM	Archivo Histórico de la Ciudad de México (Mexico City)
AHN	Archivo Histórico del Archivo General de Notarías (Mexico City)
AP	Archivo Parroquia de la Asunción Sagrario Metropolitano (Mexico City)
BNM	Biblioteca Nacional de México (Mexico City)
FILMOTECA	Subdirección de Acervos, Filmoteca de la UNAM (Mexico City)
FN	Familias Novohispanas: Un sistema de redes, Javier Sánchiz and Victor Gayol, https://gw.geneanet.org/sanchiz
FS	Family Search (Church of Jesus Christ of Latter-day Saints), http://www.FamilySearch.org
UT	Benson Latin American Collection, University of Texas, Austin

WORKS CITED

Agüeros, Victoriano, comp. *Episodios históricos de la Guerra de la Independencia.* 2 vols. 1910; repr. Mexico City: Instituto Nacional de Estudios Históricos de las Revoluciones de México, 2008.

Aguirre Salvador, Rodolfo. *El mérito y la estrategia: Clérigos, juristas y médicos en la Nueva España.* Mexico City: UNAM, Centro de Estudios sobre la Universidad / Plaza y Valdés, 2003.

Alamán, Lucas. *Historia de México desde los primeros movimientos que prepararon su independencia en el año de 1808 hasta la época presente.* 5 vols. 1849–1852; repr. Mexico City: Publicaciones Herrerias, 1938.

Alaniz, Sebastián. *Mujeres por la Independencia.* Mexico City: Lectorum, 2009.

Album mexicano: Retratos de los personajes ilustres de la primera y segunda época de la Independencia mexicana y notabilidades de la presente. Mexico City: Julio Michaud y Thomas, ca. 1840.

Alessio Robles, Vito. "Introducción bibliográfica: El Barón Alejandro de Humboldt, su vida y su obra." In Alejandro de Humboldt, *Ensayo político sobre el Reino de la Nueva España,* vol. 1, 9–121. Mexico City: Editorial Pedro Robredo, 1941.

Alonso, Ernesto, and Carlos Sotomayor, prods. *La antorcha encendida: Independencia de México.* Telenovela presented by Televisa from May 6 to November 15, 1996. DVD distributed by Xenon Pictures, 2005.

Alvarado, Lourdes. *Educación y superación femenina en el siglo XIX: Dos ensayos de Laureana Wright.* Mexico City: UNAM, Centro de Estudios sobre la Universidad, 2005.

Álvarez, José Rogelio, ed. *Enciclopedia de México.* 12 vols. Mexico City: Editora Mexicana, 1977.

Amador, Elías. *Noticias biográficas de insurgentes apodados.* Mexico City: SEP, 1946.

Amador, María Luisa, and Jorge Ayala Blanco. *Cartelera cinematográfica, 1970–1979.* Mexico City: UNAM, Centro Universitario de Estudios Cinematográficos, 1988.

Arnold, Linda. *Bureaucracy and Bureaucrats in Mexico City, 1742–1835.* Tucson: University of Arizona Press, 1988.

Arrioja Vizcaíno, Adolfo. *El águila en la alcoba: La Güera Rodríguez en los tiempos de la independencia nacional.* Mexico City: Grijalbo, 2005.

Arrom, Silvia Marina. *La mujer mexicana ante el divorcio eclesiástico (1800–1857).* Mexico City: SepSetentas, 1976.

———. *The Women of Mexico City, 1790–1857.* Stanford, CA: Stanford University Press, 1985.

———. *Containing the Poor: The Mexico City Poor House, 1774–1871.* Durham, NC: Duke University Press, 2000.

"Avisos: Gran Concierto." *El Monitor Republicano*, December 25, 1846, 4.

Barba, Guillermo. *La conspiradora: La historia desconocida de la Güera Rodríguez*. Mexico City: Planeta, 2019.

Barrios Gómez, Agustín. "Ensalada Popoff." *Novedades*, May 3, 1959, 2nd section, 8.

Bastien, Remy, Dolores Plaza, and José L. Echave. "La Güera Rodríguez: Bella conspiradora mexicana." *Hombres y Héroes* 158, año IV (August 29, 1990).

Batista, Jesús. "La célebre 'Güera' Rodríguez." *Tierra de historia* (blog). August 3, 2010. http://tierradehistoria.blogspot.com/2010/08/la-celebre-guera -rodriguez.html, accessed January 9, 2019.

Bautista, Eduardo. "La 'Güera' Rodríguez, la feminista desconocida." *El Financiero*, March 19, 2019. https://www.elfinanciero.com.mx/culturas /la-gueera-rodriguez-la-feminista-desconocida, accessed July 22, 2020.

Bazant, Mílada. *Laura Méndez de Cuenca: Mexican Feminist, 1853–1928*. Trans. and foreword by Mary Kay Vaughan. Tucson: University of Arizona Press, 2018.

Beruete, Miguel de. *Elevación y caída del Emperador Iturbide*. Transcription, prologue, and notes by Andrés Henestrosa. Mexico City: Fondo Bruno Paglio, 1974.

Blanco, José Joaquín. *Álbum de pesadillas mexicanas: Crónicas reales e imaginarias*. Mexico City: Ediciones Era, 2002.

Bloch, Catherine. "La Güera Rodríguez y Gertudis Bocanegra." In *La ficción de la historia: El siglo XIX en el cine mexicano*, ed. Ángel Miquel, 30–33. Mexico City: Cineteca Nacional, 2010.

Briggs, Donald C., and Marvin Alisky. *Historical Dictionary of Mexico*. Metuchen, NJ: Scarecrow Press, 1981.

Brunk, Samuel. *The Posthumous Career of Emiliano Zapata: Myth, Memory, and Mexico's Twentieth Century*. Austin: University of Texas Press, 2008.

Burkholder, Mark A., and D. S. Chandler. *Biographical Dictionary of Audiencia Ministers in the Americas, 1687–1821*. Westport, CT: Greenwood Press, 1982.

Burton, Tony. "Did You Know? Mathieu de Fossey." *Mexconnect*, March 14, 2008. http://www.mexconnect.com/articles/1170-did-you-know-mathieu -de-fossey, accessed August 10, 2016.

Bustamante, Carlos María de. *Suplemento a la historia de los tres siglos de México durante el gobierno español, escrita por el padre Andrés Cavo* . . . 4 vols. Mexico City: Testamentaria de D. Alejandro Valdés, 1836–1838.

———. *Cuadro histórico de la Revolución Mexicana*. 5 vols. 2d ed. Mexico City: J. M. Lara, 1843–1846.

———. *Diario histórico de México, 1822–1848, del licenciado Carlos María de Bustamante*, ed. Josefina Zoraida Vázquez and Héctor Cuauhtémoc Hernández Silvia. CD-ROM. CD 1: 1822–1834, CD 2: 1835–1848. Mexico City: CIESAS / El Colegio de México, 2001, 2003. INAOE.

Calderón de la Barca, Fanny. *Life in Mexico: The Letters of Fanny Calderón de la Barca, with New Material from the Author's Private Journals*. Ed. Howard T. Fisher and Marion Hall Fisher. Garden City, NY: Doubleday, 1966.

Calvillo, Manuel, comp. *La República Federal Mexicana, gestación y nacimiento: La consumación de la Independencia y la instauración de la República Federal, 1820-1824*. 2 vols. Mexico City: El Colegio de México / Colegio de San Luis, 1974.

Cano, Gabriela. *Se llamaba Elena Arizmendi*. Mexico City: Tusquets Editores, 2010.

Carbajal López, David. "Tras los pasos de Ramón Cardeña y Gallardo." *Apuntes de historia del Catolicismo* (blog). June 30, 2013. http://historiadelcatolicismo.info/tras-los-pasos-de-ramon-cardena-y-gallardo, accessed October 4, 2017.

Casa Telmex Cuicuilco, prod. "La Güera Rodríguez." November 2010. https://www.youtube.com/watch?v=QsHS2qrGft4, accessed April 17, 2017.

Casasola, Gustavo. *Seis siglos de historia gráfica de México, 1325-1925*. 4th ed. Mexico City: Casasola, 1971, vol. 1.

Castillo Ledón, Luis. *Hidalgo: La vida del héroe*. 2 vols. Mexico City: Talleres Gráficos de la Nación, 1948-1949.

Castro, C., dib. y lit. *México y sus alrededores: Colección de monumentos, trajes y paisajes dibujados al natural y litografiados por los artistas mismos*. 1855; Mexico City: Decaen, 1857.

Chassen-López, Francie R. "A Patron of Progress: Juana Catarina Romero, the Nineteenth-Century Cacica of Tehuantepec." *Hispanic American Historical Review* 88, 3 (2008): 393-426.

Chust, Manuel, and Víctor Mínguez, comps. *La construcción del héroe en España y México (1789-1847)*. Valencia: Universitat de València, 2003.

Crononautas Tijerina. "Corrido a la Güera Rodríguez." December 17, 2010. http://www.youtube.com/watch%3Fv%3DsEanp16NdxU, accessed February 23, 2015.

Couturier, Edith. "Women in a Noble Family: The Mexican Counts of Regla, 1750-1830." In *Latin American Women: Historical Perspectives*, ed. Asunción Lavrin, 129-149. Westport, CT: Greenwood Press, 1978.

———. *The Silver King: The Remarkable Life of the Count of Regla in Colonial Mexico*. Albuquerque: University of New Mexico Press, 2003.

Cumplido, Ignacio, ed. *El album mexicano: Periódico de literatura, artes y bellas letras*. Mexico City: Imp. del Editor, 1849.

Curiel, Fernando. "Prólogo." In Guillermo Prieto, *Obras completas*, vol. 1, 15-47. Mexico City: Consejo Nacional para la Cultura y las Artes, 1992.

Cypess, Sandra Messinger. *La Malinche in Mexican Literature: From History to Myth*. Austin: University of Texas Press, 1991.

Dávila, Vicky. "Conozca a las 10 prostitutas más famosas de la historia." La W Radio, November 6, 2013. https://www.wradio.com.co/multimedia

/fotogalerias/conozca-a-las-10-prostitutas-mas-famosas-de-la-historia
/20131106/fotogaleria/2009008.aspx, accessed February 3, 2015.

"Denuncia del alcaide y el teniente de las cárceles secretas del Santo Oficio."
September 26, 1817. *Boletín del Archivo General de la Nación* 3: 3 (July-
September 1932): 334–335.

Díaz, Ana. "La Güera Rodríguez, la mujer detrás de la independencia de
México." *Belelu / Nueva mujer* (blog). January 8, 2013. https://www.belelu
.com/2013/01/la-guera-rodriguez-la-mujer-detras-de-la-independencia-de
-mexico/, accessed February 3, 2015.

Diccionario Porrúa de historia, biografía y geografía de México. Mexico City:
Porrúa, 1964 (1st ed.), 1995 (6th ed.).

*Episodios Mexicanos: Un recorrido por la historia de México desde Teotihuacán
hasta la Expropiación Petrolera*. Mexico City: SEP, 1981, nos. 28–35.

Escamilla Dimas, Jorge Luis. "La Güera Rodríguez y su papel en la Independencia de México" (Facebook post). September 14, 2012. https://es-la.facebook
.com/notes/jorge-luis-escamilla-dimas/la-g%C3%BCera-rodr%C3%ADguez
-y-su-papel-en-la-independencia-de-m%C3%A9xico-/415734565157629/,
accessed June 9, 2016.

Fernández, Aurora. *Mujeres que honran a la patria*. Mexico City: Imp. Zavala,
1958.

Fernández de Lizardi, José Joaquín. *Calendario para el año de 1825: Dedicado
a las señoritas americanas, especialmente a las patriotas; por el pensador
mexicano*. Repr. as *Heroínas mexicanas: Maria Leona Vicario, M.
Rodríguez Lazarín, María Fermina Rivera, Manuela Herrera y otras*.
Mexico City: Biblioteca de Historiadores Mexicanos, 1955.

Fernández de Recas, Guillermo. *Mayorazgos de la Nueva España*. Mexico City:
Instituto Bibliográfico Mexicano, 1965.

Flores Acevedo, Oscar. "Sobre *Antorcha y Cenizas*." www.oscarfloresacevedo
.com/resena-de-antorcha-y-cenizas, accessed July 13, 2017.

Flórez, Ramón de. "El México de antaño: Dos periodistas de la época." March
19, 2014. http://old.nvinoticias.com/en/node/200576, accessed June 9, 2016.

Fossey, Mathieu de. *Viage a México*. Mexico City: Ignacio Cumplido, 1844.

———. *Le Mexique*. Paris: Henri Plon, 1857.

Francois, Marie Eileen. *A Culture of Everyday Credit: Housekeeping, Pawnbro-
king, and Governance in Mexico City, 1790–1920*. Lincoln: University of
Nebraska Press, 2006.

Fuentes Aguirre Catón, Armando. *La otra historia de México: Hidalgo e
Iturbide, la gloria y el olvido*. 2 vols. 2008; repr. Mexico City: Planeta,
2014.

Fuentes Mares, José. *Las mil y una noches mexicanas*. 2 vols. Mexico City:
Grijalbo, 1984.

Galeana, Patricia. *Museo de la Mujer*. Mexico City: UNAM, 2012.

Galí Boadella, Montserrat. *Historias del bello sexo: La introducción del Romanticismo en México*. Mexico City: UNAM, Instituto de Investigaciones Estéticas, 2002.

Galindo y Villa, Jesús. *Polvo de historia*. Mexico City: E. Gómez de la Puente, 1923.

Galván, Delia. "Federico Schroeder Inclán." In *Dictionary of Mexican Literature*, ed. Eladio Cortés, 346. Westport, CT: Greenwood, 1992.

Garci, Antonio. *Más pendejadas célebres en la historia de México*. Mexico City: Diana, 2011.

García, Genaro. *Leona Vicario: Heroína insurgente*. Mexico City: Museo Nacional de Arqueología, Historia y Etnología, 1910.

———. comp. *Documentos históricos mexicanos: Obra conmemorativa del primer centenario de la independencia de México*. 7 vols. 1910; repr. Nendeln/Liechtenstein, Kraus-Thomson, 1971.

García, Rubén. "La Güera Rodríguez y el coronel Iturbide." *Todo* 799 (December 30, 1948): 27.

———. "La Influencia de la Guerra [sic] Rodríguez sobre Iturbide y la Independencia." *Todo* 800 (January 6, 1949): 43.

———. "¿Por qué hizo la independencia Iturbide? Su movimiento contrarevolucionario a favor de los absolutistas." *Todo* 801 (January 13, 1949): 27.

García Cubas, Antonio. *Diccionario geográfico, histórico y biográfico de los Estados Unidos Mexicanos*. 5 vols. Mexico City: Antigua Imp de Murguia / Tip. de la Secretaría de Fomento, 1888–1891.

García López, Ana Belén. *Las heroínas silenciadas en las independencias hispanoamericanas*. Madrid: Editorial Complutense, 2013.

García Tsao, Leonardo. *Testimonios del cine mexicano: Felipe Cazals habla de su cine*. Guadalajara: Universidad de Guadalajara, Centro de Investigación y Enseñanza Cinematográficas, 1994.

Gibbons, Eliot. "'La Güera' Rodríguez." *Mexico / This Month* (August 1959): 11, 24.

Gómez, Mathilde. *La epopeya de la Independencia mexicana a través de sus mujeres*. Mexico City: A.N.A.G, 1947.

González Obregón, Luis. *México viejo: Noticias históricas, tradiciones, leyendas y costumbres*. 2nd series. Mexico City: Tip. de la Secretaría de Fomento, 1895.

———. *México viejo y anecdótico*. Mexico City: Vda de Ch. Bouret, 1909.

———. *Las calles de México: Leyendas y sucedidos*. 6th ed., 1922. Repr. Mexico City: Ediciones Botas, 1944.

Guardia, Sara Beatriz, comp. *Las mujeres en la Independencia de América Latina*. Lima: Centro de Estudios de la Mujer en la Historia de América Latina / Universidad San Martín de Porres / UNESCO, 2010.

Guedea, Virginia. *Prontuario de los insurgentes*. Mexico City: UNAM, Centro de Estudios Sobre la Universidad / Instituto Mora, 1995.

———. "Rodríguez de Velasco y Osorio Barba, María Ignacia." In *Encyclopedia of Latin American History and Culture*, ed. Barbara Tenenbaum, vol. 4, 592. New York: Charles Scribner's Sons, 1996.

———. "Rodríguez de Velasco y Osorio Barba, María Ignacia (La Güera Rodríguez): 1778–1850 Pro-Independence Socialite." In *Encyclopedia of Mexico: History, Society & Culture*, ed. Michael S. Werner, vol. 2, 1286. Chicago: Fitzroy Dearborn Publishers, 1997.

Guzmán Pérez, Moisés. "Gertrudis Bocanegra y el proceso de construcción de la heroína en México." In Guardia, *Mujeres en la Independencia*, 59–73.

———. "Mujeres de amor y de guerra: Roles femeninos en la Independencia de México." In Senado de la República, *Mujeres insurgentes*, 17–98.

Hernández, Carlos. *Mujeres célebres de México*. San Antonio, TX: Casa Editorial Lozano, 1918.

Hernández, Francisco, dir. "La Güera Rodríguez: La mujer novohispana más ilustrada de la alcoba independiente" (monologue). October 1, 2010. https://www.youtube.com/watch?v=3ettae58umE, accessed June 9, 2016.

Hombres y Héroes. Wikipedia en español. https://es.wikipedia.org/wiki/Hombres_y_Héroes, accessed December 12, 2016.

Huerta-Nava, Raquel. *Mujeres insurgentes*. Mexico City: Lumen / Consejo Nacional para la Cultura y las Artes, 2008.

Jiménez Gómez, Juan Ricardo. "Creencias y prácticas religiosas en Querétaro al final de la Colonia." In *Creencias y prácticas religiosas en Querétaro: Siglos XVI-XIX*, coord. Juan Ricardo Jiménez Gómez, 105–151. Mexico City: Universidad Autónoma de Querétaro / Plaza y Valdés, 2004.

Kentner, Janet R. "The Socio-Political Role of Women in the Mexican Wars of Independence, 1810–1821." PhD diss., Loyola University Chicago, 1975.

Krumm-Heller, Arnoldo. "Esbozo biográfico del barón Alejandro von Humboldt." In Ernst Wittich et al., *Memoria científica para la inauguración de la estatua de Alejandro de Humboldt obsequiada por S.M. el Emperador Alemán Guillermo II a la nación mexicana, con motivo del primer centenario de su independencia, México 13 de septiembre 1910*, 3–41. Mexico City: Müller Hermanos, 1910.

Ladd, Doris M. *The Mexican Nobility at Independence, 1780–1826*. Austin: University of Texas Press, 1976.

Lavrin, Asunción, ed. *Latin American Women: Historical Perspectives*. Westport, CT: Greenwood Press, 1978.

Lizana y Beaumont, Francisco Javier. *Instrucción pastoral . . . sobre la costumbre de llevar las señoras el pecho y brazos desnudos*. Mexico City: Oficina de Doña María Fernández de Jauregui, 1808.

Lombardo de Ruiz, Sonia, and Theubet de Beauchamp. *Trajes y vistas en la mirada de Theubet de Beauchamp: Trajes civiles y militares y de los pobladores de México entre 1810 y 1827*. Facsimile. Mexico City: INAH/Turner, 2009.

López Arellano, Marcela. *Anita Brenner: Una escritora judía con México en el corazón.* Aguascalientes: Universidad Autónoma de Aguascalientes / Centro de Documentación e Investigación Judío de México, 2016.

López de Escalera, Juan. *Diccionario biográfico y de historia de México.* Mexico City: Editorial del Magisterio, 1964.

Lozano Torres, Eduardo. *Bolívar, mujeriego empedernido: Las batallas amorosas del Libertador.* Bogotá: Intermedio, 2015.

Macías Galland, José Luis. "Una Güera, que rockea y se apellida Rodríguez." *Cielo a la tierra* (blog). September 18, 2010. https://cieloalatierra.wordpress.com/2010/09/18/una-guera-que-rockea-y-se-apellida-rodriguez/, accessed July 2, 2017.

Malo, José Ramón. *Diario de sucesos notables de don José Ramón Malo.* Ed. Mariano Cuevas. 2 vols. Mexico City: Editorial Patria, 1948.

Mandrell, James. *Don Juan and the Point of Honor: Seduction, Patriarchal Society, and Literary Tradition.* University Park: Pennsylvania State University Press, 1992.

"María Ignacia Rodríguez de Velasco." Wikipedia en español. https://es.wikipedia.org/wiki/Mar%C3%ADa_Ignacia_Rodr%C3%ADguez_de_Velasco, accessed June 1, 2017, and August 8, 2018.

"María Ignacia Rodríguez de Velasco y Osorio Barba." Wikipedia. https://en.wikipedia.org/wiki/Mar%C3%ADa_Ignacia_Rodr%C3%ADguez_de_Velasco_y_Osorio_Barba, accessed June 1, 2017, and August 8, 2018.

María y Campos, Armando de. "Estreno de *Hoy invita la güera,* en el teatro Globo, por Lola Bravo." *Novedades,* April 3, 1955. http://criticateatral2021.org/transcripciones/1152_550403.php, accessed April 17, 2017.

Marston, William Moulton. "Why 100,000,000 Americans Read Comics." *American Scholar,* Winter 1943–1944. https://theamericanscholar.org/wonder-woman/#, accessed June 15, 2017.

Martín Moreno, Francisco. *Las grandes traiciones de México.* Mexico City: Joaquín Mortiz / Planeta Mexicana, 2000.

———. *Arrebatos carnales II: Las pasiones que consumieron a los protagonistas de la historia de México.* Mexico City: Planeta, 2010.

Martínez Núñez, César Alejandro. "Biografía crítica de la Güera Rodríguez, 1779–1851." Licenciatura thesis, UNAM, Facultad de Filosofía y Letras, 2010.

———. "La redención de La Güera." *BiCentenario: El ayer y hoy de México* 21 (2013): 15–21.

Martínez Serrano, Hector. "Manuel Tolsá inmortalizó el rostro de la Güera Rodríguez." Radio program, May 4, 2012. https://www.youtube.com/watch?v=dUL5ULfmdDQ, accessed June 28, 2017.

Martínez Villaseñor, Jorge. *El viento no es para siempre.* Jiquilpan, Mexico: n.d. [2011?]. E-book. http://www.lulu.com/shop/jorge-mart%C3%ADnez

-villase%C3%B1or/el-viento-no-es-para-siempre/ebook/product-17452659. html, accessed April 15, 2017.

Mateos, Juan A. *Historia parlamentaria de los congresos mexicanos de 1821 a 1857.* Mexico City: Vicente S. Reyes, 1877, vol. 1.

Mejía Chávez, Carlos Gustavo. "'¡Que le quieren dar veneno al señor Arzobispo-Virrey!' Historia de una conspiración dirimida por la Inquisición de Nueva España (agosto de 1809–enero de 1810)." *Historia Mexicana* 68: 1 (2018): 49–110.

Miquel i Vergés, Josep María. *Diccionario de insurgentes.* Mexico City: Porrúa, 1969.

Molly. "Alebrijes." *The Amazing Adventures of los von ZauRunyon!* (blog). October 31, 2010. http://vonzaurunyon.blogspot.com/2010/10/alebrijes .html, accessed February 3, 2015.

Moreno Juárez, Sergio. "Presencia, participación y representación femenina en los dos Centenarios de la Independencia nacional (1910 y 1921)." *Signos Históricos* 14, no. 27 (2012): 25–62.

Muñoz Altea, Fernando. "La Güera Rodríguez, una mexicana muy singular." In *Genealogía e historia de la familia: Vínculos familiares y métodos para su estudio,* coord. Laura Elena Dávila Díaz de León, 197–218. Aguascalientes: Universidad Autónoma de Aguascalientes, 2018.

Musacchio, Humberto, ed. *Diccionario enciclopédico de México ilustrado.* 4 vols. Mexico City: Andrés León, 1989.

Nina. "La famosa 'Güera Rodríguez.'" *De enaguas, molcajetes y armas* (blog). March 3, 2010. https://armandina1959.wordpress.com/2010/03/03/la -famosa-guera-rodriguez/, accessed June 9, 2016.

Núñez Becerra, Fernanda. *La Malinche: De la historia al mito.* Mexico City: INAH, 1996.

"El ocaso de la Nueva España: La Güera y el Caraqueñito." Episode of *Tele Historia,* July 21, 2010. http://telehistoria.wikifoundry.com/page/El+ Ocaso+de+la+Nueva+Espa%C3%B1a+-+La+G%C3%BCera+y+El+Caraque% C3%B1ito, accessed April 17, 2017.

Olmedilla, Carlos. "México, 1808–1821: Algunas aportaciones históricas." *Historia Mexicana* 9, no. 4 (1960): 586–600.

Oropeza Martínez, Roberto. *Apuntes autodidácticos para estudiantes: Artemio de Valle-Arizpe, La güera Rodríguez: con introducción y antecedentes, aspectos generales, sinopsis, comentario y análisis guiado, autoevaluaicón, bibliografía.* Mexico City: Fernández Editores, 1990.

Orozco y Berra, Manuel. *Diccionario universal de historia y de geografía . . . refundida y aumentada.* 10 vols. Mexico City: Andrade y Escalante, 1853–1856.

Ortega y Medina, Juan A. *Humboldt desde México.* Mexico City: UNAM, Facultad de Filosofía y Letras, 1960.

Ortega y Pérez Gallardo, Ricardo. *Historia genealógica de las familias más antiguas de México.* 3 vols. 3rd rev. ed. Mexico City: Imp. de A. Carranza y Cía., 1908–1910.

Padrón general de las casas que comprehenden los ocho quarteles mayores en que está distribuida esta capital, valores de sus actuales arrendamientos comparados con los que rendían el año de 1796, para deducir el diez por ciento que se paga a la Hazienda Pública Nacional de México, diziembre 31 de 1813. Mexico City: Oficina Impresora de Estampillas, 1903.

Palacio, Celia del. *Adictas a la insurgencia: Mujeres en la guerra de Independencia.* Mexico City: Punto de Lectura, 2010. Kindle edition.

Pani, Erika. "El proyecto de estado a través de la vida cortesana y del ceremonial público." *Historia Mexicana* 45, no. 2 (1995): 423–460.

Parbst, Rodolfo E. "La Güera Rodríguez." *Conozcamos la historia* (blog). March 28, 2016. https://rodolfoparbst.blogspot.com/2016/03/la-guera-rodriguez.html, accessed June 27, 2017.

Peral, Miguel Ángel. *Diccionario biográfico mexicano.* Mexico City: Editorial P.A.C., 1944.

Peza, José Miguel de la. "La bella 'Güera' Rodríguez: Un episodio romántico de la agitada vida del libertador de nuestro país, el Generalísimo Don Agustín de Iturbide." *Excelsior,* September 27, 1921, 5th section, 6.

Pi y Margall, Francisco, and Francisco Pi y Arsuaga. *Historia de España en el siglo XIX: Sucesos políticos, económicos, sociales y artísticos.* Vol. 2. Barcelona: Miguel Seguí Editor, 1903.

Poinsett, Joel R. *Notes on Mexico, made in the Autumn of 1822.* 1824; repr., New York: Praeger, 1969.

Pouwels, Joel Bollinger. *Political Journalism by Mexican Women during the Age of Revolution, 1876–1940.* Lewiston, NY: Edwin Mellen Press, 2006.

Presente amistoso dedicado a las señoritas mexicanas. Mexico City: Ignacio Cumplido, 1851.

Prieto, Guillermo. *Memorias de mis tiempos (1828–1853).* 2 vols. Mexico City: Vda de C. Bouret, 1906.

Reyes, Alfonso. "Rumbo a Goethe." *Sur: Revista trimestral,* año II (summer 1932): 7–85.

Reyes Hernández, Itzeel. "'La Güera Rodríguez' eterna seductora." *Quién,* April 29, 2010. http://www.quien.com/espectaculos/2010/04/29/la-guera-rodriguez-eterna-seductora, accessed June 9, 2016.

Reznik, Nicoletta. "¿Quién fue la Güera Rodríguez?" *La máquina de la verdad: Situaciones e historias casuales, inéditas, curiosas, extremas, a veces insólitas, sin época ni especialidad* (blog). August 6, 2011. http://lamaquinadelaverdad.blogspot.com/2011/08/quien-fue-la-guera-rodriguez.html, accessed February 3, 2015.

Ríos, Arturo. "La Güera estrenó a Simón Bolívar en las mieles del amor." *México Nueva Era: Periodismo digital de vanguardia*, August 4, 2015. http:// mexiconuevaera.com/opinion/2015/08/4/la-guera-estreno-simon-bolivar -en-las-mieles-del-amor, accessed October 17, 2017.

——. "El romance de la Güera con Humboldt." *México nueva era: Periodismo digital de vanguardia*, August 5, 2015. http://mexiconuevaera.com /opinion/2015/08/5/el-romance-de-la-guera-con-humbolt, accessed December 14, 2017.

Rippy, J. Fred. *Joel R. Poinsett, Versatile American*. Durham, NC: Duke University Press, 1935.

Rivera, Reyna Lorena. "La Güera Rodríguez, vital en la independencia." *Excelsior*, November 18, 2012. http://www.excelsior.com.mx/2012/11/18 /comunidad/870341, accessed February 3, 2015.

Robertson, William Spence. *Iturbide of Mexico*. Durham, NC: Duke University Press, 1952.

Rocafuerte, Vicente. *Bosquejo ligerísimo de la Revolución de Mégico desde El Grito de Iguala hasta la proclamación imperial de Iturbide*. 1822; facsimile, Mexico City: Porrúa, 1984.

Rodríguez, Jaime E. "From Royal Subject to Republican Citizen: The Role of the Autonomists in the Independence of Mexico." In *The Independence of Mexico and the Creation of the New Nation*, ed. Jaime E. Rodríguez, 19–43. Los Angeles: UCLA Latin America Center Publications / Mexico/Chicano Program, University of California Irvine, 1989.

——. "Los caudillos y los historiadores: Riego, Iturbide y Santa Anna." In Chust and Mínguez, *La construcción del héroe*, 309–335.

Romero de Terreros y Vinent, Manuel. *Los condes de Regla: Apuntes biográficos*. Mexico City: M. León Sánchez, 1909.

——. *Ex-antiquis: Bocetos de la vida social en la Nueva España*. Guadalajara: Jaime, 1919.

——. *La corte de Agustín I: Emperador de México*. Mexico City: Museo Nacional de Arqueología, Historia, y Etnología, 1921.

Rosas, Alejandro. *99 pasiones en la historia de México*. Mexico City: Planeta, 2012.

Rubio Siliceo, Luis. *Mujeres célebres en la independencia de México*. Mexico City: Talleres Gráficos de la Nación, 1929.

Ruvalcaba, Patricia. "La Profesa: Un estuche de lujo." *Nuevo guía del centro histórico de México*. N.d. https://www.guiadelcentrohistorico.mx/kmcero /cultura/la-profesa-un-estuche-de-lujo, accessed July 2, 2017.

Salinas Basave, Daniel. "Los mitos del bicentenario 22: La Güera." Television program, September 29, 2010. https://youtu.be/MS3hKtKPhbI, accessed July 6, 2017.

Sánchez Robles, María Guadalupe. "La Güera Rodríguez, a doscientos años de la independencia de México." In Guardia, *Mujeres de la Independencia*, 364–369.

Sartorius, Carl, and Johann Moritz Rugendas. *Mexico about 1850*. Stuttgart: Brockhaus, 1961.

Schober, Otto. "La reinvindicación de 'La Güera' Rodríguez." *Zócalo Saltillo*, October 21, 2009. http://www.zocalo.com.mx/seccion/opinion-articulo /la-reinvidicacion-de-la-gueera-rodriguez, accessed June 9, 2016.

Schroeder Inclán, Federico. *Hoy invita la Güera: Comedia antihistórica en tres actos*. 1955. In Salvador Novo and Federico S. Inclán, *La culta dama / Hoy invita la Güera*, 65–136. Mexico City: Fondo de Cultura Económica, 1997.

Senado de la República (Comisión especial encargada de los festejos del bicentenario . . .), ed. *Mujeres insurgentes*. Mexico City: Siglo XXI, 2010.

Sevilla, María Eugenia. "Las dos Güeras." *Revista Bicentenario* en *Pro Ópera*, January–February 2011. http://www.proopera.org.mx/pasadas/enefeb2 /revista/16–17bicentene2011.pdf, accessed June 26, 2017.

Singer, Armand E. *The Don Juan Theme: An Annotated Bibliography of Versions, Analogues, Uses, and Adaptations*. Morgantown: West Virginia University Press, 1993.

Solórzano, Carlos. "Hoy invita la Güera." *Ovaciones,* November 4, 1962, 5.

Sosa, Francisco. *Biografías de mexicanos distinguidos*. Mexico City: Oficina Tipográfica de la Secretaría de Fomento, 1884.

Sosa, Octavio. *Diccionario de la ópera mexicana*. Mexico City: INBA/Conaculta, 2005.

Sotomayor, Arturo. *Don Artemio*. Mexico City: UNAM, Biblioteca del Estudiante Universitario, 1967.

Stern, Steve J. *The Secret History of Gender: Women, Men, and Power in Late Colonial Mexico*. Chapel Hill: University of North Carolina Press, 1995.

Sunderland Guerrero, Javier. "Olor a almizcle." In A. Abdó et al., *Las revoltosas*, 53–61. Mexico City: Selector, 2010.

Tecuanhuey, Alicia. "La imagen de las heroínas mexicanas." In Chust and Mínguez, *La construcción del héroe*, 71–90.

TeleSur. "La Güera Rodríguez." *Misterios de la historia*, episode 36, December 9, 2016. https://www.youtube.com/watch?v=grn9LpSIgw8, accessed June 26, 2017.

Thompson, Waddy. *Recollections of Mexico*. New York: Wiley and Putnam, 1846.

Torre Villar, Ernesto de la. *Los 'Guadalupes' y la Independencia, con una selección de documentos inéditos*. Mexico City: Editorial Jus, 1966.

Torrente, Mariano. *Historia de la Revolución hispano-americana*. 3 vols. Madrid: Imp. L. Amarita, 1829–1830.

———. *Historia de la Independencia de México*. Madrid: Editorial América, 1918.

Townsend, Camilla. *Malintzin's Choices: An Indian Woman in the Conquest of Mexico*. Albuquerque: University of New Mexico Press, 2006.

Tuñón Pablos, Julia. *Women in Mexico: A Past Unveiled*. Trans. Alan Hynds. Austin: University of Texas Press, 1999.

———. "¿Pueden existir las heroínas en celuloide? La representación de las mujeres insurgentes en el cine mexicano (1934–1991)." In Guardia, *Mujeres en la Independencia*, 303–315.

Twinam, Ann. *Public Lives, Private Secrets: Gender, Honor, Sexuality, and Illegitimacy in Colonial Spanish America*. Stanford, CA: Stanford University Press, 1999.

Urena, Carlos. "La Güera Rodríguez, la mujer que sedujo a una nación y cambió la historia de México." *Cultura colectiva* (blog). January 4, 2017. https://culturacolectiva.com/historia/la-guera-rodriguez-y-la-independencia-de-mexico, accessed December 12, 2018.

Valle, Rafael Heliodoro, comp. *Bolívar en México*. Mexico City: Secretaría de Relaciones Exteriores, 1946.

———. *Cómo era Iturbide*. Mexico City: Imp. del Museo Nacional de Arqueología, Historia y Etnografía, 1922.

———. "Redescubriendo a Iturbide." *Excelsior*, January 2, 1951, 7.

———. "Deudas de la Güera Rodríguez." *Excelsior*, January 19, 1951.

Valle Arizpe, Artemio de. *La Güera Rodríguez* [selection]. In *Cuadernos Mexicanos*, año 1, núm. 15. Mexico City: SEP/CONASUPO, n.d., ca. 1982.

Valle-Arizpe, Artemio de. *La Güera Rodríguez*. 1949; 2nd ed., Mexico City: Porrúa, 1950.

———. *La Güera Rodríguez*. 1949; 9th rev. ed., Mexico City: Porrúa, 1960.

———. *La Güera Rodríguez: Relatos reales del sorprendente y divertido personaje de la historia de México*. Mexico City: Lectorum, 2011.

Vargas, Ángel. "Después de casi tres décadas, *La Güera* reaparece en escenarios nacionales." *La Jornada*, September 12, 2010. http://www.jornada.unam.mx/2010/09/12/cultura/a03n1cul, accessed June 26, 2017.

Vázquez Santa Ana, Higinio. *Bosquejos biográficos de hombres ilustres nacionales*. Mexico City: Secretaría de Gobernación, 1920.

Veinte mujeres notables de la vida de México. Mexico City: Instituto Mexicano Norteamericano de Relaciones Culturales, 1974.

Velasco, Karina. "Enredos amorosos y políticos con La Güera Rodríguez." *Crónica*, August 13, 2010. http://www.cronica.com.mx/imprimir.php?id_nota=525296, accessed April 7, 2017.

———. "La Güera Rodríguez." *Crónica*, August 21, 2010. http://www.cronica.com.mx/notas/2010/527014.html, accessed April 7, 2017.

Velasco, Sherry. *The Lieutenant Nun: Transgenderism, Lesbian Desire, and Catalina de Erauso*. Austin: University of Texas Press, 2000.

Velázquez Moreno, Rodrigo. "'La Güera' Rodríguez (1778–1850)." *Algarabia* (blog). February 12, 2014. http://algarabia.com-fue/la-guera-rodriguez -1778–1850/, accessed February 3, 2015.

Vigil Talavera, Arturo. *La puta libertadora: Relatos de la Güera Rodríguez.* Tacna, Peru: Arturo Vigil Talavera, 2019. Kindle edition.

Villalpando, José Manuel. *Amores mexicanos.* Mexico City: Planeta, 1998.

Villaseñor y Villaseñor, Alejandro. *Biografías de los héroes y caudillos de la Independencia.* 2 vols. 2nd rev. ed., Mexico City: Editorial Jus, 1962.

Ward, H. G. *Mexico in 1827.* London: Henry Colburn, 1828.

Weeks, Charles A. *The Juárez Myth in Mexico.* Tuscaloosa: University of Alabama Press, 1987.

Wolcott, Roger, ed. *The Correspondence of William Hickling Prescott, 1833– 1847.* Cambridge, MA: Riverside Press, 1925.

Wright de Kleinhans, Laureana. *Mujeres notables mexicanas.* Mexico City: Tip. Económica, 1910.

Xakan, Jaime M. "María Ignacia Rodríguez: La 'Gúera' Rodríguez." *Revista Discover,* January 29, 2015. http://revistadiscover.com/profiles/blogs /biografia-de-la-guera-rodriguez-resumen, accessed June 9, 2016.

Yolo Camotes. "La Güera Rodríguez: La seductora de la Independencia." Television program, June 12, 2017. https://www.youtube.com/watch?v=hkC5qVTU _qk, accessed July 2, 2017.

Yorch. "La Güera Rodríguez: Heroína olvidada." *El Mundo según Yorch* (blog). September 20, 2010. http://elmundosegunyorch.blogspot.com/2010/09 /la-guera-rodriguez-heroina-olvidada.html, accessed February 3, 2015.

Zamora Plowes, Leopoldo. *La comedia mexicana Quince Uñas y Casanova aventureros: Novela histórica picaresca.* 2 vols. Mexico City: Talleres Gráficos de la Nación, 1945.

———. *Quince Uñas y Casanova aventureros: La novela sobre Santa Anna y la guerra con Estados Unidos,* condensed and annotated by Pilar Tapia. Mexico City: Terracota, 2007.

Zárate Toscano, Verónica. *Los nobles ante la muerte en México: Actitudes, ceremonias y memoria (1750–1850).* 2000; repr. Mexico City: Colegio de México / Instituto Mora, 2005.

———. "Los privilegios del nombre: Los nobles novohispanos a fines de la época colonial." In *Historia de la vida cotidiana en México III: El siglo XVIII; entre tradición y cambio,* coord. Pilar Gonzalbo Aizpuro, 325–356. Mexico City: Colegio de México / Fondo de Cultura Económica, 2005.

Zeuske, Michael. *Simón Bolívar: History and Myth.* Trans. Steven Rendall and Lisa Neal. Princeton, NJ: Markus Wiener Publishers, 2013.

Index

Valdivielso Vidal de Lorca, José María (Marqués de San Miguel de Aguayo), 47, 70, 103
Valle, Rafael Heliodoro, 142, 156–157
Valle-Arizpe, Artemio de: career of, 136, 221n2; as source for history texts, 165–166; as source of future legends about La Güera, 2, 154–155, 158, 161, 167; viewing of La Güera's items, 107, 108. See also *La Güera Rodríguez* (Valle-Arizpe)
Vega, Rafael, 65, 80, 170
Velasco, Francisco Lorenzo de, 65, 170
Velázquez de la Cadena, José Manuel, 70, 213n17
Verduzco, José Sixto, 65, 211n56
Vicario, Leona: "afterlife" of, 131, 174, 188–189; education of, 14; as independence heroine, 2, 114, 131; intelligence of, 188; La Güera's correspondence with, 66, 170; notable contributions by, 81–82; potential feminist icon, 188; punishment of, 68, 80
Victoria, Guadalupe, 77
Villahermosa, Marquesa de, 47–50
Villalpando, José Manuel, 172
Villamil Alvarado, José Gerónimo López de Peralta de Villar: lawsuit with his son, 16–17; objection to his son's marriage, 15, 120
Villamil y Primo, José Gerónimo López de Peralta de Villar: courtship with La Güera, 119–120; death of, 27; debts left by, 28; divorce suit against La Güera, 19–27; jealousy of, 19, 22, 23, 139; La Güera's marriage to, 15; lawsuit with his father, 16–17; physical abuse allegations, 22–23; reputation concerns of, 25; Valle-Arizpe account of, 140; wealth and status of, 15–18
Villar Villamil Rodríguez, Agustín Gerónimo, 18
Villar Villamil Rodríguez, Gerónimo Mariano: birth of, 18; children of, 50; custody of, 20; death of, 107; godparents of, 18; in Iturbide's court, 70; La Güera's closeness with, 103–104; La Güera's debt to, 86, 88; as *mayorazgo* inheritor, 28, 29, 50; Molino Prieto woes, 78–79; properties of, 50, 53; quoted, 90; *regidor* inheritance, 43, 57; in republican politics, 50, 78, 98, 104; residence of, 104, 210n49, 218n51; signature of, 89; wedding of, 50

Villar Villamil Rodríguez, María Antonia: birth of, 18; children of, 50, 103; death of, 107; dowry of, 58; La Güera's closeness with, 104; marriage of, 47; possible Iturbide affair, 74, 141; residence of, 218n53
Villar Villamil Rodríguez, María de la Paz: birth of, 18, 27; children of, 50, 102; death of, 102; dowry of, 58; marriage of, 47, 67; as model for Tolsá sculpture, 116, 155
Villar Villamil Rodríguez, María Guadalupe: birth of, 18; illness and death of, 27–28, 34, 42–43, 46–47; La Güera's custody of, 20
Villar Villamil Rodríguez, María Josefa: birth of, 18; Bustamante on, 102; children of, 50, 102; death of, 102; education of, 20, 47; marriage of, 47–50; mother-in-law's acceptance of, 49–50; opinion of the Iturbide court, 76; portrait of, 49; in republican politics, 76–77; separation from her husband, 99–102

Ward, Henry G., 77, 92, 101, 209n31
Weeks, Charles, 189
widowhoods of La Güera: after Briones's death, 29–30, 121; property management in, 28–29, 32–33; trials of second, 58–60; after Villamil's death, 27–28
women in the late colonial period: dearth of biographical information on, 2; importance of inheritances to, 57; independence war involvement, 68, 80–82, 220n29; La Güera as typical, 3, 108–109, 189–190; La Güera in histories of, 160; misunderstanding of, 3, 186; Museo de la Mujer, 2, 179; perils of motherhood for, 34; political involvement by, 32, 62; property management by, 33; protection for wives and widows, 24, 28; smoking by, 54; Valle-Arizpe's depiction of, 149–150; vulnerable social position of, 59–60
Wright de Kleinhans, Laureana, 115

Xala, Conde de, 48

Yermo coup, 36, 39, 63

Zamora Plowes, Leopoldo, 132
Zavala, Lorenzo, 75
Zerecero, Anastasio, 75
Zorrilla, José, 144–145

Founded in 1893,
UNIVERSITY OF CALIFORNIA PRESS
publishes bold, progressive books and journals
on topics in the arts, humanities, social sciences,
and natural sciences—with a focus on social
justice issues—that inspire thought and action
among readers worldwide.

The UC PRESS FOUNDATION
raises funds to uphold the press's vital role
as an independent, nonprofit publisher, and
receives philanthropic support from a wide
range of individuals and institutions—and from
committed readers like you. To learn more, visit
ucpress.edu/supportus.